Praise for the First Edition of *Five Big Ideas for Effective Teaching*

Included in the *UK Times* Higher Education Suggested Reading List (2013) as a recommended read for educators.

This is an interdisciplinary book like no other currently in publication. The bridge to practice is articulated clearly, setting the stage for a new paradigm in teacher education and how we consider learning.

—Deborah Schussler,
Department of Education and Counseling, Villanova University

This book is easy to read, understand, and use to apply what we know about learning in the brain and translate that knowledge into educational practice.

—Daniel C. Miller, Diplomate in School Neuropsychology,
Department of Psychology and Philosophy, Texas Woman's University

Offers a "big idea" framework that helps professionals consume and apply critical funds of knowledge efficiently. It could be used as required reading for a preservice teacher education course.

—Tanner LaBaron Wallace,
Applied Developmental Psychology in Education, University of Pittsburgh

This inspirational book merges brain science and pedagogy by generating a powerful congruity between the science of learning and the art of teaching through strategies that have a profound impact on student learning.

—Reem Kobrsi, president, International Educational Organization

Every school of education should make this book mandatory reading and deans should hop on-board and make it a required roundtable text for their faculties.

—Douglas Stewart, O'More College

One of the best books on neuroscience and education. Given the new core standards, topics in the book are just what teachers need.

—Debby Zambo,
Division of Leadership and Innovation, Arizona State University

In their most interesting and instructive book, the authors appear to me as guides leading readers on a fascinating journey of discovery.

—Reuven Feuerstein, cognitive psychologist,
International Center for the Enhancement of Learning Potential

The theme woven throughout *Five Big Ideas* cannot be overstated: ALL children can learn. This book is a must-read for everyone who interacts with children and young adults!

—Martha H. Hopkins,
School of Teaching, Learning, and Leadership, University of Central Florida

D1603535

This promising paradigm that applies theory to classroom challenges offers hope for our schools struggling with outdated practices.

—Ruth V. Burgess, emeritus professor,
School of Teacher Education, Missouri State University

This text provides a treatise to move teachers and their students from an educational paradigm preparing them for a world rapidly ceasing to exist to the flexible thinking for adaptation to whatever the future may hold.

—Marjorie S. Anderson, coordinator of field experience,
director of Secondary Education Program, Cumberland University

The five big ideas presented in this book summarize current research findings that are important for all effective educators, teacher educators, administrators, policymakers, and parents.

—Brett D. Jones, Educational Psychology, Virginia Tech

I found this book uplifting and inspiring. It integrates established research and theory with myth-busting and insightful presentation of the latest research.

—Susan M. Benner,
associate dean of Professional Licensure, College of Education,
Health, and Human Services, University of Tennessee, Knoxville

An excellent volume that has multiple applications for classroom teachers, researchers, preservice teachers, and policymakers.

—David S. Martin, professor/dean emeritus, Gallaudet University

This text is a wonderful choice for student teaching seminars or PLCs in schools. If your goal is to establish a culture of continuous improvement, this book is for you.

—Lisa J. Lucas,
educator, coach, and consultant, West Chester University

I particularly appreciated the emphasis on providing workable ideas and strategies for classroom practitioners. I look forward to sharing this book with my students.

—Keith Nikolaus, Educational Leadership, Lipscomb University

As a classroom teacher, I can say that these five interconnected big ideas have enhanced the way I teach and the way my students take charge of their own learning potential.

—Kelly D. Rose, classroom teacher, Bristol, Virginia

The concepts in this book have helped me become a more effective teacher. My students have become metacognitive learners who know that learning changes their brains, and their motivation has soared!

—Diane Dahl,
classroom teacher and edublogger of *For the Love of Teaching*

Five Big Ideas for Effective Teaching

Connecting Mind, Brain,
and Education Research
to Classroom Practice

SECOND EDITION

Donna Wilson
Marcus Conyers

Foreword by Robert Calfee

TEACHERS COLLEGE PRESS

TEACHERS COLLEGE | COLUMBIA UNIVERSITY

NEW YORK AND LONDON

Published by Teachers College Press, 1234 Amsterdam Avenue, New York, NY 10027

Cover image by CLIPAREA / Shutterstock.

Library of Congress Cataloging-in-Publication Data

Names: Wilson, Donna (Psychologist), author. | Conyers, Marcus, author.
Title: Five big ideas for effective teaching : connecting mind, brain, and education research to classroom practice / Donna Wilson, Marcus Conyers ; Foreword by Robert Calfee.
Description: Second edition. | New York : Teachers College Press, [2020] | Includes bibliographical references and index.
Identifiers: LCCN 2020001572 (print) | LCCN 2020001573 (ebook) | ISBN 9780807763773 (hardcover) | ISBN 9780807763766 (paperback) | ISBN 9780807778500 (ebook)
Subjects: LCSH: Learning, Psychology of. | Learning—Physiological aspects. | Brain.
Classification: LCC LB1060 .W553 2020 (print) | LCC LB1060 (ebook) | DDC 370.15/23—dc23
LC record available at https://lccn.loc.gov/2020001572
LC ebook record available at https://lccn.loc.gov/2020001573

ISBN 978-0-8077-6376-6 (paper)
ISBN 978-0-8077-6377-3 (hardcover)
ISBN 978-0-8077-7850-0 (ebook)

Printed on acid-free paper
Manufactured in the United States of America

Contents

Foreword

Most people believe that the brain has something to do with learning. Views of the connection among brains, minds, and learning vary widely, however, especially with regard to schooling. Perhaps the most important distinction is the "grading vs. growing" contrast. The grading perspective views students' minds as varying in capacity, from gallon to teaspoon size; schooling is about determining the size of an individual student's mind and then filling it up. The growing perspective begins with a focus on cultivating each mind to the fullest extent, assuming that every individual has substantial and perhaps unlimited potential.

This book is about brains, minds, and schooling, but it is not at all what I expected. Since the advent of brain-imaging techniques in the 1980s, most writing on these topics has focused on the brain, for reasons that are understandable. Innovative imaging techniques take snapshots of blood flow in the brain, the assumption being that areas of mental activity require energy and oxygenation. We can actually see where the brain is working on a particular task! The process is much less intrusive than early studies by Penfield and Jasper (Hebb, 2009) on epileptic patients, who poked around in live and open skulls to see what happened when various areas were stimulated. In any event, I expected lots of fMRI images showing hot and cold regions, and so on.

This book does feature recent advances in brain research, but the "five big ideas" build on more than a century of research across a broad spectrum of disciplines—neurologists and psychologists, cognitivists and computer scientists, researchers and practitioners. The title promises ideas for effective teaching, and the book delivers on this promise, in clear, compelling, and believable prose. This is a book for educators, for policymakers, for parents, and even for presidents. The five big ideas are distributed over five chapters, but I think that the main message can be captured in a single sentence: "Virtually every newborn possesses immense intellectual potential, which can be fully realized given conditions that appropriately engage and support learning."

This claim has been made by other psychologists, generally without reference to the neurophysiology of the brain (e.g., Bloom, 1964; Bruner,

1977). In my presentations to teachers and others (Calfee & Patrick, 1995), I always make the point that "our brains all have unlimited capacity." To be sure, some afflictions run counter to this claim—brain injuries and diseases such as Alzheimer's. But virtually every kindergartner who enters the classroom in our country has a growing, active organ in his or her skull eager to learn from experience. When I make this claim, I am aware that many in my audience may have trouble with this proposition, which I often accompany with a cartoon of an adolescent pleading with a teacher: "Ms. Smith, I'm sorry, but my brain is full!" In fact, however, if you give even passing attention to an event, you will be able to recognize it later. With some deliberate practice, you can come to own it.

A Foreword is supposed to set the stage for readers, to offer suggestions about what to look for. Let me propose that, as you page through this book, you consider implications of the messages for educators, for policymakers, for parents, and for citizens. What would our country and our world look like if the challenge in these pages were accepted? What would it take to make the necessary changes?

The authors build around a few seminal themes—neural plasticity, malleable intelligence, and the role of teachers as shapers of minds for the new worlds that are ahead of us (Martinez, 2000, 2010).

If you are a teacher, a school administrator, or a parent of school-age children, think about the meaning of this work for the pragmatics of the school experience. If students are engaged in compelling projects, if they are learning "really new stuff," if they are working together on demanding tasks, if they respond enthusiastically when you ask "what did you do in school today," if the teacher can tell a good story about progress (formative assessment), then several brains are growing like crazy.

The Flat World (Darling-Hammond, 2010, Friedman, 2007) now appearing on the horizon poses both challenges and opportunities. For some, the question is about who will win the competition: the United States, China, India, the Muslim world? The better question is, who will manage collaboration? We need to take better care of our brains (an important message in the book is attention to the physical well-being of the brain) and of our minds. And notice that, although the book focuses on the schooling of young people, we all have brains and minds that are marvelously malleable, including teachers and even administrators.

—Robert Calfee, Stanford University

Acknowledgments

Many thanks to our colleagues at universities, colleges, and other educational institutions across the country and internationally who generously agreed to preview this book: Tracey Tokuhama-Espinosa, Daniel C. Miller, Reuven Feuerstein, Marcia Stewart, Brett D. Jones, Karin Harman James, Keith Nikolaus, Ruth Burgess, Reem Kobrsi, and Nancy Romain. With some reviewers, we feel as if we are continuing conversations that began at the Brain, Neurosciences and Education Special Interest Group sessions of the American Educational Research Association (AERA) 2012 meeting with Debby Zambo; at the AERA Teacher Education (Division K) Workgroup meeting in 2011 with Susan Benner and Tanner LeBaron Wallace; at Donna's presentation at the American Association of Colleges for Teacher Education (AACTE) 2012 conference with Deborah Schussler, Lisa J. Lucas, and Marjorie Anderson; at our presentation at the International Association for Cognitive Education and Psychology 2011 conference with Linda Rittner, David Martin, and Katherine Greenberg; and with Martha Hopkins, with whom Marcus has presented at National Board for Professional Teaching Standards conferences. We would like to thank graduates of the brain-based teaching programs at Nova Southeastern University who teach at the K–12 and community college levels and took time to serve as reviewers: Diane Dahl, Kelly Rose, and Douglas Stewart. In addition, we appreciate the work of the two anonymous reviewers who looked over our manuscript early in its development.

The pioneering work of theorists Reuven Feuerstein and Robert Sternberg has informed and inspired our own. We also share what we have learned in these pages from Robert Sylwester, who has brought clarity to the field of education in connecting the implications of brain science to classroom practice and who worked with us on our Scholarships for Teachers in Action Research with the Florida Department of Education.

We gratefully acknowledge the hundreds of teachers who earned their graduate degrees in brain-based teaching and then shared with us the positive results they and their students are achieving in their classrooms. Their stories inspire us. Throughout this book, you will find passages from thoughtful teachers who are applying their knowledge of the five big ideas presented here in their professional practice. They teach in public, private, and virtual K–12 schools and in community colleges throughout the United States. The remarkable teachers whose stories are featured include Diane Dahl, Theresa A. Dodge, Paul Farmer, Donna Garland, Edna Gibson, Allison Groulx, D'Jon McNair, Tonya S. Moore, Margaret (Meg) Norris, Kelly D. Rose, Melissa M. Smith, Douglas Stewart, and Gretchen Vermiglio.

We are enormously thankful for contributions from our amazing editor, Karen Bankston, and associates Diane Franklin and Elizabeth Johnson. They always get the job done well, on time, every time, despite our obsession with adding new research all along the way! We had the privilege to work with Acquisitions Editor Jean Ward and Managing Production Editor Karl Nyberg, and we thank them and their colleagues at Teachers College Press for the care they have taken in presenting our work.

Finally, we acknowledge the significance of being able to work together on this project. Writing this book has reminded us how much we both enjoy constantly learning together, celebrating findings, and grappling with how best to share them to contribute to forward movement in this profession we both love.

Preface

We are pleased to launch this second edition of *Five Big Ideas for Effective Teaching: Connecting Mind, Brain, and Education Research to Classroom Practice*. Since our book was first published 7 years ago, it has been assigned as required reading in teacher education (including educational psychology courses across the United States and Canada), used in professional development programs, shared in teacher reading groups, and cited in many education texts, journals, blogs, and websites. We have shared insights from these pages in presentations in North America, Europe, Asia, South Africa, the Middle East, and Australia. Key concepts from this text have been applied in a national teacher-training initiative across Jamaica.

We are gratified and inspired by responses from educators, who have shared with us how the five big ideas framework—which connects practical applications to foundational research on neuroplasticity, learning potential, malleable intelligence, body-brain connections, and metacognition—informs and guides their work.

Central to this framework is neural plasticity, the fact that learning changes the structure and function of the human brain (Mateos-Aparicio & Rodríguez-Moreno, 2019). The capacity for our brains to evolve throughout our lifetimes is something we have been sharing with students and educators for 20-plus years. Explicitly teaching learners about their own brain plasticity and the malleability of intelligence can support the development of growth mindsets and can lead to better student outcomes (Dweck, 2019).

In conjunction with neural plasticity, we also stress the importance of metacognition—an awareness of how we think as a means of improving how we learn. Importantly, there has been a considerable rise in interest in research on metacognition and the need to translate this research into practice (Kleitman & Narciss, 2019). There is an ever-increasing range of evidence supporting that metacognition has a significant impact on student achievement (Perry, Lundie, & Golder, 2019). To bring this concept to life in the classroom, we share several practical strategies for teaching students to "drive their brains."

There is an increasing understanding about the positive impact of supporting the whole learner—what we describe as the Body-Brain System. Bolstering this view is recent research confirming the beneficial effects of physical activity on brain function and performance (Doherty & Miravalles, 2019). Additionally, creating classroom environments and experiences that support social and emotional learning can have a positive impact on student learning and well-being outcomes. As researchers Immordino-Yang, Darling-Hammond, and Krone state, "When given adequate opportunity, support, and encouragement, children naturally think, feel emotions, and engage with their social and physical worlds. And these patterns of thoughts, feelings, and engagement organize brain development" (2018, p. 1).

Publishing this second edition, therefore, provides an opportunity to share current findings in ever-expanding fields of research connected to how people learn, and to expand discussions on practical teaching and learning strategies that recent studies have found to be effective in enhancing students' learning:

- We've added new sections on social and emotional learning to Chapters 4 and 5 to explore exciting findings on how guiding students to develop cognitive, affective, and behavioral competencies can improve their personal relationships, peer and teacher interactions, and academic outcomes.
- We explain recent advances in understanding how brain plasticity extends over the life span, how working memory supports students to think quicker and tackle more complex learning tasks, and how teaching students about growth mindsets can power learning.
- We weave in our own work over the past 6 years to synthesize the science behind the power of positivity, learning potential, metacognition, the social aspects of cognition, and the Body-Brain System for classroom and school applications.
- We've taken note of feedback and input from readers and reviewers in some structural revisions to make this text more reader-friendly.
- The reference list has been expanded with relevant new publications.

As with the first edition of this book, we hope you enjoy exploring the five big ideas framework and applying it in your professional practice—and we look forward to hearing from you!

Introduction

Over the past 20-plus years, we have worked with tens of thousands of practicing and prospective teachers, all seeking to discover more about how students learn so that they may become better teachers. Some are pursuing undergraduate degrees to establish a firm pedagogical foundation as they begin their teaching careers. Others, many in graduate programs, are veteran educators looking to find answers to persistent challenges in their classrooms and to rekindle the inspiration and motivation that steered them into their profession in the first place.

These teachers chose their vocation with the aim of making a positive difference in the lives of their students but have come to realize that the path to teaching and learning is arduous and full of obstacles and potential detours. They remain committed to this endeavor and understand how necessary it is—both for the futures of their students individually and for what they will contribute to society—and they want to equip themselves with the most effective tools and strategies to accomplish this work.

TEACHER EDUCATION AND PROFESSIONAL DEVELOPMENT: PREPARING, DEVELOPING, AND SUPPORTING TEACHERS BY PROVIDING THEM WITH A FIRM FOUNDATION

The big ideas presented in this text constitute some of the core elements of a framework for learning and teaching that supports all students to become self-directed learners capable of developing 21st century competencies to achieve their full potential in school and in life. The framework and ideas presented in this text are in alignment with a new direction for education proposed by Darling-Hammond, Flook, Cook-Harvey, Barron, and Osher in the article "Implications for Educational Practice of the Science of Learning and Development" (2019). What we do in school changes the way children think and may well determine what choices they have throughout life, so how we go about it is of paramount importance.

Effective teaching takes advantage of our framework of five big ideas, which are explored in this text:

1. Neurocognitive plasticity, renewed attention to the discovery that learning changes the physical structure of the brain as it changes the way students think;
2. The learning potential of every child, or the recognition that nearly every child can learn and improve his or her academic performance;
3. The modifiability of intelligence, which stands at odds with the persistent myth that intelligence is fixed;
4. The role of emotions, the body, and the brain in learning;
5. The need for explicit instruction on metacognition, or thinking about one's thinking with the aim of enhancing learning.

These big ideas are closely interconnected. They form a synergy that provides firm grounding for the implications of mind, brain, and education research in classroom practice. The transdisciplinary field of mind, brain, and education brings together research from psychology, neuroscience, and educational practice. In this text we also present research on the importance of social and emotional learning, physical activity, nutrition, and the development of a growth mindset as key factors that support learning.

Along with the essential concepts at the center of this text, our goal is to underscore that, more than any other school-based component—more than the choice of curriculum, the age and condition of the school building, and the socioeconomic background of the student population—the effectiveness of teachers makes the biggest difference in how well and how much students learn (Committee on the Study of Teacher Preparation Programs in the United States & National Research Council, 2010; Darling-Hammond & Rothman, 2011; OECD, 2018; Spector, 2019). Thus, preparing, developing, and supporting educators with the tools to guide every child to achieve more of his or her potential must be a foundational part of the system of learning. Tokuhama-Espinosa suggests that integrating findings from neuroscience and psychology into teacher education and professional development can help teachers develop valuable understandings about learning, teaching, and the cognitive and emotional aspects of education: "Teachers who can use information from neuroscience and psychology will be the real game changers in the decades to come" (2011b, final paragraph).

This research must be translated into practical applications and strategies for classroom use. As Barber and Mourshed note in their 2007 international study of high-performing school systems, educational reforms cannot succeed without "knowledge precise enough for teachers to understand how to apply it in their own classroom" (p. 27). Berliner (2009) has called for closing what he calls the "great disconnect" between the abundance of cognitive theory and research and its application in the classroom. A researcher-practitioner gap in the field of mind, brain, and education science continues to be a challenge (Hobbis et al., 2019). The aim of this text is to empower teachers with our original framework and practical strategies for realizing a new vision for education. Since the first edition publication of this book in 2013, other researchers, such as Darling-Hammond and colleagues (2019), also advocate for an approach to education grounded in the science of learning and human development. In this text, we present a practical guide to some of the most essential implications of mind, brain, and education research that teachers can use to increase their understanding of how students learn and to explore ways to enhance student achievement. Furthermore, an understanding of these big ideas can be used by policymakers and those who influence and advocate for educational changes that support 21st century teacher education and practice.

Every day, teachers walk into the classroom as the most influential school-related factor in helping students achieve academic success. It's important that they be equipped with tools that will enhance learning opportunities for all students. By using effective practices and strategies, teachers can inspire students not only to think but also to innovate, to reflect, and to work in collaboration with others. They key is to stimulate and guide students' development so that they achieve even more than expected (OECD, 2018). Educational reforms likely to have the most significant impact on student achievement focus on recruiting the best candidates to become teachers (i.e., people with high literacy skills and a commitment to pursue and put into practice a rigorous, research-based teacher education program) and on preparing and supporting teachers with opportunities for continuous learning and career development. Educators in training and those just beginning their careers must be willing to work continually to improve their teaching practice and to collaborate with colleagues in supportive professional learning communities. This is true for all teachers, but especially for the newest generation joining the profession, who especially value feedback, opportunities to interact with their peers, and professional development geared to their needs (Coggshall, Behrstock-Sherratt, & Drill, 2011).

If teacher education and schools and districts aim to increase student achievement, they must strive to ensure that all elements of the educational system work together productively in support of that goal, all firmly grounded and united in an understanding of how learning happens.

This book is primarily written for teachers, teacher educators, professional developers, administrators, and policymakers. We hope it will guide you to look for ways to enhance your practice and to advocate for necessary systems changes in your school, district, and state and at the national level, as well as in your own practice. Add your voice to the local and national conversations about what works in education.

TEACHERS AS LEARNERS: ENHANCING MINDSET AND METHODS

Everything in these pages about how students learn also applies to teachers. Improving your teaching practice is a continuous process of learning from and applying research, learning from and with colleagues, engaging in professional development, and taking on instructional leadership roles so you can learn even more as you mentor others about what works in the classroom. Many of the most effective teachers continue to learn throughout their careers and apply what they learn with their students.

As they continue their journey of learning, effective teachers embody what has been termed the *growth mindset* (Dweck, 2016, 2019), a belief system that has been shown to result in successful learning outcomes among those who personify it.

The importance of teachers as learners also relates to the core concept of metacognition, or thinking about your thinking as a path to improve learning. In teacher education, metacognition is embodied in the need for reflection on your teaching and a willingness to identify weaknesses or gaps in your teaching practice as a first step toward improvement (Wilson & Conyers, 2016). Thinking about your teaching is best accomplished through a combination of self-reflection and collaboration with colleagues sharing what they have found to be challenging and what strategies seem to be most successful.

A useful metaphor that captures why we teach is the joy we experience when we see the lightbulbs pop on above students' heads in that instant when learning occurs. Growth-minded teachers who believe in the power of lifelong learning have those "Ah-ha!" moments too. During a weeklong workshop at a national gathering of teachers, a director of curriculum and instruction from a Louisiana parish described the workshop as "a laboratory for learning." Drawing on Piaget's conception about how humans deal with internal conflict, the educator went on to say, "We're in this disequilibration of learning and are learning how to be vulnerable together and how to describe the process of learning itself." That was indeed our goal—to problem-solve aloud together as a community of learners the issues teachers faced alone in their classrooms. Each of the teachers in the workshop had gotten to some seemingly insurmountable challenge in his or her practice. Together, they all put aside the notion that, as teachers, they must have all the answers, and they acknowledged the value of sharing with and learning from each other. The teachers walked away from the workshop invigorated and inspired, with useful new ideas and strategies and a renewal of their belief in the power of learning—of guiding their students' potential to learn something new by activating their own. This example demonstrates two more big ideas in action that we will explore in this text, that of metacognition and social cognition, or the power of learning together.

FIVE BIG IDEAS FROM RESEARCH TO APPLICATION

This text begins with an overview of the challenges and opportunities facing teachers today as they develop their skills in the "adaptive expertise" needed to keep pace in their ever-evolving profession (Prologue). Synthesizing research from the field of mind, brain, and education studies, we have distilled five big ideas that can help all teachers—both new and veteran—become more effective in the classroom and increase student achievement. We have joined relevant research of recent years with the theories of previous decades, translating it all into practical approaches that can be implemented immediately in the classroom. These big ideas include brain plasticity (Chapter 1), learning potential (Chapter 2), theories of intelligence (Chapter 3), the interrelationship of emotions, the body, and the brain in support of academic gains (Chapter 4), and metacognition (Chapter 5). Each of these chapters incorporates additional elements—from the impact of teacher expectations on student performance, to research on learning motivation, to the power of learning together (for students and in support of teachers' professional development)—that form a conceptual framework for teaching and learning in ways that reflect implications of mind, brain, and education research. Chapter 6 addresses and debunks the "myths" associated with the big ideas explored in earlier chapters, and Chapter 7 emphasizes the importance of teachers continuing to learn about advances in research and applications through formal and informal professional learning communities.

Throughout this text you will find examples of the practical theory presented here in action, in the classrooms of teachers who have graduated from a graduate degree program in brain-based teaching. As Miller and DeFina state, "The goal of brain-based education is to translate brain research into the optimization of the school learning environment" (2010, p. 142). Many teachers have shared their stories with us of implementing what they learned in their graduate studies with their own students. In Georgia, special education teacher D'Jon McNair speaks of being "stunned" by the discovery that children can be taught cognitive strategies to improve their thinking and school performance. Texas teacher Diane Dahl demonstrates how blogging and sharing reflections on and results of reading strategies can result in networking on a global scale. California teacher Edna Gibson describes cognitive strategies her 8th-grade students find useful in making meaning and aiding in recall of science concepts. These real-life adaptive experts are wielding powerful tools to help each of their students realize his or her full potential.

We consider it our privilege to have worked with teachers like these. Our interactions with educators, especially with teachers in the graduate degree program in brain-based teaching that we designed with Nova Southeastern University, provide many opportunities for conversations about what works in their classrooms, about their professional challenges and successes. Our approach to teacher education has been collaborative, allowing us, as one teacher put it, to "practice what we teach" in translating implications of mind, brain, and education research into practical theory and classroom strategies for learning and teaching.

In addition to the stories and examples from practicing teachers, presented in the "From Teachers for Teachers" boxes, several other special features of this text are designed to help you apply in your teaching practice the research and educational theory explored in these pages:

- Each chapter begins with a question intended to guide readers to activate and examine their prior knowledge and beliefs about the subject matter at hand.

- The "In Sum" boxes are not chapter summaries but instead emphasize key points in each section.
- If you would like to explore the subject matter presented in each chapter in more depth, the "To Learn More" boxes suggest helpful books, professional journal articles, and other resources on theory and practice.
- The "From Teachers for Teachers" features provide real-life examples of practicing teachers' perspectives and use of the principles and strategies set out in this text in their classrooms.
- Several chapters include a focus on applications based on mind, brain, and education research in special sections titled "From Research to Classroom Practice."
- These chapters conclude with a "What's the Big Idea?" summary, drawing on the title of this book and our aim to explore five big ideas from mind, brain, and education research that matter most to teachers.
- The chapters end with a list of useful terms and "Questions for Reflection" on the subject matter.

And now on to five truly big ideas in education!

Challenges and Opportunities in 21st Century Schooling

Teachers make a difference. Indeed, of all the factors that education leaders can control, the quality of teaching has perhaps the greatest potential effect.

—Committee on the Study of Teacher Preparation Programs in the United States and the National Research Council, *Preparing Teachers: Building Evidence for Sound Policy*, p. 9

What do you think represents the most significant challenge and greatest opportunity in education today?

Every day we are inspired by stories of teachers who are applying the implications of research and the latest strategies in the classroom, and by the students who are benefiting from these innovative approaches. These teachers' commitment to their students' success is exemplary, and their enthusiasm is evident in the stories they share: the Oklahoma 2nd-graders who demonstrate their favorite reading comprehension strategies for students in New Zealand through a video blog, the Georgia middle-schoolers who are excited to show how metacognition helps them take charge of and improve their academic performance, or the California 8th-graders who use various strategies to aid in meaning-making and recall of key science concepts. The best teachers also share how they apply what they have learned about the science of learning to their own professional and personal lives.

But these kinds of stories too seldom make their way into the public discourse about education. Instead, we are told by policymakers and news organizations that our school system is not what it once was: The United States lags far behind other countries, the achievement gap for poor and minority students continues to widen, and schools cannot meet rigorous new standards. Yet the teachers in the classrooms described here and throughout this book are committed to making a positive difference in guiding their students to achieve more of their academic potential. They approach their work with confidence and enthusiasm because they know they have the tools needed to improve their practice, and they are committed to ongoing learning necessary to keep pace with the changing demands of their profession.

In 2000, the National Research Council report *How People Learn* (Bransford, Brown, & Cocking, 2000) highlighted the ways in which learning changes the brain and suggested approaches for increasing student achievement. Since then, a few universities have begun offering degree programs for educators that combine mind, brain, and education research; among them are Harvard University; Nova Southeastern University; and The University of Texas, Arlington (Sparks, 2012). Recently, a collaborative group of teacher educators, Deans for Impact, launched The Learning by Scientific Design Network, a 2-year initiative (2019–2021) bringing together six educator-preparation programs designed to ensure that novice teachers understand basic principles of learning science and incorporate them into their teaching practice (Deans for Impact, 2015–2020). Journals such as *Scientific American Mind* and *Mind, Brain, and Education* share research from this new field. This transdisciplinary approach is transforming the way we think about education.

Efforts to consider teaching and learning in modern scientific terms have of late been referred to as the "science of learning" (Blakemore, 2018). As a component of growing scholarship in the learning sciences, mind, brain, and education studies began to develop around the world in the early 21st century (Tokuhama-Espinosa, 2017). The International Mind, Brain, and Education Society (IMBES) was formed in 2007, in part, to provide "support for the interest in brain-based education" (Miller & DeFina, 2010, p. 142); the IMBES website (imbes.org) sets out its mission to "facilitate cross-cultural collaboration in biology, education and the cognitive and developmental sciences." Major conferences in countries like Japan, the United States, and the United Kingdom provide opportunities for researchers and practitioners across disciplines, including the cognitive sciences, neurobiology, and education, to share knowledge and establish new ways of working together (Battro, Fischer, & Lena, 2008).

To Learn More

In the article "Applying the Science of Learning in the Classroom," Paul Howard-Jones and his colleagues (2018) share some ideas related to the science of learning that can be applied in the classroom. This article is retrievable from impact.chartered.college/article/howard-jones-applying-science-learning-classroom/

Scholars working in the field of mind, brain, and education are often characterized by a willingness to share knowledge with others outside their original disciplines, a recognition of the need to adapt professional language in order to communicate with others outside their immediate field, and a belief that linking information across disciplines is beneficial for themselves and others (Tokuhama-Espinosa, 2011a).

The mind, brain, and education field includes findings from educational neuroscience, sometimes referred to as *neuroeducation*, which has been defined as "an emerging effort to integrate neuroscience methods, particularly functional neuroimaging, with behavioral methods to address issues of learning and instruction" (Varma, McCandliss, & Schwartz, 2008, p. 140). Practitioners may also draw from the discipline of school neuropsychology, an emerging area within school psychology (Miller, 2010). Research and principles from these fields have practical implications for classroom instruction. Especially as complementary insights continue to emerge from across neuroscience, psychology, and education, this is an incredibly exciting time to be an educator. While we do face challenges, the knowledge we need to overcome them is within our grasp—and we have every reason to hope and believe that, given the proper approach, our schools and classrooms can fulfill their promise of helping every child learn and succeed.

IN SUPPORT OF A GOLD STANDARD
FOR EDUCATIONAL PROFESSIONALS:
TEACHERS AS ADAPTIVE EXPERTS AND LIFELONG LEARNERS

Educational researchers Hatano and Inagaki describe the best teachers as "adaptive experts" (National Academies of Science, Engineering, and Medicine, 2018). The beginning of a school term brings a new group of students, each with a unique set of individual talents and learning needs. The teacher's job is to maximize each student's academic progress by identifying his or her strengths and weaknesses and implementing the appropriate learning and teaching strategies, all while keeping pace with new educational materials and innovations and staying on the lookout for "teachable moments." As Hattie notes:

> It is surely easy to see how it is tempting for teachers to re-do the successes of the previous year, to judge students in terms of last year's cohort, and to insist on an orderly progression through that which has worked before. It is required of teachers, however, that they re-invent their passion in their teaching; they must identify and accommodate the differences brought with each new cohort of students, react to the learning as it occurs (every moment of learning is different), and treat the current cohort of students as if it is the first time that the teacher has taught a class—as it is for the students with this teacher and this curricula. (2009, p. 1)

Instilling the flexibility and commitment to continuous learning required of an adaptive expert has been called "the gold standard for teacher education" (National Academies of Science, Engineering, and Medicine, 2018). Effective teacher training should prepare educational professionals for a lifetime of learning as they, over time, become more efficient and innovative in their work, willing to rework their core thinking, beliefs, and competencies in order to adapt proven strategies for use with their students.

CHALLENGES IN THE CURRENT SYSTEM
OF TEACHER EDUCATION AND SCHOOLING

Our aim is to help set aside two primary obstacles that may keep preservice and practicing teachers from achieving the highest standards of their profession (Hammerness et al., 2005): (1) deeply ingrained misconceptions about effective teaching that may go uncorrected, a problem Lortie (1975) called "the apprenticeship of observation," and (2) overly simplistic conceptions of the complex act of teaching.

Young people who head to college to study geology, accounting, or medicine expect to start at the beginning and learn a whole new set of knowledge, skills, and behaviors required of their profession. In contrast, many students of education, having already spent 12 years in classroom, begin their training with preconceived and often simplistic notions about what it means to be a teacher, and those core beliefs may persist throughout their undergraduate years and into practice even if they are incorrect or outmoded (Hattie, 2009; Lortie, 1975; Pajares, 1992). Kennedy contends that many people—future teachers among them—believe that "teaching is fundamentally a self-evident practice" (1999, p. 54), that educators who know their subject matter should be able to pass it on to students easily once they learn a few simple classroom management techniques and adapt those tactics to suit their own personal styles.

In reality, teaching is an endlessly complex endeavor, and much of what we know now about student learning and effective instruction is based on implications from psychology, neuroscience, and education research that has been reported in recent decades. That means that educational practices that date back to the childhoods of many current preservice and practicing educators, such as tracking students based on perceived potential to learn and learning through rote memorization and filling out worksheets, has since been demonstrated to be ineffective.

Putting behind perceptions about teaching you have learned in your own "apprenticeship of observation" allows you to base your practice on what is understood by the profession as a whole, rather than just one's own experience. Moving from assumptions based largely on personal experiences as a student to an understanding of teaching based on professional standards and research requires that teachers become effective learners able to go beyond earlier conceptions of what it means to learn and teach. Our aim in this text is to help support the development of an understanding of and appreciation for effective instruction—and for the pursuit of knowledge that must become an enduring part of your career as a teacher as you put these instructional philosophies and strategies to work in your classroom. Feiman-Nemser evokes the power of big ideas like those presented in this text to inspire teachers and teachers-in-training to set aside outmoded perspectives about teaching and learning:

> The likelihood that professional study will affect what powerful early experiences have inscribed on the mind and emotions will depend on its power to cultivate images of the possible and desirable and to forge commitments to make those images a reality. (2012, p. 32)

The need for preservice and practicing teachers to reexamine any possible preconceptions about the nature of intelligence exemplifies this necessary and continual pursuit. We will explore the still-unfolding research and theories about intelligence as malleable, modifiable, and multifaceted, which stands in clear contrast to previous and persistent views of fixed intelligence. Clearly, this about-face has far-reaching implications for classroom practice, but an adequate introduction to these findings and classroom applications may be lacking in teacher preparation and professional development programs. Lusk and Jones (2011) examined educational psychology textbooks with the aim of comparing how they covered various theories of intelligence as a basis for classroom practice; the researchers identified the need for more in-depth coverage of both theory and application to provide educators with a solid foundation to guide their teaching. Our aim is to help fill that gap and to link a practical understanding of intelligence, potential, and plasticity with functional frameworks for increasing student achievement, putting the brain and body to work in learning, and powering learning through metacognition.

TOOLS FOR LEARNING AND TEACHING IN THE 21st CENTURY

Not only have the research and theory about effective instruction evolved in recent years, but so have the challenges for which we need to prepare today's students. When our current system for schooling was designed in the early 1900s, "only 5 percent of jobs required specialized knowledge and skill; today about 70 percent of jobs are 'knowledge work' positions" requiring the capability to acquire and apply specialized information, creatively manage tasks, and use advanced technologies (Darling-Hammond & Oakes, 2019, pp. 1–2). A common lament in communities is that "kids are different today." That is certainly true, but then so is the world around them, as is indicated by a massive change in the job market. In addition to gaining the classic reading, writing, and arithmetic skills at the core of traditional education, children who are coming of age in the 21st century must be equipped with the social-emotional, critical thinking, and problem-solving skills they will need to continue learning and adapting to the demands of their work and personal lives. In the early to mid-20th century, 1 in 20 jobs required specialized knowledge and thinking skills, compared with 14 in 20 jobs today; yet many schools continue to rely on a curriculum designed for that earlier era (Darling-Hammond, 2010). As defined by the international group of stakeholders involved in the OECD Future of Education and Skills 2030 project, skills are "the ability and capacity to carry out processes and to be able to use one's knowledge in a responsible way to achieve a goal" (OECD, 2019, p. 1). In that regard, skills are an integral part of achieving competency, a holistic concept that also includes the mobilization of knowledge, attitudes, and values to meet complex demands (OECD, 2019).

The OECD Learning Compass 2030 identifies three different types of skills (OECD, 2018):

- cognitive and metacognitive skills, which include critical thinking, creative thinking, learning-to-learn, and self-regulation;
- social and emotional skills, which include empathy, self-efficacy, responsibility, and collaboration; and
- practical and physical skills, which include using new information and communication technology devices (OECD, 2019).

Significant changes in the American education system are needed so that virtually all students can learn these skills. Practical understandings for teaching these skills are among the big ideas examined in this text.

BRAIN PLASTICITY, POTENTIAL, AND INTELLIGENCE

Chapters 1, 2, and 3 explore individually three of the teaching essentials presented in this text. It may be useful to consider them initially together because they are closely interrelated, all drawing support in research amassed in recent years. "More has been learned about the brain in the last 10 years than in the previous 200 years," Restak asserted in 2009 (p. 5), and new technologies continue to shed light on how the brain develops, functions, and recovers from injury. This research has overturned a long-held assumption that the brain is a finished product at birth or at least by early childhood. Rather, the brain is plastic—its physical structure changes as a result of learning and experiences *across the entire life span* (Merzenich, 2013; Mateos-Aparicio & Rodríguez-Moreno, 2019; National Academies of Science, Engineering, and Medicine, 2018). Furthermore, learning novel and complex skills may help keep the brain healthy

(Nussbaum, 2010). We explore the science behind brain plasticity in further detail in Chapter 1.

An understanding of brain plasticity has profound implications for the classroom. New knowledge can help all teachers set aside any preconceived ideas they may have brought to their teacher training from their own days as students in Lortie's "apprenticeship of observation." Hardiman and Denckla argue that "growth in understanding about brain plasticity has created a completely new way to think about how learning and achievement take place in the education of children and youth" (2010, p. 4). We propose that this new way of thinking can and should lead to positive changes in the way teachers operate in the classroom. An understanding of plasticity helps teachers understand that every brain is unique and that current performance on a task simply reflects what that unique brain has acquired thus far—not its ultimate potential to succeed at that task (Wilson & Conyers, 2016, 2020).

In fact, an understanding of plasticity forces us to rethink what we mean when we talk about student potential, or indeed anyone's potential in life. As we discuss in Chapter 2, *potential* can be thought of as the neurocognitive capacity to improve one's performance in a particular area. Several factors influence whether an individual achieves his or her potential, including the environment (nurturing relationships, encouragement, and high expectations from teachers help maximize student potential), opportunities to practice, and a willingness to put in hard work. These factors—not genetics alone—make an enormous difference in an individual's capacity to succeed at a task.

Similarly, plasticity may help us to reconceptualize intelligence. While genes certainly play a role, research indicates that intelligence, like potential, is not fixed at birth; on the contrary, intelligence is malleable and can increase (Dweck, 2019; Feuerstein, Feuerstein, & Falik, 2010; Sternberg, Jarvin, & Grigorenko, 2015). When teachers align instruction to the ways in which students learn, virtually every student can progress to higher levels. We define intelligence and examine theories of intelligence and strategies through which teachers may be able to increase students' intelligence in Chapter 3.

When teachers have an accurate understanding of plasticity, potential, and intelligence, they may be more likely to embody growth mindsets and a belief system that all their students can learn—and, therefore, to implement strategies that focus on improving knowledge and skills. Furthermore, students who understand that learning changes the brain and that they can get smarter demonstrate higher levels of motivation, growth-mindedness, and academic achievement (Dweck, 2016, 2019). Formative assessments facilitate this incremental learning, or the steady academic progress achieved by purposefully building on what students have learned and providing support when they struggle.

From Teachers for Teachers

Joining in Dana Foundation's annual observance of Brain Awareness Week (dana.org/brainweek), Diane Dahl and her class of 2nd-graders explored the senses as the gateway of information input to the brain. They learned how the brain interprets visual input and discovered from brain scan images how different parts of the brain work during different tasks. They also created protective "helmets" for eggs, tested in a 10-foot drop, to underscore the importance of preventing brain injury. At the end of the week, student Josh reported, "I learned what our brain is and that it can help you learn. It's fun to make connections in your brain."

THE BODY-BRAIN SYSTEM

The fourth big idea explored in this text focuses on how the body and brain work together to support school performance. An understanding of this interaction equips teachers and students with a powerful tool to increase learning motivation and achievement and attain more of their potential—and to make the case against efforts to cut back physical education to carve out more time for academic learning and test preparation. In this text we primarily focus on factors that that are more school-based, rather than home-based. For example, there is relatively less emphasis on nutrition and sleep, although these are very important influences on learning.

Body-Brain System refers to the ways in which the brain and body work together to enhance learning. All emotions, thoughts, and behaviors flow from this system. This concept actually encompasses several systems—the nervous system, the cardiopulmonary system, even the digestive system—that contribute to readiness to learn, attention, retention, motivation, and a positive outlook about one's ability to achieve. Chapter 4 presents research on several aspects of the Body-Brain System, including the impact of students' emotions and social lives, physical activity, nutrition, and sleep on learning.

Many believe that emotions are the gateway to learning and thinking (Davidson, 2012; Frederickson, 2009; Immordino-Yang, 2016; Sylwester, 2005). As affective neuroscientist Mary Helen Immordino-Yang (2016) points out, an emotional connection is essential to learning, and emotions have a powerful influence on the cognitive system. For example, students in a low-stress, high-challenge, positive, and collaborative environment tend to learn well. Hardiman and Denckla note that "teachers who understand that the brain's emotional wiring connects with the prefrontal cortex—the center for higher-order thought—would appreciate the need to provide their students with a positive emotional connection to learning" (2010, p. 6).

The power of positive emotions has become a focus of positive psychology, a field that has emerged in the past 2 decades and aims to help children and adults flourish (Seligman, 2011, 2018b). The role of positivity, or the process of experiencing positive emotions, in enhancing creative thinking and problem solving has been explored in the education literature (Frederickson, 2009; Gilman, Huebner, & Furlong, 2009; Woolfolk Hoy, Hoy, & Kurz, 2008). By developing heartfelt positivity, teachers and students alike can experience more growth and creativity and become far more resilient in difficult times. Frederickson asserts:

> The potential for life-draining negativity lies within you just as does the potential for life giving positivity. You have more say than you think about which you feel and when. The treasure of your own positivity is waiting. You can tip the scales to unleash your life's potential to flourish. (2009, p. 11)

Studies in positive psychology demonstrate the importance of modeling and fostering optimism in the classroom; positivity can result not only in increased student achievement but also in greater capacity for teachers to flourish (Germuth, 2012b; Harman & Germuth, 2012; Seligman, 2011; Conyers & Wilson, 2016). In fact, a 2011 meta-analysis by Durlak,

Weissberg, Dymnicki, Taylor, and Schellinger found that students whose schooling incorporated instruction to develop competencies in social and emotional learning (SEL) experienced significant academic gains (of 11 percentile points) over students who did not receive this type of instruction.

Regular physical activity and proper nutrition are also key components of the Body-Brain System (Conyers & Wilson, 2015b), helping to improve learning and enhance positive changes in the brain. Exercise is a powerful medicine for mood. In fact, a study by Duke University researchers suggests that exercise may be more effective than medication as a long-term solution to alleviate mild to moderate depression (Traver & Sargent, 2011). Exercise also stimulates the production of brain-derived neurotrophic factor, or BDNF, which helps neurons and synapses grow (Liu & Nusslock, 2018). Students exposed to a systematic exercise program not only achieved high levels of wellness but also performed among the best in the world in math and science. Proper nutrition similarly has a powerful influence on cognitive performance. Studies indicate that good nutrition can enhance student achievement, reduce classroom behavior problems, and increase the quality of higher-order thinking (CDC, 2014; Nussbaum, 2010).

METACOGNITION

The fifth big idea is metacognition, which we unpack in Chapter 5. By guiding students to "think about their thinking" with the aim of improving learning, teachers can give their students a gift that lasts a lifetime (Wilson & Conyers, 2016). Hattie (2012) describes teaching as a process of creating change in the student's cognitive system. Indeed, a good deal of evidence indicates that going to school has a positive effect on students' cognitive abilities—even when the emphasis is only on basic skills like reading and writing: "American research from the first half of the 20th century . . . showed schooling's influence on children's general cognitive abilities beyond specific skills and factual knowledge" (Baker, Salinas, & Eslinger, 2012, p. 7). When one considers the dramatic expansion of schooling in this country—only half of school-aged children were enrolled in school 100 years ago (Baker et al., 2012)—it seems clear that a larger population is developing cognitive skills than ever before.

In fact, research has shown that IQ scores have increased from one generation to the next in 30 countries around the world, including the United States. Called the "Flynn effect" for the researcher who first reported this trend (Flynn, 1987), the exact cause of this rapid increase is unknown, but scholars speculate that education has played a significant role:

> It seems likely that the ultimate cause of IQ gains is the Industrial Revolution, which produced a need for increased intellectual skills that modern societies somehow rose to meet. The intermediate causes of IQ gains may include such factors as a more favorable ratio of adults to children, better schooling, more cognitively demanding jobs, and more cognitively challenging leisure. (Nisbett et al., 2012, p. 12)

Such findings provide hope that education is already doing a great deal to build students' cognitive skills. Yet, as we discuss in greater detail later in this chapter, the demands of today's educational and workforce systems require students to continue developing ever more advanced thinking skills. A foundation in plasticity, potential, and intelligence reinforces the fact that these skills can be taught—that all students have the potential to become better thinkers. Furthermore, an explicit focus on teaching metacognitive skills along with cognitive skills can help students get smarter about their own learning. As we describe in Chapter 5, metacognitive skills can be developed early in school—not just in later grades, as previously assumed. Students can learn how to gather information, explore and elaborate on it, and communicate what they have learned,

---

From Teachers for Teachers

For Paul Farmer, who teaches middle school students with moderate to severe and multiple disabilities in the Coachella Valley Unified School District in California, "The idea of systematically teaching cognitive skills within the context of core subject matter has certainly been useful." Mr. Farmer explains:

> My students have varying degrees of intellectual impairment. The idea that they can learn valuable cognitive skills is an intriguing notion. The brain is not a lump of concrete—it has plasticity and is moldable throughout a lifetime. This must be true not only for the general population, but for the intellectually disabled community as well. The accumulation of small incremental changes over time might result in measurable and meaningful functional outcomes.

applying metacognition to assess how they reach solutions. Such skills are particularly valuable in helping students develop into more sophisticated, self-directed learners in all content areas and in demonstrating their mastery of current standards. In short, improving metacognition empowers students to take control of their learning, or "drive their brains" as we say in our work in teacher education (ASCD, 2018; Wilson & Conyers, 2016).

Taken together, the five essential ideas that form the core of this book provide research-based approaches and a sampling of strategies that can guide new teachers and reinvigorate the classrooms of veteran teachers. They provide educators with reason to expect that they can make a positive difference in the learning of virtually every student they encounter and provide a framework for their own continued learning as well. The final two chapters of this text lend further support to these aims by identifying persistent myths about learning and teaching that educators may encounter in their professional practice and by exploring ways that teachers can continue their own lifelong journey of learning in collaboration with their colleagues and other peers.

THE CHALLENGES OF TEACHING TODAY

At the beginning of this chapter, we alluded to some of the challenges that our educational system faces today. The five big ideas we describe may not enable educators to address every problem they will encounter in their careers, but they will help to overcome two pervasive, systemic challenges that touch many classrooms and schools in the United States:

Outdated assumptions and information perpetuate inequalities in our educational system. Because the connections between research on brain plasticity and learning and teaching are not widely known, many teachers practicing today may have been trained at a time when it was assumed that the brain could change in only one direction—degenerating from aging, injury, or disease. These teachers, therefore, may not fully comprehend the capacity students have to achieve at higher levels. Furthermore, "few teacher preparation programs include courses on cognition and learning" (Hardiman & Denckla, 2010, p. 7). As a result, some educators believe that intelligence is fixed (Halvorson, 2012; Lusk & Jones, 2011; Nisbett, 2009); they have what Dweck (2016, 2019) calls a "fixed mindset," as opposed to a "growth mindset," the latter of which focuses on a person's ability to improve.

Many people still operate under the false assumptions that the brain does not change, that ability is fixed, and that little can be done to help teachers enhance their effectiveness (Darling-Hammond, 2010; Dweck, 2019; Hardiman & Denckla, 2010). If students are not performing well, people commonly assume that the problem lies in deficits within the students rather than in factors such as quality of instruction, motivation, or organizational issues (Rueda, 2011). Various proposals, including charter schools, school vouchers, merit pay for teachers, and smaller schools, have been put forward as solutions to improve student learning; however, research shows that these propositions may have a minimal, or even negative, impact (Hattie, 2009, 2012).

At the same time, students in poverty and minority students often have less access to high-quality education than do their more fortunate peers. In 2009, 19% of all school-age children in the United States were living in poverty, and greater percentages of Black, Hispanic, and American Indian/Alaska Native students attended high-poverty schools (defined by the percentage of the student population eligible for free or reduced-price lunch) than did White and Asian students (Aud et al., 2011). Students in poverty are more likely to be taught by educators who are teaching outside the field in which they have training and experience and by 1st-year teachers, who are generally less effective than their more experienced colleagues (Almy & Theokas, 2010); this situation holds true around the country, "so whether they are growing up in cities, suburbs, small towns, or rural communities, students in higher poverty schools everywhere are getting shortchanged when it comes to access to better qualified teachers" (p. 2).

When one considers additionally that students arrive at school with varying levels of readiness—including, for example, a potential 6-year spread in reading ability (Fielding, Kerr, & Rosier, 2007)—it is easy to see how a fixed mindset could be particularly detrimental for those students who seem to be a little bit "behind" or who attend high-poverty schools and lack the opportunity to experience excellent teaching. Opportunity gaps for these children can quickly lead to achievement gaps.

In the context of reading, for example, lower-income and minority students often need a highly effective school system to ensure that they are taught by educators with substantial expertise, where they are supported by small-group sessions and one-on-one tutoring until they are reading on grade level (Allington, 2011b). Without this additional support, many students—especially English-language learners, students in poverty, and minority youth—may doubt their own potential to achieve well at school. Students may not know that learning changes the brain and that effort makes the difference, and they may arrive at school without many of the school readiness factors that contribute to academic success. Such students see little reason to try, and teachers with a fixed mindset give them little reason to hope for improvement.

Schools and students are being held to standards that are higher than ever before and that emphasize new skills for the 21st century. Current rigorous standards are designed to provide educators with targets for helping students progress in the development of expertise in key domains of knowledge. The challenge for today's education system is that the goal is now to ensure that virtually all students achieve at high levels of cognitive achievement. Such an undertaking has never been attempted:

> Contemporary American educators confront the most daunting challenge in the history of public schooling in the United States: they are called upon to raise academic standards to the highest level in history with common core standards that are so rigorous and include such challenging cognitive demands that they align with the highest international benchmarks. (DuFour & Marzano, 2011, p. 5)

These new standards mark a departure from schooling in much of the 20th century, which was focused more heavily on basic skills like reading, writing, and math. There is widespread agreement today that such skills, while necessary, are insufficient for the 21st century (World Economic Forum, 2018). A report from the National Research Council on "Education for Life and Work" (Pellegrino & Hilton, 2012) identifies three domains of 21st century competencies: cognitive (thinking and reasoning), intrapersonal (regulating one's behaviors and emotions to achieve goals), and interpersonal (relating to others and understanding others' points of view). This report supports the need for explicit instruction to help students master these competencies, which are addressed in more detail in Chapters 5 and 7.

In short, students today must learn effective thinking and learning strategies, and they must be prepared for a more collaborative, ever-evolving work environment (World Economic Forum, 2018). Having good problem-solving skills in addition to basic reading, writing, and math skills will be necessary to get and perform well in interviews, and the ability to constantly reinvent one's work skills will be required to maintain job security (Friedman & Mandelbaum, 2011). Rueda asserts that for students to thrive in the new global economy, they need to learn how to be "self-regulated learners, who have acquired expertise and can transfer their knowledge and skills to real-world problems" (2011, p. 7). Baker and colleagues (2012) further explain that "the substantive complexity of jobs requiring analytical reasoning (i.e., combinations of mathematics, language, and reasoning skills) and synthetic reasoning (i.e., putting different ideas and concepts together in new ways, effortful thinking, and new problem solving) have increased significantly" (p. 12).

The job marketplace for today's students will be more competitive than ever; new technology now means that 2 billion more people compete for jobs online with students in the United States (Friedman & Mandelbaum, 2011). The landscape in which we live, work, and communicate has changed dramatically in just a few years; as author Thomas Friedman noted, "Facebook didn't exist; Twitter was a sound; the cloud was in the sky; 4G was a parking place; . . . applications were what you sent to college; and Skype for most people was a typo" (NPR, 2011).

Never in human history has there been such an ambitious agenda for empowering virtually all students with the skills and knowledge they need to become self-regulated learners who have content expertise, solve problems and create solutions, and succeed in a highly competitive global economy.

OPPORTUNITIES KNOCK FOR LIFELONG LEARNERS

The teacher education programs from which many teachers graduate have traditionally not focused on the adult or professional as learner; in fact, the focus has most often been primarily on teaching, not learning. We have found in our work that teachers are excited to reflect on how they themselves learn and that doing so helps them better understand the needs of other learners, the difficulty of learning, and the value of an effective teacher. They become better teachers of their students and are also better equipped to share their expertise with their colleagues.

From Teachers for Teachers

In an ethnographic study of teachers (Germuth, 2012b; Wilson, 2012), one participant explained how her graduate studies have helped her work more effectively with other teachers to facilitate their continued learning:

> If we can continue to help new and experienced teachers learn more about brain-based teaching, I believe they will be happier and more effective. New educators also need a strong socio-emotional support group from their peers rather than a competitive stance. . . . Often, I get to see the school, our staff, and students from a new perspective when mentoring. I have to remember to be positive and open-minded. I do believe that using what works well for students in the classroom will work well for my mentees. . . . I always learn something from them as well and continue to apply my signature strength of life-long learning in doing so. (p. 15)

Furthermore, advances in technology have made it possible for teachers to learn from each other in ways never before imagined. Teachers can find lesson plans and network online with other teachers around the globe to share knowledge. Teachers now entering the field have grown up in the digital age and are accustomed to making online connections; they may even have more of a growth mindset orientation. In fact, more and more teachers today have less and less experience; in the 2007–08 school year classrooms were most likely to be led by teachers with 1 or 2 years of experience, reflecting the fact that many experienced teachers are retiring and others are leaving the field (Omer, 2011). The knowledge gap being created may be bridged in part with technology and a willingness among teachers to learn from one another (Wilson & Conyers, 2016).

All this is to say that the opportunity to meet the challenges in education lies with teachers—with you. Research shows that teachers are keen to learn about the brain (Pickering & Howard-Jones, 2007; Serpati & Loughan, 2012; Wilson, 2012a; Wilson & Conyers, 2016, 2020; Zambo & Zambo, 2009). Teachers can use plasticity research to inform their colleagues and students about the meaning of potential and intelligence, counteracting the fixed mindset. Teachers can transform classroom instruction and teach 21st century skills by emphasizing cognitive and metacognitive skills and preparing lessons that account for the ways in which the body and brain may interact in the learning process. Student diversity does not have to translate into educational inequalities or stand in the way of all children achieving their potential.

New and veteran teachers alike can be excited and inspired that they can keep learning through new experiences in their professional and personal lives, and they should share and model for their students the excitement that comes from learning. Research suggests that students may benefit when their teachers model a love of learning (Feuerstein, Feuerstein, & Falik, 2010). In essence, we must all strive to be the passionate, engaged, and thoughtful learners we want our students to become.

Of course, to be most successful, teachers must be supported by effective school systems and leaders—a theme to which we will return many times in this text. Educational leaders and policymakers often focus on external factors like standards, data analysis, and governance accountability to the point that some may lose sight of the learners themselves (Hardiman & Denckla, 2010). Yet studies (Barber & Mourshed, 2007; Fullan, 2016) have shown that effective school systems focus on improving instruction and teacher education. District resources should focus on supporting teachers with professional opportunities to learn about the latest research and time to work with colleagues locally to develop lessons. Indeed, there can be dramatic increases in student achievement when teachers are given the opportunity to work together to improve instruction (Conyers & Wilson, 2016; Fullan, 2016).

Finally, schools need to be supported in these efforts by the larger community. Given that children spend most of their time at home and in their neighborhoods rather than in school and have the equivalent of about 185 days away from school each year (Neuman, 2009), it's no surprise that factors beyond the scope of the classroom have a tremendous impact on student achievement. For instance, a study of 900 students in Baltimore, Maryland, revealed that the achievement levels of poor and middle-income students who had made similar gains while at school diverged outside school: The middle-income students continued to make gains after school and over the summer holiday, while poor students fell behind (Entwisle, Alexander, & Olson, 1998). Neuman (2009) describes cost-effective and well-researched programs that support healthy brain development and academic achievement. With community leaders' support for such programs, educators will be further empowered to help all students reach their potential.

CONNECTING THE SCIENCE OF
LEARNING TO THE ART OF TEACHING

The teachers we described at the beginning of this prologue represent the hope of what public education in the 21st century can be. They are pioneers in applying implications of psychology, neuroscience, and education research in ways that increase the motivation and enhance the academic achievement of the students in their classrooms. Although their students are diverse, they do not hold some to higher standards than others; they believe in the potential of all their students to make academic gains supported by their teaching.

Although there are substantial challenges, this is an exciting time to be in education. The science of learning is being connected ever more closely to the art of teaching. We are in a time when more is known about how the brain functions, how people learn, and what can be done to enhance learning than ever before. This means that teachers have greater opportunities than they had previously to test different strategies and lessons, constantly enhancing their skills and experiencing the thrill of seeing their students gain in understanding. Through these opportunities, teachers can find greater levels of satisfaction and joy in their work. In short, this is a time for hope and optimism about the ability of effective teaching to empower students with the skills and knowledge they need to achieve at higher levels of success, both academically and in life outside school.

Questions for Reflection

- Who is the greatest teacher you have ever encountered? What made him or her so effective?
- What is it about the field of education that most inspires you with hope and optimism?
- What do you consider to be the greatest challenges you face as a teacher? Do you see ways in which the five big ideas introduced in this chapter might help you meet this challenge? If so, how?
- What opportunities do you have to continue learning new skills or to learn from colleagues? How can you better take advantage of such opportunities?

CHAPTER 1

Big Idea 1

Implications of Neural Plasticity for Learning and Teaching

> One of the most striking advances in learning sciences in the past 15 years has been in understanding the protracted course of brain development, which begins in utero and continues well into adulthood.
>
> —National Academies of Science, Engineering, and Medicine,
> *How People Learn II: Learners, Contexts, and Cultures*, p. 55

What is your familiarity with the terms* neural plasticity *or* brain plasticity? *What do you know about this concept?

Over the past half century, neuroscientists have learned a great deal more about the way our brains process new information. For much of the 20th century, neuroscientists believed that the brain was largely a finished product by early adolescence. With the development of brain-imaging technologies, however, has come the understanding that the brain can change and adapt throughout life. The emerging field of educational neuroscience shows that the brain is *plastic*, or malleable; makes new cellular connections; and changes in structure and function as learning occurs. The National Academies of Science, Engineering, and Medicine explains the process:

> As people acquire knowledge, there are significant changes in their brain activity, brain structure, or both that complement the rapid increase in processing speed and effort needed to use the acquired knowledge. Changes that can be detected in grey and white matter provide one form of evidence for this connection between knowledge acquisition and brain structure (2018, p. 63).

Hinton, Fischer, and Glennon make the point that "arguably the most important insight for education is that the brain is highly adaptive, a property called plasticity" (2012, p. 3). In recent years, other scholars across the world have likewise begun focusing on educational neuroscience. Researchers in Paris created the Learning Sciences and Brain Research project at the Centre for Educational Research and Innovation of the Organisation for Economic Co-operation and Development; scientists in Tokyo created the Baby Science Society of Japan; and education professors at Harvard launched a graduate program called Mind, Brain, and Education. These various groups came together to form the International Mind, Brain, and Education Society, and a number of other universities and research centers in the United States and abroad have begun to focus on this exciting transdisciplinary field (Fischer, 2009).

We still have an enormous amount to learn about how the brain changes as it is exposed to new information and experiences—and what that means for education. In the *Handbook of Educational Psychology II*, the late Robert Calfee, author of our Foreword, identified research on plasticity and other aspects of brain studies as one of four "really important problems" that we must learn more about in education (2006, p. 35) to further assist teachers. Even as this research continues, we can draw a number of broad principles useful for educators from an understanding of brain plasticity and even make a few specific recommendations for the classroom. However, Calfee cautioned that studies based on brain imaging must be analyzed and interpreted carefully to move beyond anecdotal evidence and unsupported conclusions about cause and effect.

Perhaps most important, plasticity research allows us to rethink our mindsets about human potential and ability. Educational philosopher Israel Scheffler (2010) identifies a persistent and pervasive assumption in American education that the academic ability of students is a stable and internal trait, relatively impervious to school-based intervention. This notion that ability is fixed and that many students are unable to achieve

---

In Sum

Studies showing that learning changes the brain's structure and function supports the view that the academic ability of almost all students can be improved with the appropriate educational conditions. This has major implications for educational practice.

academic success because of some internal, inflexible deficit needs to be reconsidered in light of current evidence about the brain's ability to change in the proper learning environment. In other words, knowing that the brain's architecture continually adapts as we learn points to the fact that "belief in a growth mindset is scientifically accurate, whereas belief in a fixed mindset is a misconception" (Harvard Graduate School of Education, 2015, p. 2).

UNDERSTANDING THE SCIENCE OF NEURAL PLASTICITY

The terms *neural plasticity, neuronal plasticity, neuroplasticity,* and *brain plasticity,* which are typically used interchangeably, can be defined as "the ability of the nervous system to change its activity in response to intrinsic or extrinsic stimuli by reorganizing its structure, functions, or connections" (Mateos-Aparicio & Rodríguez-Moreno, 2019, para. 1). Our brains create new synapses through a process called *synaptogenesis* and also eliminate synapses through a process called *pruning.*

Building chiefly on the work of Greenough and Black (1992) and Bruer and Greenough (2001), scientists have further defined plasticity by differentiating between two different types: experience-*expectant* and experience-*dependent.* Experience-expectant plasticity refers to experiences that are common to all humans and are important for typical development, such as learning to walk and talk. These types of experiences happen early in life and are apt to take place during "sensitive periods" of brain and body development (Black, 2018). A commonly cited example of these sensitive periods at work is the fact that people who learn a new language later in life may not be able to master the same nuances of pronunciation as people who began hearing and speaking the language as infants. Similarly, as adults we often retain the accent of the region where we grew up, even if we move and live for long years elsewhere.

Lightfoot, Cole, and Cole explain that

> evidence for experience-expectant brain development is found in an interesting pattern of synaptic proliferation and elimination. At several points during development, different portions of the brain undergo an explosive increase in synapse formation, called exuberant synaptogenesis, which produces far more synapses than would be required by the particular experiences the growing organism is likely to encounter. In other words, the profusion of synapse at

different points in development would seem to prepare the brain for a range of possible experiences. (2008, p. 129)

The first few years of a child's life are one such period of rapid synaptic growth. Woolfolk Hoy states that at birth

each neuron has about 2,500 synapses. . . . By age 2 to 3, each neuron has around 15,000 synapses; children this age have many more synapses than they will have as adults. In fact, they are *oversupplied* with the neurons and synapses that they will need to adapt to their environments. (2010, p. 29, emphasis in original)

These synapses decrease through pruning of neuronal connections that are not used repeatedly; concentrated periods of synaptic pruning have been identified in infancy, middle childhood, and adolescence (Giedd, 2015; Giedd et al., 1999).

In contrast, experience-dependent plasticity describes changes in the brain that are based on experiences that occur throughout life and are not common to people as a whole; "in experience-dependent development, individual differences in brain development depend on the idiosyncratic experiences that are encountered across the life span. . . . Experience-dependent brain development is a source of enduring plasticity and of adaptability to the demands of everyday life" (Shonkoff & Phillips, 2000, p. 190). One example of experience-dependent plasticity is vocabulary development, which has been shown to continue throughout life but to vary based on individuals' exposure to language. People who read regularly for pleasure or as a work requirement develop an ever-expanding vocabulary. Skills that are developed through practice, like playing a musical instrument or a sport, are also examples of this type of plasticity.

A crucial aspect of experience-dependent plasticity is that "such development is invariably tethered to one's immediate environment" (Baker et al., 2012, p. 12). Children who grow up in poverty or are deprived in various ways, therefore, can experience long-lasting negative effects on their brain development. These effects may not be irreversible, but they require intensive concerted effort to remediate. One conclusion is clear—and supported by cognitive psychology: Experience matters, for both children and adults.

While brain plasticity research holds promise for understanding and treating brain injuries (for example, see Immordino-Yang, 2016;

Immordino-Yang & Fischer, 2007, who report on two case studies demonstrating that when one hemisphere of the brain is removed the other can take on some of its functions), it also sheds new light on the age-old nature-versus-nurture debate. Scientists now generally agree that a person develops as a result of complex interaction between genetic and environmental factors—not the dominance of one over the other.

Sylwester cites the intertwined impact of nature and nurture on development: "Thirty thousand genes are enough to direct the development and initial operation of a basic birth body, but they're not enough to provide specific directions for living out our complex extended life" (2010, p. 15). He goes on to suggest:

> It's probably best to think of genes as phenomena that *enable* rather than *constrain* behavior. Genes provide the mechanisms for biological possibility, but the challenges we confront and the decisions we make determine which genes are expressed to facilitate our responses—and so to affect such human properties as character and intelligence. . . . Parents and educators can't change the genetic history of a child, but they can do the kind of nurturing that will provide the child with the best possible adaptations of whatever nature provided. (p. 18; emphasis added)

A key conclusion that teachers can take away from these discussions is that plasticity relates directly to learning and to how we think about education (Burns, 2019). Zull describes teaching as "the art of changing the brain" and goes on to highlight the teacher's role in "creating conditions that lead to change in a learner's brain" (2002, p. 5). Indeed, brain plasticity is what makes it possible for students to learn. Furthermore, researchers have shown that the brain can continue changing throughout our lives—well beyond the childhood years spent in the classroom.

In Sum

Experience-dependent synaptogenesis is the mechanism that can turn what we do into what we know—inside and outside the classroom. This type of neuronal development results from the experiences students have in school, at home, and in the community.

BRAIN DEVELOPMENT OVER THE LIFE SPAN

Current and emerging neuroscientific findings suggest little support for the once-popular notion that most important brain development occurs from birth to 3 years of age (Bruer, 1999; Tokuhama-Espinosa, 2018). No one disputes that a loving, supportive, language-rich environment in these early years is beneficial, but there is no evidence currently that a high level of synapse or neuron development in infancy predicts learning ability later in life. John Bruer, summing up the research on early neural plasticity, concludes that "brainpower does not depend on the number of synapses formed before age 3" (1999, p. 99).

Moving Toward Ever-Greater Independence

Plasticity is intrinsic to the function and development of the brain, and it is essential for memory and learning processes. Furthermore, the time windows for plasticity that occur during development shape the connections in the brain and its activity (Pérez-Rodríguez et al., 2018).

For most, the majority of the brain's development occurs over the course of the first 20 years of life. Sylwester segments this development into two 10-year periods. From birth to around age 10, we learn "how to be *a human being*—learning to move, to communicate, and to master basic social skills" (2010, p. 60). We form ties with our families and learn how to interact with non–family members; we also gradually develop fluency in basic skills such as reading and math, and our motor skills improve steadily as well. During this period, the brain's sensory lobes develop, allowing us to understand and react to our environment. Sylwester suggests that beginning school

> ratchets up the motor, language, cultural, and social knowledge and skills [children] have to master. . . . By the time they reach fifth grade (about age 10) and their sensory lobes are at a reasonable level of maturity, most have learned a lot about how the world works. (p. 61)

From approximately ages 11 to 20, we learn "how to be *a productive reproductive* human being—planning for a vocation, exploring emotional commitment and sexuality, and achieving autonomy" (Sylwester, 2010, p. 60). Development during the 2nd decade is focused particularly in the prefrontal region, which is responsible for solving problems and making decisions. Although adults typically have more patience for the lapses of toddlers than of adolescents, Sylwester notes that "demanding adults tend to forget that the mastery of something as complex as reflexive thought . . . didn't occur instantly and without error in their lives" (p. 61). Parents and teachers of adolescents should be supportive of teenagers as they assume more control of their thinking abilities even as they also begin to disengage from adults and become more independent. In the classroom, this support may take the form of an explicit emphasis that students are in charge of their learning. Teachers may empower middle and high school students to set their own learning goals and choose subjects for learning projects while simultaneously teaching cognitive and metacognitive skills (see Chapter 5) they can use to achieve the goals they set for themselves.

Research has shown that the frontal lobes appear to undergo significant changes through late adolescence and that the prefrontal cortex, key to impulse control, is among the last of the brain regions to mature in the 20s (Giedd, 2004; 2015). Brain images indicate that adolescents' brains work differently than adults' when they solve problems and make decisions. Their behaviors are guided more by emotions and less by the logical, thoughtful prefrontal cortex. Based on the stage of adolescents' brain development, they are more likely to behave impulsively, get into accidents, and engage in behaviors that are unsafe, and less likely to think before taking action (American Academy of Child & Adolescent Psychiatry, 2016). The aim of guiding the learning of teenagers entails recognizing their need to become independent while providing guidance as they mature during this period of the pruning of synapses and the possibility of cognitive changes of great magnitude with new connections in the brain.

The Mechanics of Lifelong Learning

Young brains are more malleable and changeable than older brains, which have developed efficient processing systems over time to address life's typical challenges. Nevertheless, the adult brain can continue to change throughout life; while it doesn't get bigger, it doesn't lose a large percentage of neurons either, as was once thought.

A longstanding assumption was that the creation of brain cells peaked in childhood and early adolescence and then steadily declined. However, animal experiments in the 1990s established that adult brains generate new neurons in response to novel stimuli such as songbirds learning new songs; advances in brain-imaging techniques have since allowed researchers to detect neurogenesis in the brains of adult humans as well (Fotuhi, 2013; Mateos-Aparicio & Rodríguez-Moreno, 2019). In fact, Stine-Morrow and Chui (2012) propose that lifestyle factors such as personal agency and engagement may contribute to cognitive resilience and brain growth in elders.

The hippocampus, the region of the brain responsible for memory and spatial navigation, can continue to create and prune neurons throughout life. In one well-known study, Professor Eleanor Maguire of University College London compared the brains of 16 cab drivers with those of people from other walks of life and found that the posterior hippocampus was much larger in the taxi drivers. Furthermore, the hippocampus was larger in those taxi drivers who'd been in the business longer. London cabbies study the city at length and must pass an oral and driving test covering 25,000 streets and 400 routes. As one taxi driver shared, "You can't just be good at driving around. . . . You also have to be good at getting information in your head and keeping it there" (Brown & Fenske, 2010, p. 158). Maguire and her research team (2000) concluded from the study that the adult brain can indeed change in response to the environment (National Academies of Science, Engineering, and Medicine, 2018). It is fortunate that Maguire's team conducted this study before cabbies could rely on GPS system to navigate unfamiliar areas; repeating this study today might generate quite different results!

Brain-imaging technology has provided other glimpses of plasticity in action. Conducting brain scans of representatives of selected populations—including future physicians studying for medical exams, professional musicians who practice for hours each day, and children with dyslexia receiving intensive reading intervention—scientists have documented changes in gray matter volume in specific areas of the brain that correspond to learning gains. In the first example, researchers captured brain images of 38 German students at the beginning of 3 months of study for their preliminary medical exams and again on the 1st or 2nd day of the exams. MRI scans detected small but significant increases in gray matter volume in the posterior and inferior parietal cortex, which is associated with information transfer into long-term memory, and in the hippocampus, which appears to play a role in semantic and spatial knowledge acquisition (Draganski et al., 2006; National Academies of Science, Engineering, and Medicine, 2018).

Experts in disciplines including sports and music "have an increase in the density of both gray matter [containing neurons] and white matter [containing neurons' connections to other neurons] that connect task-related regions of their brains in comparison with nonexperts" (Chang, 2014, p. 64).

Their commitment to intensive practice has made musicians a popular target of this type of research. In his 2009 research review, Lutz summarizes the results of more than 40 studies connecting increases in neuronal volume and density to musical training over months, even years. The subjects of this research include children as young as 5 and 6 years old and older adults who have been playing and practicing music all their lives. Some studies showed a "positive transfer" of the resulting brain development from musical expertise to enhanced reading and linguistic perception and executive function such as more focused attention and self-discipline. (For more information on executive function, see Chapter 5.)

An essential aspect of this research is that practice and regular exposure to the content and skills to be learned are responsible for the changes to the brain, not just some genetic predisposition for academic or musical success. These findings have important implications for teachers, as does other mind, brain, and education research underscoring that the brain is always learning. The message for students struggling with subjects they find difficult is that they *can* learn if they keep practicing and studying. Working with their teacher, with peers, and on their own, they may need to break complex material down into simpler content and try out different tactics to understand and solve problems. Protests that "I'm not smart enough!" or "I can't do this!" should be gently but firmly challenged with a reminder they can learn if they are willing to keep trying. Metaphors may be a useful way to reinforce this point: Great musicians spend hours every day in rehearsal. Professional athletes practice, practice, and practice so they can be the best. Academic success requires the same commitment to hard work and persistent effort.

There is no off switch when the school day ends. Thus, teachers should advocate for supporting classroom education with a variety of nontraditional learning experiences through after-school enrichment and community programs offering active opportunities that are relevant to students' lives and interests (Hinton et al., 2012).

From Teachers for Teachers

In an ethnographic study of teachers earning advanced degrees (Germuth, 2012b), several participants noted that research on neurocognitive plasticity has implications for teachers as well as their students. For example, a kindergarten teacher in a Title I school suggested that "educators and leaders will benefit as they recognize learning never stops, regardless of an individual's age." Another educator teaching English as a Second Language to K–5 students said, "One of the fascinating things [we learned] was brain plasticity—the finding that the brain is pretty elastic even as you get old. In essence, you can teach an old dog new tricks."

In short, the brain changes as a result of learning throughout life. The connection between learning and neural plasticity can be summed up in this way: (a) learning changes the physical structure of the brain; (b) structural changes alter the functional organization of the brain (in other words, learning organizes and reorganizes the brain); and (c) different parts of the brain may be ready to learn at different times (National Academies of Science, Engineering, and Medicine, 2018.

In Sum

Brain plasticity is not merely a function of the very young. It is the engine that powers lifelong learning.

PLASTICITY RESEARCH AND THE CLASSROOM

Research on experience-dependent plasticity suggests that environment has a profound impact on how people develop and what they learn (Burns, 2019). For educators, the positive implication of this research is that all students should be able to learn, regardless of their ability level when they enter school. In broad terms, then, plasticity research can provide the basis for teachers to rethink what we mean when we talk about the potential and intelligence of our students—topics treated in subsequent chapters.

Explicitly teaching students about their brain's plasticity can support student motivation and engagement in learning (ASCD, 2018; Wilson

& Conyers, 2016; 2020). Dweck's research suggests that when students learn about neuroplasticity, it can lead to improved academic outcomes (Dweck, 2019). The research into the importance of brain plasticity is ongoing. As this book goes to press, Stanford Graduate School of Education Professor Bruce McCandliss is leading a project in collaboration with a school in Menlo Park, California, that is helping researchers better understand how young learners' brains transform with the acquisition of new skills (Donald, 2019).

In time, research on plasticity may be able to provide teachers with specific knowledge and tools to guide their work. Because educational neuroscience is such a new field, researchers today are rightly cautious about our ability to bridge the gap between scientific studies in neuroscience and the realities of the classroom. Some studies, however, have focused on reading and, to a lesser extent, mathematics (Varma et al., 2008).

Reading

Research that combines brain imaging with intensive support for beginning and struggling readers is becoming more sophisticated in further supporting studies from psychology and education to inform instruction. McCandliss notes that "changes in functional circuitry within and between systems that support vision and language have been linked to progressive cognitive developments in reading ability" (2010, p. 8049). Researchers are applying findings like these to design and assess the effectiveness of specific reading instruction strategies with students with dyslexia and other reading problems. These and other findings may have implications for improving reading instruction for all students (e.g., American Psychological Association, 2014).

In one study, researchers provided intensive 8-week training to 11 dyslexic children, focusing on skills like mental imagery and articulating and tracing letters. Students demonstrated significant gains in their reading ability, and scans showed that gray matter volume had increased in the hippocampus and other areas of the brain. Scans taken after a subsequent 8-week period during which students received no training indicated that the gray matter volume had stayed the same, indicating that the brains of dyslexic children had changed and developed as a result of the reading instruction in using these strategies (Krafnick, Flowers, Napoliello, & Eden, 2011).

Working with preschool children in a 1-month study, James (2010) found that children who engaged in the sensorimotor activity of learning to print letters had more activity in certain areas of the brain than did children who named the letters verbally. These and other studies are identifying different areas of the brain that correspond to specific reading difficulties as well as the parts of the brain that are activated during different cognitive functions involved in the act of reading. For example, Yoncheva, Wise, and McCandliss (2015) found that beginning readers who focus on letter-sound relationships, or phonics, instead of trying to learn whole words, increase activity in the area of their brains best wired for reading. In a review summarizing what is known about the structural and functional brain bases of dyslexia, researchers stress that there is evidence of brain differences in early childhood, before formal reading instruction begins, which confirms the importance of early diagnosis and intervention (D'Mello & Gabrieli, 2018).

Additionally, researchers are also exploring the different pathways in the brain that are involved in *literacy*, an umbrella term that encompasses the ability to identify, understand, and use the symbols of written language to communicate. For example, it appears that there is one pathway for phonological processing and another for processing meaning or semantics (CERI, 2007). Further research may reveal additional understanding of the brain structures and neuronal connections that facilitate literacy, supporting the potential for continuing gains in creating effective new teaching strategies. This pathways perspective is consistent with the metaphor of "wiring the brain to read," which is grounded in findings from the work of Dehaene (2009) and the hypothesis of neuronal recycling. Dehaene's hypothesis holds that our capacity to read and to perform symbolic arithmetic relies on "recycling" existing brain circuitry that evolved for other purposes, such as processing and producing spoken language.

Goswami (2019) reports that developmental imaging studies are showing promise in identifying the neural systems responsible for learning to read and for demonstrating the impact of intensive instruction with children with developmental dyslexia. Specifically, activity in the left temporal and parietal areas of the brains of children with dyslexia seems to "normalize" following targeted remediation in phonological skills and letter-sound correspondence. In other words, children with dyslexia have a harder time than their peers distinguishing the sounds of language and connecting letters to the sounds they represent. Intensive instruction in these areas helps these children make gains in reading, and those gains are reflected in physical structural changes in the brain. Goswami cautions that more research is needed to help identify what works in classroom instruction, but it seems clear that an environment rich in spoken language, both at home and at school, benefits all children. Repeating nursery rhymes, reading aloud poetry and children's stories that play with language, and sharing songs and rhyming wordplay offer joyful opportunities for children to recognize and employ the sounds and rhythm of language (Wilson & Conyers, 2013).

Math

As with reading research, studies of children learning mathematics indicate that different areas of the brain are activated based on what type of math they are learning and whether they are engaged in hands-on learning activities or pencil-and-paper calculations. Applying what we know about brain plasticity to this research may lend support to teaching math in ways that engage multiple learning pathways. For example, Varma and colleagues (2008) cite research indicating that students who learn new math operations through memorization rely on areas of the brain that are activated when retrieving verbally coded information, while students who learn to employ an algorithm to conduct the same operations showed more brain activity in areas associated with visual-spatial processing.

As a means of developing mathematical proficiency, a significant amount of instructional time needs to go beyond a traditional focus on procedural fluency. Teachers should dedicate time to developing strategies and concepts, discussing math problems, and practicing with feedback. Classroom discussions should build on students' thinking, focus on the relationship between problems and solutions, and attend to the nature of justification and mathematical argument (Bransford, Brown, & Cocking, 2000; National Academies of Science, Engineering, and Medicine, 2018).

Another study indicates that younger children solving basic math problems activate areas of the brain associated with general memory and reasoning, while older teens who can work through math problems more quickly rely more on visual and verbal areas of the brain (Rivera, Reiss, Eckert, & Menon, 2005). This research suggests the benefits of designing math lessons that help students shift "from domain-general to domain-specific modes of thought" to speed up their math-processing abilities (Varma et al., 2008, p. 144).

Studies have shown that infants are born with a basic ability to differentiate magnitudes (8 dots versus 16 dots, for example) and to keep track of and differentiate between one, two, and three items (Feigenson, Dehaene, & Spelke, 2004). Furthermore, the brain uses a variety of specialized pathways in mathematical processing that may be responsible for different types of mathematical knowledge (Dehaene, 1997). The implication for teachers is that ability in other areas of learning does not imply ability in math and that ability at a particular math skill does not imply ability in another math skill. These findings emphasize the need for differentiated instruction and formative assessment to identify each student's range of math skills and to target instruction where additional learning support may be needed.

There appears to be a relationship in the brain between numbers and space. We seem to intuitively understand numbers existing along on a number line that we visualize running left to right, with small numbers on the left and large numbers on the right. In cultures that read right to left, the mental number line seems to run right to left (Dehaene, 1997). Studies comparing cultural differences in teaching and learning math suggest that varying areas of the brain are activated. For example, Chinese-speaking children who learn basic math concepts using an abacus tend to activate motor areas of the brain when solving arithmetic problems, while English-speaking children who learn math by calculating on paper are more reliant on areas of the brain associated with language. These findings may point to the need for additional research on the best way to incorporate hands-on learning activities alongside more traditional approaches to teaching math (Varma et al., 2008).

FROM RESEARCH TO CLASSROOM PRACTICE: PLASTICITY IN ACTION

The Centre for Educational Research and Innovation (CERI) pulled together major studies on the implications of brain plasticity on reading and math instruction in a 2007 publication called *Understanding the Brain*. Here we draw on recommendations from CERI editors and others (Berninger & Richards, 2002; Bransford, Brown, & Cocking, 2000; National Academies of Science, Engineering, and Medicine, 2018) that are particularly significant for educators:

- Because we know it is easier to learn grammar and master an accent at a younger age, it makes sense for foreign-language instruction to begin as early as possible. At the same time, new instructional materials need to be developed with younger children in mind.
- Brain plasticity research points to the benefits of using formative assessments for reading (see Chapter 3 for a discussion of formative assessment). Literacy development is guided by experience rather than only by brain maturation. Since literacy is created in the brain through developmental progression over time, it would be most useful for teaching and learning to utilize ongoing assessments that support the development of literacy.
- The fact that the brain employs different pathways in reading supports a balanced approach to literary instruction.
- Similarly, because different neural pathways are used for mathematics, math teachers need to use multiple means of conveying mathematical knowledge, and researchers need to track the effects of different forms of instruction to understand better the various learning pathways. In both reading and math instruction, facilitating hands-on activities and providing many opportunities for practice and reinforcement of key concepts recognizes variations among students and makes the most of multiple modalities of representing lesson content.
- Mathematics teaching that focuses on drill or memorization creates different, less robust neural pathways than does teaching that focuses on learning by strategy, conceptual learning, or following a sequence of mathematical operations. This reliance on understanding strategies is reflected in many current state standards for mathematics, which specify that instruction should guide students to identify the structure of mathematical concepts well enough to apply them to similar problems. Similarly, our experience has shown that students learn better when instruction emphasizes conceptual learning over rote memorization.
- Because number and space are linked concepts in the brain, use of the number line in teaching and manipulatives such as an abacus and base 10 blocks build on students' inherent process for understanding these basic math concepts. Concrete objects, pictures, and diagrams like a number line help younger students conceptualize math operations and develop the understanding

they can then apply to increasingly complex and abstract problems.

- As with literacy, a different assessment process for math could better reflect the way the brain learns; assessments that focus on understanding the learning pathways (i.e., problem-solving processes) students are using, rather than on solely whether an answer is right or wrong, can give teachers a better picture of student learning.

- Because different mathematical skills may be processed in different areas of the brain, students who understand one area of mathematics well or poorly may be at the other end of the range in another area of mathematics. These findings underscore the need to rethink or eliminate tracking students into different academic tracks leading to rigid career and vocational paths.

- Modeling for students that there are a variety of ways to puzzle out the meaning of an unfamiliar word or solve a math problem, for example, and inviting them to share their own strategies underscores that there is no one right way to learn and that students can take charge of using the cognitive strategies that work best for them.

- For children and adults, emphasizing that learning changes the brain throughout our lives conveys that we can get better and achieve the goals we set for ourselves. The message that learning may keep our brains "younger" is particularly exciting for adult learners and has dramatic implications for teachers as they seek to achieve the "gold standard" of teaching—that of becoming an adaptive expert.

As we conclude this chapter, one final recommendation is that teachers should stay informed about classroom applications for teaching reading and math from researchers across the fields of mind, brain, and education to identify effective instructional approaches:

The past several years have brought about a virtual explosion of cognitive neuroscience investigations into multiple neural systems that may modulate learning and brain plasticity. Attention, working memory, social cognition, anxiety, motivation, and reward each represent functional domains that have been studied extensively in educational contexts as well as through neuroscience approaches. Combining these approaches via interdisciplinary work

---

To Learn More

For an overview of research and theories underlying current understandings about the brain, learning, and factors that support it, see *How People Learn II: Learners, Contexts, and Cultures* by the National Academies of Science, Engineering, and Medicine (2018). This text summarizes current research about the way people learn and implications for individual learning, schooling, professional development, and policy.

---

opens up opportunities to recast critical educational questions through the lens of developmental cognitive neuroscience. (McCandliss, 2010, p. 8050)

For example, a key area for study is the "sensitive periods" that characterize experience-expectant development and whether instruction is aligned properly with these periods. Importantly, understanding the extent to which higher-level math does or does not affect the brain may help educators rethink the high priority given to training in math over that in other disciplines. Our educational system has made mathematics a gatekeeper to higher education, and it is a gate that prevents many students with otherwise high potential from moving forward in their education. It also causes many freshman who fail remedial math courses in junior college to drop out, again because of what may be an unnecessary math requirement. If mathematical learning does not change the brain in ways that are critical to other kinds of thinking, this policy may be unfair. In the area of reading, neuroimaging may be able to show us which students are experiencing phonological sensitivities and may have reading difficulties later on (Goswami, 2019). On a broader scale, a better understanding of how different types of learning affect the brain's development (learning to read versus learning to perform math functions, for example) could help dictate when to teach various subjects (Baker et al., 2012).

In Sum

Low test scores are not a sign that students can't learn but an indication of the need for more informative assessments and intense expert teacher interventions in a positive classroom environment that supports students' beliefs that they can get smarter.

WHAT'S THE BIG IDEA?

The finding that learning changes the brain is a huge contribution from neuroscience to the field of mind, brain, and education research and its application in classrooms and schools. As we look to the future, we are hopeful that understanding research about brain plasticity can result in fundamental shifts in educators' outlooks about their students' ability to learn and improve their academic performance. Consider a simple example: A teacher who is unaware of current brain research might wrongly assume that a low grade on a math test indicates the student's inability to master the material, whereas a teacher who accepts the student's potential to learn based on brain plasticity would look on the test results as a sign that the student requires more practice and support to grasp the concepts being taught (Hardiman & Denckla, 2010).

Teachers can take heart knowing that all students can benefit from effective instruction and that "assertions that the die has been cast by the time the child enters school are not supported by neuroscience evidence" (Shonkoff & Phillips, 2000, p. 216). Teachers are interested in brain research and in how they can use it to inform their practice. In a survey of teachers enrolled in a teacher education program in the southwestern United States, researchers found that the majority of students thought brain research would be useful for educators; 95% agreed with the statement "I believe findings from brain research will lead to a better education for all students"; and 98% agreed that "information from brain research should be used to improve instruction" (Zambo & Zambo, 2009, p. 45). However, more than three-fourths of respondents also agreed that there are misunderstandings among educators about how brain research applies to their profession. Those concerns point to the need to clearly understand the neuroscientific evidence of brain plasticity and the implications for teaching so that all students can learn. In another study of educators from around the world, the authors found that "the majority of respondents reported an interest in learning more about the brain and its influence on learning" and that they "indicated they found scientific knowledge about the brain and its influence on learning to be interesting and valuable to their teaching practice, course development, and professional development" (Online Learning™ Consortium, 2019, p. 8)

Educators are eager to learn as much as they can about how the brain changes through learning as one pathway to improve their practice. As mind, brain, and education research continues, we look forward to exciting new developments and implications ahead for educators. Researchers in psychology and education have developed a large base of knowledge on student cognition and learning; this knowledge is now being complemented and supplemented by neuroscientists. As researchers learn how to work more closely together, they will be able to develop joint research questions that can draw on the expertise of each field and produce results that will eventually be useful for teachers in the classroom (Varma et al., 2008). In working together, they can also help create a network of individuals who can bridge the current gap between education and neuroscience by providing useful information in a digestible form (Goswami, 2019). These findings will be useful not only for teachers but also for policymakers and school leaders to evaluate different approaches for helping all students learn and addressing achievement gaps.

Key Terms

Brain imaging: The process of using technology, such as functional magnetic resonance imaging (fMRI), to measure and analyze the structure and function of the brain.

Brain plasticity: Also called *neural plasticity*; the ability of neurons (cells) in the brain and synapses (the structures that allow neurons to pass information to one another) to change throughout the life span.

Experience-dependent synaptogenesis: The process through which the brain creates new synapses based on one's unique experiences in school, at home, and throughout life.

Experience-expectant synaptogenesis: The process through which the brain creates new synapses based on experiences that are common to virtually all humans and important for development, such as walking and talking.

Genetic and environmental influences on development: The various influences that affect the way in which an individual's brain develops. Scientists now agree that both genes and environmental influences—nature and nurture—play a role in development and interact with each other in complex ways.

Lifelong learning: The brain's ability to change and develop as a result of new experiences throughout the life span—not just during childhood.

Pruning: The process through which the brain eliminates synapses.

Synaptogenesis: The process through which the brain creates new synapses.

One could make the case that the vast majority of students come to school with the potential to perform on grade level academically and that brain plasticity may be seen as one of the processes by which they develop these skills in response to high-quality instructional support. When educators recognize that learning changes the physical structure of the brain, there is a shift in their perceptions about the academic potential of their students. Thus, the concept of brain plasticity provides a vision for teachers that what they do in the classroom makes a difference for their students. This concept is also intertwined with an understanding of human potential, which is the subject of the next chapter.

Questions for Reflection

- How does the understanding that the brain changes throughout life as a result of our experiences relate to the profession of teaching?
- How do research findings about brain plasticity undermine assumptions about students' academic ability as a stable trait that is relatively impervious to change through education?
- How are classroom studies finding literacy gains as the result of intensive instruction for struggling readers consistent with neuroplasticity research?
- Is the viewpoint that some people are born with a "math gene" and others are not supported by research? Explain.
- How might an understanding of experience-dependent synaptogenesis influence teaching practice and policy development at the district level?

CHAPTER 2

Big Idea 2
Recognizing Human Potential

Americans are fascinated by stories of geniuses, prodigies and the "naturally gifted." We celebrate people who we believe have special abilities and tend to see those who work hard to succeed as less innately capable.

—Heidi Grant Halvorson,
Succeed: How We Can Reach Our Goals, p. 215

What is your view of a person's potential for learning?

In Salon.com, novelist Dave Eggers writes about the death of one of his high school English teachers, Jay Criche, and the influence Mr. Criche had on his decision to pursue a writing career. Eggers remembers that Mr. Criche wrote the following on a paper Eggers had written about *Macbeth*: "Sure hope you become a writer." Eggers writes that:

> Over the next 10 years, I thought often about Mr. Criche's six words. Whenever I felt discouraged, and this was often, it was those six words that came back to me and gave me strength. When a few instructors in college gently and not-so-gently tried to tell me I had no talent, I held Mr. Criche's words before me like a shield. I didn't care what anyone else thought. Mr. Criche, head of the whole damned English department at Lake Forest High, said I could be a writer. So I put my head down and trudged forward. (2011, para. 7)

Many of us can relate to Eggers's experience: A teacher at some point in our lives helped us understand that we could achieve more than we imagined we could. Indeed, young people are not able to assess their own capabilities and are guided on this point by "taking in" the beliefs of their elders as to what they can do; children tend to be grounded in the present and are unable, without adult help, to realize what their potential could be in the future. By the same token, teachers see the thrill children have when they master a task and show potential they didn't know they had. Such accomplishment is supported when the teacher shows faith in the student's potential. For all children—and especially those who haven't been encouraged at home to believe in their capabilities—such faith can make an enormous difference in their lives.

Eggers's teacher recognized his potential and encouraged him when others did not—and as a consequence, he worked hard to develop his abilities. But imagine if he had listened instead to those instructors who discouraged him in later years. If he had believed that he did not have the innate ability to be a writer, would he ever have persevered or succeeded in that profession?

Educators, like others in society, exhibit very different viewpoints on potential: Those with fixed mindsets believe that students come to the classroom with their capabilities largely fixed, while those who embody a growth mindset can have an enormous impact on student achievement if they set high expectations and deliver effective instruction and support for *incremental learning*. This term refers to the acquisition of knowledge that begins with learning basic skills and then making steady improvements in one's knowledge and skills. An incremental learning approach facilitates the academic progress of all students, whatever their knowledge and skill set when the school year begins.

Since the days of Plato and Confucius, people have differentiated between innate abilities, or nature, and environmental influences, or nurture. We know now that this distinction is false and that there is an interplay between these influences. As Sternberg reminds us, we are born with many basic biological structures in place, but it is through nurture that they develop: "The existence of the cerebral cortex is a result of nature, but the memories stored in it derive from nurture" (2009, p. 71). Rather than trying to parse the ratio of influence between nature and nurture, enlightened policymakers, administrators, and teachers turn their energy to creating policies and instructional practices that cultivate potential. Shonkoff and Phillips (2000) report that "an emphasis on whether hereditary constraints or environmental incentives are the preeminent influence in human development can still be observed not only in scholarship in psychology but also, more significant, in public discourse" (p. 40).

Often this continued discourse allows for a mistaken belief to persist: that behavior is based primarily on fixed, inherited abilities and only in small part on education, the environment, and individual decisions—or, in other words, that potential is fixed (Dweck, 2016). As emphasized in the previous chapter, however, an understanding of the brain's plasticity helps to dispel the pervasive myth of fixed potential and related false beliefs about ability. In this chapter, we explore the ways in which potential is misunderstood, offer a new definition for the concept, and discuss how classroom teachers and the larger educational system can help all students realize their academic potential.

MISUNDERSTANDING POTENTIAL: THE FIXED MINDSET

It is a pervasive belief in our society that some people are born with innate talent in one area or another and can excel in their particular field without much effort. Howe, Davidson, and Sloboda (n.d.) describe this idea:

> It is widely believed that the explanation for the differences between individuals is that the likelihood of people becoming unusually competent in certain fields of accomplishment depends upon the presence or absence of attributes that have an inborn biological component, and are variously labeled "gifts" or "talents" or, less often, "natural aptitudes." It is thought that a young person is unlikely to become an exceptionally good musician, for example, unless he or she is among the minority of individuals who are, innately, musically "talented" or "gifted." (p. 2)

Fortunately, research does not support the idea that success depends primarily on inborn traits that are beyond one's control. Although genetics undoubtedly play a role in determining one's abilities, a large body of scholarship has demonstrated that hard work and one's environment have a significant effect on achievement as well. Brown and Fenske (2010) argue that resilience, motivation, and hard work are more important for achieving one's potential than other commonly cited factors.

Additionally, Ericsson has proposed that thousands of hours of deliberate practice are necessary to become an "expert" in any endeavor (Ericsson & Pool, 2016). Effective teachers we know agree that becoming an expert teacher requires commitment and effort over time but offers great rewards.

Carol Dweck (2019) is well known for her research on the beliefs individuals hold about the relative importance of talent and effort—and the impact those beliefs may have on academic performance and other endeavors. Her position is that people generally approach their lives from one of two basic outlooks: a "growth mindset," which assumes that intelligence and ability can be developed and improved through hard work, and a "fixed mindset," which assumes that intelligence and ability are largely unchangeable (see Chapter 3 for a more extensive discussion of research from Dweck and Ericsson).

Dweck's work has shown that a fixed mindset has a detrimental effect on the achievements of both children and adults. Those who regard talent as innate often believe that the need to work hard at something indicates a lack of potential and are therefore reluctant to "waste" their effort. Thus, the fixed mindset prevents individuals from achieving their potential in life—or even acknowledging what their true potential might be. People with a growth mindset, on the other hand, are more likely to keep trying until they achieve their goals, more confident that they will succeed.

In Sum

Although genetics may play a role in determining one's "natural abilities," hard work, persistence, a supportive environment, the development of a range of learning strategies, and belief in one's ability to succeed can have a powerful influence on achievement in school and other endeavors.

DEFINING POTENTIAL IN THE CLASSROOM

Reuven Feuerstein developed a theory of dynamic intelligence and a specific cognitive methodology for assisting children with disabilities such as Down syndrome and with emotional and environmental challenges. Some of the children with whom Feuerstein had worked were Holocaust survivors who had lost all their loved ones. He developed ways to help teachers better reach students who were performing poorly—that is, to help teachers maximize students' potential by applying new strategies with their hard-to-reach students and to make a difference in students' lives when driven by a belief in every student's potential.

It is a commonly held assumption in the field of education that all teachers should believe in their students' potential. The Interstate Teacher Assessment and Support Consortium identifies 10 teaching standards and related "critical dispositions" necessary for teachers to attain the standards; one such disposition states, "The teacher believes that all learners can achieve at high levels and persists in helping each learner reach his/her full potential" (Council of Chief State School Officers, 2011, p. 11). Additionally, the National Council for Accreditation of Teacher Education (NCATE) notes that "the two professional dispositions that NCATE expects institutions to assess are *fairness* and the belief that all students can learn" (2010, "Professional Dispositions"). But what constitutes fairness with regard to the belief that all students can learn? Do schools need different types of policy, structures, and instruction in place to achieve fairness for all students?

If we are to embrace the concept of students' potential in educational contexts, we must first free the term from common constraints and misperceptions. Bredo (2006) writes that conceptual confusion on the most important of matters is sometimes hard to identify because those matters are so familiar and seemingly straightforward. He cites Jammer's (1953/1969) insistence in Jammer's book *Concepts of Space* that scientists must continually revisit and critique fundamental theories and constructs to ensure that they remain valid in light of continuing research; in his foreword to Jammer's book, Albert Einstein writes that "in the interests of science it is necessary over and over again to engage in the critique of . . . fundamental concepts, in order that we may not be unconsciously ruled by them" (pp. xi–xii). Because these beliefs about potential are so deeply ingrained in our social consciousness, we are unlikely to take the time to sort through any problems with our perceptions.

To help redefine *potential*, Scheffler proposes that:

> Potential may be understood as a subtype of *capacity*—the capacity to become a being with certain characteristics, to acquire a feature of some sort.

. . . Attribution of potential, thus understood, refers explicitly or implicitly to features comprising some designated outcome. (2010, p. 51)

We define *potential* as "the neurocognitive capacity for acquiring the knowledge, skills and attitudes to achieve a higher level of performance in any domain" (Conyers & Wilson, 2015a, p. 4). When we speak of potential as capacity, we must be clear that we are not speaking of behaviors, traits, or skills that someone has intrinsically, nor are we predicting that the potential will necessarily be realized. Rather, potential represents the power to improve one's skills and knowledge through *hard work* and *persistence* in environmental conditions that provide *opportunities* to do so.

To understand how this definition can be applied in an educational setting, let's consider that a 1st-grader named Cheri is a potential reader. In calling her a *potential* reader, we are making the point that while she does not currently know how to read, she has the *capacity* to learn how to read. We cannot predict whether she will realize her potential to read, because that depends on what her environment provides her. If she has an excellent teacher, opportunities to practice reading, and supportive parents, for example, she's much more likely to reach her potential than she will be if her teacher and family assume she is a low achiever and provide little guidance or encouragement for her to work hard.

In short, educators should consider reexamining their own subconscious beliefs about student potential. When a teacher creates a classroom environment that is based on the belief that all students have the neurocognitive capacity to improve their performance, they have an equal opportunity to maximize their academic potential.

In Sum

Potential can be defined as the capacity for acquiring the knowledge and skills to achieve to a higher level of performance in any domain when provided the proper conditions. In education, those conditions include effective instruction and support in a positive learning environment.

TEACHER EXPECTATIONS ABOUT
THEIR STUDENTS' LEARNING POTENTIAL

Rosenthal and Jacobson (1968) caused quite a stir when they published their classic study *Pygmalion in the Classroom*, which demonstrated that teacher expectations influence student performance (though they were criticized for their methodology, the study has nonetheless had a significant impact in the field). Today, it is a broadly accepted principle that teachers' expectations make a difference in student achievement and changes in teacher expectations can produce changes in student learning. When teachers expect that students will do well, students tend to do well; when teachers expect students to fail, they tend to fail. Hattie (2012) notes that "if teachers have high expectations, they tend to have them for all students; similarly, if they have low expectations, they have them for all students" (p. 82)—and students tend to perform to the level of those expectations. Hattie goes on to cite studies in which researchers

asked teachers (after about a month of working with students) to predict where the students would end up at the end of the year in math, reading, and physical education—and when the students were tested at the end of the year, the teachers proved to be reasonably accurate. The problem is that even though some teachers set targets below where the students began the year, some set targets with little improvement, and some set targets

---

From Teachers for Teachers

An elementary school teacher participating in qualitative research on a graduate degree program (Germuth, 2012b) discussed how her studies influenced her views of students' learning potential. All 2nd-graders at her school are assessed to determine whether they would benefit from inclusion in the district's program for gifted students. In the past, the teacher had offered opportunities for "enrichment" learning only to students identified as gifted in the assessment. However, after studying research that all students have the potential to make learning gains, she now offers some type of meaningful and enriching activities to all students regardless of their assessment scores.

reasonably randomly—the students met whatever expectations the teachers had. (p. 82)

This "expectations effect" has been shown at the positive end of the spectrum as well as the negative. In analyzing Rosenthal and Jacobson's work, Achor notes that when teachers expected their students to make significant academic gains, "the belief the teachers had in the students' potential had been unwittingly and nonverbally communicated. More important, these nonverbal messages were then digested by the students and transformed into reality" (2010, p. 84).

Research on the impact of teacher expectations highlights the critical importance of the foundational beliefs about learning and teaching that educators bring to the classroom. Yet teachers must do more than just believe in their students' potential; they must act on that belief by creating a classroom environment that fosters potential and helps each student grow. They must develop the capacity and the conviction in their ability to teach every child. An analysis of research on effective instruction and high-performing classrooms highlights several key elements that enable students—indeed, all people—to achieve their potential:

- The capacity to learn new knowledge and skills, facilitated by neuroplasticity
- Access to opportunities for learning
- Experience appropriate pedagogy
- Willingness to devote the necessary effort required to achieve one's goals
- Support and encouragement from parents, teachers, and other caring people

Capacity Facilitated by Neuroplasticity

As discussed in the previous chapter, experiences change the brain. Learning changes the physical structure of the brain, organizing and reorganizing it (National Academies of Science, Engineering, and Medicine, 2018). In fact, the foundations of human potential are built permanently into the brain's readiness for learning from infancy throughout one's life and in the ability of the brain and body to continually adapt to new challenges.

As the research cited in Chapter 1 demonstrates, teachers who embrace the power of plasticity are less likely to conclude from low test scores that students are unable to learn and more likely to view assessment results productively as a means to identify where further teaching and learning must occur.

Thus, learning about brain plasticity can have a positive effect on teacher expectations for their students (Germuth, 2012b; Harman & Germuth, 2012; Wilson & Conyers, 2016, 2020)—and on students' perceptions of their own abilities. In a study in Texas, 7th-grade students in an experimental group were assigned college student mentors who told them that intelligence is expandable. They were also taught how the brain can make connections across the life span. The students accessed a webpage that reinforced the messages delivered by the mentors; the page had animated graphics showing neurons and dendrites and featured a commentary about the brain making new connections when new problems are solved. The mentors also supported students as they created a presentation in words and pictures about what they had learned. Reporting on this study, Nisbett noted that the students in the experimental group demonstrated a higher performance in math than students who did not take part in the experiment. The girls in the study outperformed their female counterparts at a particularly high rate—a positive finding, since girls "tend to have worries about whether their gender makes them less talented in math" (2009, p. 144).

Access to Opportunity

Opportunity includes the environment, education, structure, and time required to cultivate one's potential. Returning to Cheri and the reading example, we can see that if Cheri is to realize her potential to read, there must be a lack of constraints—her environment cannot block her from learning. As Scheffler puts it, in our thinking about the environment, our efforts need to include "the study of conditions that block learning, prevent development, necessitate failure to attain some designated outcome"; for example, it is important to "inquire into cultural factors that are preventive for learning, in particular, belief systems, institutions and policies that may impede acquisition" (2010, p. 49). This may be especially true for disadvantaged students who come from backgrounds where education may not be valued and expectations for academic performance are low.

Furthermore, the environment must *require* Cheri to be changed, instead of assuming she cannot change; "if the environment does not require the person to be modified but adapts itself to him or her . . . meaningful and sustained change will not occur" (Feuerstein et al., 2010, p. 127). For example, Cheri's environment will not support her progress in learning to read if her teacher has low expectations of her potential to become a reader. From a philosophical perspective, Scheffler (2010) suggests there is a propensity for success if the proper conditions are present in the environment. If given the opportunities, Cheri is much more likely to learn how to read.

Effort and Persistence

Effort in the form of persistent practice is a necessary element of achieving potential. Returning to Cheri's process of learning to read, if she has been read to, spoken to, and encouraged to speak at home since infancy, she is more likely to be comfortable with language. Children in high-income families are exposed to an estimated 30 million words at home by age 3, compared with 10 million words in low-income households (Bergland, 2014; Start Early, Finish Strong, 1999); the achievement gap between wealthy and poor children may be connected to this early exposure to language. Allington (2011a) contends that while only about one-third of students in the United States read at or above the proficient level, studies indicate that the vast majority of students could be reading on grade level if provided intensive instruction by expert teachers—in other words, if the right conditions for achieving their potential were met.

Support and Encouragement

Dave Eggers might never have taken himself seriously as an aspiring writer without the encouragement of his growth-minded high school English teacher. We know from a great body of educational research that children learn better in a positive environment where they feel safe, secure, accepted, and encouraged to take intellectual risks. In synthesizing more than 800 classroom studies, educational researcher John Hattie found a great deal of evidence for the role of positive teacher-student engagement in supporting learning. Hattie writes that creating a positive learning environment requires teachers to enter the classroom with certain conceptions about progress, relationships, and students. It requires them to believe that their role is that of a change agent—that all students *can* learn and progress, that achievement for all is changeable and not fixed, and that demonstrating to all students that they care about their learning is both powerful and effective. (2009, p. 128)

The power of plasticity, access to opportunity, persistent effort, and support from caring others are the necessary building blocks of potential. The achievement of academic potential requires hard work and commitment on the part of students and teachers and the provision of proper learning conditions—opportunities to succeed. Teachers must bear in mind that the conditions needed for students to achieve their potential differ from student to student and for each student over time. For example, our developing reader Cheri needs certain types of instructional support as she is learning to read, but once she has developed basic reading skills, she will benefit from different strategies as she aims to develop fluency and enhance her reading comprehension skills. With regard to this type of academic maturation or growth, Scheffler (2010) suggests that in developmental sequences conditions may vary and need to be timed appropriately. What should never be assumed is that this learning will simply happen on its own, or that it will happen when the wrong conditions are present or the right environment is not provided for a child.

The vast majority of students have the potential—or, as we say, the neurocognitive capacity—to make the academic gains necessary to achieve at grade level. The challenge and opportunity are that as students arrive in kindergarten, for example, their cognitive performance presents a broad range of manifest skills. In such cases, standard assessments of their skill level at a static moment are inadequate for predicting their future abilities

---

In Sum

Realizing one's potential is the result of making the most of neuroplasticity, access to opportunities, persistent effort, use of appropriate strategies, and support and encouragement from caring others.

and stand "in contradiction to the unpredictable essence of the human being" (Feuerstein et al., 2010, p. 86). The use of formative assessment to measure incremental progress toward skill mastery will more easily allow educators to measure students' potential and development over time. After all, as Dweck reminds us, "an assessment at one point in time has little value for understanding someone's ability, let alone their potential to succeed in the future" (2016, p. 29); instead, we should focus on measuring progress. We will explore the use of formative assessments in more depth in Chapter 3.

To Learn More

The Woman Who Changed Her Brain: How I Left My Learning Disability Behind and Other Stories of Cognitive Transformation by Barbara Arrowsmith-Young tells the story of a woman who overcame severe learning disabilities by building a better brain and used her experience to develop a program that has helped others do the same (2012, Free Press, a division of Simon & Schuster Inc.).

EDUCATIONAL LEADERSHIP: BEYOND THE CLASSROOM

To support all students in achieving their potential, policymakers, principals, and curriculum and assessment developers may need to first "revise their frameworks to reflect new models of children's thinking and take better advantage of children's *capabilities*" (Duschl et al., 2007, p. 5). Lyman (2016) has found that neuroscientifically literate principals have the potential to level the playing field for students with learning challenges through an application of findings from educational neuroscience. Principals can and are using the newest information about learning and the brain to help teachers transform classrooms and to help schools address the way students actually learn. Allington's (2011b) point, supported by studies, that every student could be reading on grade level by the end of 1st grade if they experience high-quality instruction and support could lead to a guiding question for educational psychologists and other school professionals: If the vast majority of students are not reading on grade level, is it a result of (a) a lack of academic potential, which as we have defined it would mean that there is a deficit in the neurocognitive system that cannot be changed, or (b) the fact that the students did not experience an effective, intensive system of reading instruction and support?

The greater question may then be on what basis decisionmakers at all levels, from state and federal policymakers to classroom teachers, assess academic success or failure. If we armed educators with a practical theory of potential and plasticity, the guiding question among all key stakeholders might well become: How do we adapt our instructional support system to effectively help more students fulfill their potential over time?

Indeed, supporting effective instruction is where many high-performing educational systems around the world have put their focus (Conyers & Wilson, 2016; Fullan, 2016), whether or not these systems directly acknowledge the concept of neurocognitive plasticity. There are a number of real-life examples in which virtually all students have become more successful within various academic domains (Cunningham & Allington, 2010; Walberg & Haertel, 1997). It should be noted, too, that significant academic gains have been made in educational systems with a large percentage of disadvantaged youth, which provides further evidence of the significant academic potential of children across all demographics. Findings from the PISA 2018 study continue to demonstrate that school systems can produce good outcomes among disadvantaged students. The most important school-based factor for doing so is teacher effectiveness (OECD, 2019).

Therefore, we advocate for systemic changes to focus on instruction and support student achievement. Scheffler (2010) implies that teachers, school and community leaders, and policymakers must actively set forth the conditions that provide students with the opportunity to actualize their potential; that is to say, it is an active rather than passive proposition to establish and support a learning environment that nurtures students' academic potential. Feuerstein and colleagues support specific training for parents and professionals to cultivate "a human modifiability perspective" (2010, p. 130); they argue that schools should be organized to allow teachers to observe and support each other and engage in ongoing training and peer learning.

In schools, the perspective that students' potential for academic achievement is fixed and immovable supports the argument that certain students have permanent deficits that cannot be surmounted. This view relieves policymakers and educators of the responsibility to teach and support struggling learners. On the other hand, an understanding of human potential can provide a foundation for educators to better recognize and accept their responsibility for their students' development. When driven by a belief that all children deserve the chance to reach their potential, educators can do much to advocate for these kinds of changes and shift the focus to support for effective education within our communities. What we do outside the classroom—the ways in which we make our voices heard and draw on our expertise to persuade those in a position of power—can have as profound an impact as what we do directly with our students.

In Sum

Teachers, school and community leaders, and policymakers work together to establish and support the conditions that provide students with the opportunity to actualize their potential.

FROM RESEARCH TO CLASSROOM PRACTICE: GUIDING STUDENTS TO ACTUALIZE THEIR LEARNING POTENTIAL

Teachers can use a variety of instructional strategies and approaches to guide students to achieve more of their learning potential in the following ways:

Plasticity-powered capacity to learn: Consider teaching students about how the brain changes as they learn—for example, by having students create models in class to learn how synapses form or by drawing on online resources that illustrate the brain's ability to grow through learning. By developing their understanding that learning changes the brain, students are more likely to persist through learning challenges, more confident in their abilities to succeed.

Access to opportunity: Challenge students and hold them to high expectations so that they are required to improve and reach their potential. Use formative assessments to determine when children need additional support and provide those opportunities at the appropriate time (see Chapter 3 for a discussion of formative assessments).

Persistent effort: Continue to provide additional support and interventions so that students are constantly challenged to practice. Helping students identify what motivates them internally is also a great way to get them to keep working.

Support and encouragement: Offer every student support, making sure that you communicate that you appreciate their effort, not just results. This type of praise helps students develop persistence. Offer encouragement to students throughout a project, helping them to understand that the process in addition to the results are part of the learning experience. Offer them an opportunity to assess their work so they can improve in the future. Share stories about other students and discuss role models who succeeded through hard work and persistence. Take the time to continually assess student progress, celebrating improvements and making changes in instructional strategies as needed to keep pace with students' learning.

WHAT'S THE BIG IDEA?

Research suggests that virtually all people have the capacity to learn, to grow, and to improve at the goals they set for themselves through hard work, persistence, and the use of effective strategies (Dweck, 2019). Effort, not just innate ability, is what often distinguishes successful people. When teachers help students believe in their ability to learn, these students are more likely to persist until they master challenges. Those initial successes then provide the motivation to keep learning and progressing. The same transformation is possible for people of all ages, including teachers; the realization that we have the potential to build skills in any new area can change our lives (ASCD, 2018; Wilson & Conyers, 2020).

To Learn More

To learn more about how to support students to reach their potential and achieve at higher levels, see *Developing Growth Mindsets: Principles and Practices for Maximizing Students' Potential* (Wilson & Conyers, 2020).

Key Terms

Incremental learning: Ensuring that all students begin with the basic skills and knowledge they need to continue to make steady academic progress through progressively more complex lessons.

Manifest skills: The skills and abilities that students demonstrate at a particular moment in time—for example, on starting a new school year.

Neurocognitive capacity: The brain's capacity to learn and change given the right conditions for learning to occur.

Potential: The neurocognitive capacity for acquiring the knowledge, skills, and attitudes to achieve to a higher level of performance in any domain.

Questions for Reflection

- When you were a student, did you have a teacher like Mr. Criche who particularly inspired or encouraged you? What did that teacher do or say to support you?
- Did you have a teacher who discouraged you from trying something? How did you respond?
- Do you know anyone who seems to have an innate talent for something? How much time and practice do you think that person has put into his or her particular area of expertise?
- What are some specific activities or strategies you are using or could use in your classroom that align with the elements described in this chapter to actualize potential? For example, how could you challenge students to commit to the hard work of learning by varying the lessons by which they practice new learning skills?
- What are some ways in which you could advocate for administrators and policymakers in your community to focus their dialogue and actions on cultivating all students' potential?

CHAPTER 3

Big Idea 3
Understanding Intelligence

Although genetics play a role, "a significant part of students' intelligence is attributable to environmental influences."

—Robert Sternberg and Wendy Williams,
Educational Psychology, p. 138

How do you define intelligence?

Intelligence—and our perceptions about it—clearly plays a role in student achievement and success throughout life. Virtually everyone has an opinion about his or her own level of intelligence as well as, in many cases, that of others. Often, too, people believe they are smarter in one area than another. Sternberg and Williams define intelligence as "goal-directed, adaptive behavior" (2010, p. 121). Gottfredson offers a similarly broad definition of intelligence, noting that it

> involves the ability to reason, plan, solve problems, think abstractly, comprehend complex ideas, learn quickly and learn from experience. It is not merely book learning, a narrow academic skill, or test-taking smarts. Rather it reflects a broader and deeper capability for comprehending our surroundings—"catching on," "making sense" of things, or "figuring out" what to do. (1997, p. 13)

These definitions allow wide scope for a variety of theories and ideas about the meaning of the concept. For example, to what degree is intelligence determined by nature and to what degree by nurture—genetics or the environment? Can people increase their intelligence? And most important, can teachers help students become smarter?

In the previous two chapters, we have learned that it is the interplay of nature and nurture that informs how people develop, in contrast to the myth of fixed potential. We discovered that the environment and instruction have a profound effect on the way children's brains develop and whether they will reach their potential in different fields. Extending that line of reasoning, evidence indicates that the same is true of intelligence—that is, while genetics play a role, "a significant part of students' intelligence is attributable to environmental influences" (Sternberg & Williams, 2010, p. 138).

In 1996, a review by a group of leading scholars (Neisser et al.) outlined what experts believed about intelligence at that time. The field called for an update to these findings, and a follow-up article was published in 2012 (by Nisbett et al.). While both reports are in agreement in many respects, there were several differences, including in the most recent report a strong emphasis on the role of the environment and the interaction between genes and the environment. The Nisbett report stated that

> much more is known about the effects of environment on intelligence, and a great deal of that knowledge points toward assigning a larger role to the environment than did Neisser and colleagues and toward a more optimistic attitude about intervention possibilities. (p. 2)

How did researchers arrive at this conclusion? They compared the academic performance and assessments of intelligence of twins and other siblings adopted by families of differing socioeconomic circumstances. Children growing up in wealthier families were found to have more consistent exposures to learning experiences and supports—in effect, environments more supportive of their cognitive development. Therefore, researchers concluded that genetic factors played a larger role in IQ differences among children raised in these environments. In other words, because these children had in common more support for developing their intellectual capacity and fewer environmental barriers, genetic differences became the most significant variable in explaining differences in achievement.

On the other hand, children with the same genetic background who were raised in lower-income families experienced a wider range of cognitive environments; some families put great emphasis on their children's learning, while others were less supportive. Given these variations in exposures to learning opportunities and support, the researchers proposed that variations in intellectual performance were more closely connected to the environments in which these children were raised. In many cases, these differences were subtle and difficult to quantify, but Nisbett and colleagues found sufficient evidence to suggest as one explanation that "children in poverty do not get to develop their full genetic potential" (p. 5), because environmental influences are less supportive of their cognitive development. An important implication for educators is that disadvantaged children may benefit even more than their peers from access to effective instruction and a positive learning environment.

Households of varying socioeconomic status (SES) also vary greatly in the number of encouraging statements versus reprimands children receive (Nisbett et al., 2012). Nisbett and his colleagues assert:

> We can be confident that the environmental differences that are associated with social class have a large effect on IQ. We know this because adopted children typically score 12 points or more higher than comparison children (e.g., siblings left with birth parents or children adopted by lower SES parents), and adoption typically moves children from lower to higher SES homes. (p. 7)

Interventions by teachers in the early grades can do much to help address these types of disparities between students when they first arrive at school. Allington (2011a) cites a variety of school-based studies showing that effective, intensive instruction in kindergarten and 1st grade can close the school readiness gap and prepare virtually all students to be reading on grade level by the end of 1st grade. Fielding and colleagues (2007) report on educational reforms that increased the percentage of students achieving reading and math goals from 57% in 1995 to 89% in 2006. Listening to children, talking with them, and reading with them are simple acts that can help bring their literacy skills up to speed, particularly when teachers coach parents on the importance of making these efforts at home as well.

In this chapter, we discuss the role of environment in intelligence, highlight different theories of intelligence, and explore how these various conceptions have an impact on student learning in the classroom. We do not present the full range of views on intelligence, nor do we focus particularly on IQ, which is just one way of evaluating intelligence. Instead, we concentrate on what we believe to be some of the best current and practical thinking on the subject, in terms of its application for teachers. We focus particularly on conceptions of changeable or malleable intelligence, which align well with the current views of brain plasticity and human potential discussed in this text. We then explore how teachers can structure their classrooms in ways that may increase intelligence and help students believe in their own capacity to get smarter, thereby increasing students' motivation, effort, and achievement levels. Ultimately, the concept of malleable intelligence allows teachers, students, and parents to focus on continual learning and improvement, a mindset that is particularly useful for helping those students who come to school without the prerequisite skills, content, and strategies needed to excel academically.

CONCEPTIONS OF INTELLIGENCE

In *Teaching for Wisdom, Intelligence, Creativity, and Success* (2015), Sternberg, Jarvin, and Grigorenko segment the various theories on intelligence into two major categories: "single-faceted" or general theories of intelligence (also known as *g*-factor) and "multifaceted" theories, "which emphasize the importance of multiple and distinctive aspects of intelligence" (p. 4).

The *g*-factor theory defines intelligence as a single ability that applies to many different kinds of tasks (Sternberg & Williams, 2010); those who believe in this theory generally assume that intelligence is a fixed, predetermined attribute (Sternberg et al., 2015). The theory was originally developed by Charles Spearman in the early 20th century, and some psychologists continued to believe that intelligence was a fixed attribute even after research showed that genetics only partially explained a person's level of intelligence. In fact, some psychologists and educators still believe in this theory of single intelligence (Sternberg & Williams, 2010).

In the 1930s, Louis Thurstone suggested that intelligence consisted not of one general factor but instead of seven primary mental abilities: verbal comprehension, verbal fluency, inductive reasoning, spatial visualization, and number, memory, and perceptual speed (Sternberg & Williams, 2010). Other researchers tried to synthesize elements of the general factor theory with Thurstone's theory. For example, Cattell (1971) and Horn (1968) offered their views that a general factor of intelligence exists but is made up of two major subfactors—fluid intelligence and crystallized intelligence. *Fluid intelligence* refers to abstract thinking, such as using logic, identifying patterns, and applying problem-solving skills in new situations. *Crystallized intelligence*, on the other hand, refers to all the knowledge and skills one possesses and the ability to apply those knowledge and skills; it generally increases with age.

More recent research supports this distinction between fluid and crystallized intelligence; in fact, brain imaging research has suggested that the prefrontal cortex is involved in fluid thinking (Nisbett et al., 2012). Furthermore, studies have shown that fluid intelligence can be enhanced by building working memory—the system that stores and uses information in the short term while disregarding distractions (see the discussion on cognitive strategies in Chapter 5). These findings further support the idea that intelligence is not a single factor or dimension, suggesting instead that "IQ is best represented by at least two dimensions rather than one" (p. 3). In other words, the research and latest thinking on intelligence point toward multifaceted theories of intelligence. This way of thinking about intelligence may help educators to consider how children with a learning difficulty in one area may well have strengths in other areas.

In Sum

General factor (*g*-factor) theories of intelligence envision intelligence as a fixed, predetermined attribute that applies to many different kinds of tasks, while multifaceted theories hold that intelligence encompasses a variety of abilities, including verbal comprehension and fluency, inductive reasoning, spatial visualization, and memory.

Theories that emphasize multifaceted conceptions of intelligence, and that assume intelligence can be changed or modified, can be particularly helpful for teachers. Indeed, researchers who believe in multifaceted conceptions of intelligence, according to Sternberg and colleagues, "generally agree that intelligence is the flexible capacity to learn from experience and to adapt to one's environment. . . . They also tend to agree that intelligence can be developed, whether through formal explicit instruction or in informal educational situations" (2015, pp. 4–5).

Howard Gardner's (2006) theory of multiple intelligences is perhaps the most well-known theory in U.S. schools that falls into this multifaceted category and is cited in many other works, including *Multiple Intelligences in the Classroom* (Armstrong, 2017). Gardner posited that there are eight distinct and separate types of intelligence: linguistic, logical-mathematical, spatial, musical, bodily-kinesthetic, interpersonal, intrapersonal, and naturalist.

Sternberg (1988) makes a strong case that people can make themselves smarter. His triarchic theory of intelligence postulates a set of three processing components: metacognitive components for planning and evaluation, performance components for implementing whatever you have decided upon, and knowledge-acquisition components that help you learn how to solve problems (Sternberg & Williams, 2010). These components then lead to three different aspects of intelligence: analytical, creative, and practical. A person does not need to be strong in each of these aspects to be intelligent: "Rather, intelligent persons know their own strengths and weaknesses. They find ways to capitalize on their strengths and either compensate for or correct their weaknesses" (p. 132). Recently, other researchers have agreed that Sternberg's work on practical and creative intelligence "showed that measuring nonanalytic aspects of intelligence could significantly improve the predictive power of intelligence tests" (Nisbett et al., 2012, p. 2).

Indeed, Sternberg, Kaufman, and Grigorenko argue that "being intelligent is more than just being book-smart; it is knowing how to apply it [intelligence]" (2008, p. 1). "Successful intelligence," in Sternberg's view, is "the ability to achieve success in life, given one's personal standards, within one's sociocultural context" (1999, pp. 292–293). Teaching for successful intelligence involves teaching four different thinking skills—memory, analytical, creative, and practical skills (Sternberg et al., 2015). Sternberg and colleagues have created a model that is meant to help teachers implement these theories and ideas in the classroom. This model—abbreviated as WICS, for Wisdom, Intelligence, and Creativity, Synthesized—builds on and expands traditional instructional models that emphasize memory and analytical skills while also incorporating the other important skills encompassed within successful intelligence. As Sternberg describes WICS:

> The basic idea is that citizens of the world need creativity to form a vision of where they want to go and to cope with change in the environment, analytical

Conversation with a Father

Soon after Donna Wilson became a school psychologist, her father drew on his own experience and urged his daughter to do what she could to ensure that test results were never used as a way to limit a child's opportunities. Like many of his generation, Charles Wilson rarely spoke of his military service during World War II. But he believed that the army's reliance at that time on the Army General Classification Test to award officer promotions was not the best way to identify the soldiers who were best equipped to lead under the pressure of battles.

The Army General Classification Test is described on a website about the history of military testing as "a test of general learning ability . . . used by the Army and Marine Corps to assign recruits to particular jobs." Charles Wilson felt that he had not performed particularly well on the test—perhaps because parts of the exam tested knowledge he had never had the opportunity to learn as a poor boy growing up in rural Oklahoma. But however he performed on that test, Private First Class Wilson used his practical and creative intelligence to save the lives of fellow soldiers in the jungles of the Pacific theater, for which he was awarded a Bronze Star. When he came home, Charles Wilson became a small-town entrepreneur who served on the school board for 25 years and wrote articles for local, regional, and state newspapers. He never spoke about his military award or the experiences that led to it, but the citation issued on December 10, 1945, tells the story:

> On 16 February 1945, Private Wilson was a rifleman in a cavalry troop. When the squad leader was cut down by enemy fire at the height of the bitter battle for Manila, he unhesitantly assumed command of his squad. In the face of mounting fierce resistance his squad was unable to advance, and unflinchingly he crawled forward in the face of deadly fire to locate and pinpoint an enemy machine gun nest that was taking a heavy toll of lives. After securing the information, he crawled back, briefed his men, and led them in a daring maneuver across fire lanes blanketed with barrages from artillery and mortar shells and through a minefield to the enemy's flank from where he brilliantly led an attack that annihilated the enemy's machine gun nest. Private Wilson's intrepid bravery and exceedingly outstanding display of leadership under fire reflects great credit upon him and the 1st Cavalry Division.

intelligence to ascertain whether their creative ideas are good ones, practical intelligence to implement their ideas and to persuade others of the value of these ideas, and wisdom in order to ensure that the ideas will help achieve some ethically based common good, over the long and short terms, rather than just what is good for them and their families or friends. (2010, pp. 603–604)

The WICS model can help students develop skills necessary for progressing in the school and work environments of the 21st century. The model is discussed in more detail in the "From Research to Classroom Practice" section later in this chapter.

The various conceptions of intelligence described here include some of the major theories in the field today. In the rest of this chapter we focus specifically on multifaceted conceptions of intelligence like Sternberg's; these can be particularly useful for educators because they emphasize the variations in intelligence and the ways in which intelligence can be developed. Researchers who have focused specifically on ways in which intelligence is changeable, dynamic, or malleable can offer a number of insights for teachers who wish to increase learning and achievement for all students in their classrooms. For all types of intelligence, Sternberg and colleagues note, "The brain functions in much the way muscles do. The more you exercise it, the better it functions" (2008, p. ix).

To Learn More

Robert Sternberg has written widely, on his own and with colleagues, on multifaceted conceptualizations of intelligence. *Applied Intelligence* (Sternberg, Kaufman, & Grigorenko, 2008, Cambridge University Press) and *The Triarchic Mind* (Sternberg, 1988, Viking) fully explain these theories of intelligence. For a practical guide to understanding and implementing Sternberg's work for 21st century classrooms, see *Teaching for Wisdom, Intelligence, Creativity, and Success* (Sternberg, Jarvin, & Grigorenko, 2015, Skyhorse Publishing). Finally, Sternberg's article for *The Chronicle of Higher Education*, "Finding Students Who Are Wise, Practical, and Creative" (July 6, 2007), describes how Tufts University implemented his ideas on its application for undergraduate admissions to identify students with a wider range of academic skills.

DYNAMIC, CHANGEABLE INTELLIGENCE

Reuven Feuerstein is a pioneer in the field of researchers who focus particularly on ideas of dynamic or changeable intelligence (Feuerstein, Falik, & Feuerstein, 2015; Feuerstein, Falik, Rand, & Feuerstein, 2006; Feuerstein, Rand, Hoffman, & Miller, 1980; Feuerstein et al., 2010). He worked primarily with adolescents and young adults with a history of environmental deprivation related to the Holocaust and with people with Down syndrome and other neurobiological challenges. His work is based on the belief that intelligence is a "dynamic energetic agent" (Feuerstein et al., 2010, p. 17) or a "dynamic self-regulating process that is responsive to external environmental intervention" (Feuerstein et al., 1980, p. 2), and that cognitive processes can be modified so that people become better learners and thinkers through effective teaching. Feuerstein is among researchers and practitioners who use dynamic assessment procedures that have the core purpose of increased thinking and learning capacity by measuring responsiveness to feedback.

To Learn More

Four books provide excellent overviews of Reuven Feuerstein's theory of dynamic intelligence and descriptions of his methods for cognitive modifiability: *Beyond Smarter: Mediated Learning and the Brain's Capacity for Change* (Feuerstein, Feuerstein, & Falik, 2010, Teachers College Press), *Creating and Enhancing Cognitive Modifiability: The Feuerstein Instrumental Enrichment Program* (Feuerstein, Falik, Rand, & Feuerstein, 2006, ICELP), *What Learning Looks Like: Mediated Learning in Theory and Practice, K-6* (Feuerstein & Lewin-Benham, 2012, Teachers College Press), and *Changing Minds and Brains—The Legacy of Reuven Feuerstein* (2015, Teachers College Press).

MALLEABLE INTELLIGENCE,
GROWTH MINDSETS, AND STUDENT LEARNING

Another conceptualization of dynamic intelligence comes from Carol Dweck (1999, 2016), who has distinguished between an "incremental" and an "entity" view of intelligence. The incremental view treats intelligence as changeable or malleable; individuals with this viewpoint gain

> **In Sum**
>
> Teaching students that intelligence is dynamic, malleable, and changeable is the first step toward developing the belief that they can get smarter through hard work and persistent effort.

satisfaction from the process of learning and often see opportunities to improve. In contrast with the incremental view, the entity view treats intelligence as fixed and stable. Individuals with an entity view have a high desire to prove themselves to others and to avoid looking unintelligent. Those views can be aligned with Dweck's (2016) work on mindsets; those with an entity view have a "fixed mindset" about people's ability to improve their intellectual capacity, and those with an incremental view have a "growth mindset" about the ability to get smarter.

The concept of flexibility in intelligence allows teachers, parents, and policymakers to focus on improvement with greater confidence in the outcome, especially in the case of low-achieving students. Teachers' views on malleable intelligence have significant implications for their students' academic performance, as teachers' beliefs on this subject influence students' beliefs and consequently students' motivation; unfortunately, about one-fourth of preservice and in-service teachers believe that intelligence is fixed (Jones, Bryant, Snyder, & Malone, 2012).

Likely as a reflection of the beliefs of their parents, teachers, and others, many students also believe that intelligence is fixed. Dweck conducted a study that followed students for 2 years as they transitioned from grade school to junior high, a challenging period for many students. Before the study began, she determined whether each student had a fixed or growth mindset: "Did they believe their intelligence was a fixed trait or something they could develop?" (2016, p. 57). The students had similar academic

> **To Learn More**
>
> For a description of the "fixed" and "growth" mindsets, as well as practical strategies and tips to cultivate a growth mindset in the classroom and in life, refer to Carol Dweck's *Mindset, the New Psychology of Success: How We Can Learn to Fulfill Our Potential* (Ballantine Books, 2016).

records at the start of the study, but over the next 2 years those with a fixed mindset showed a steady decline in grades while their peers with a growth mindset improved their grades. "With the threat of failure looming," Dweck writes, "students with the growth mindset instead mobilized their resources for learning. They told us that they, too, sometimes felt overwhelmed, but their response was to dig in and do what it takes" (pp. 57–58). Other studies yield similar results indicating that, in fact, students with a growth mindset are more apt to continue in the face of setbacks (Moser, Schroder, Heeter, Moran, & Lee, 2011; Nussbaum & Dweck, 2008), and, for some students, this mindset results in higher levels of achievement as shown on measures such as grades and test scores (Blackwell, Trzesniewski, & Dweck, 2007).

The growth mindset motivated these students to put forth greater effort in the face of challenges. Teachers with a growth mindset understand that beliefs about intelligence can drive *motivation* and *effort*, two critical components that allow anyone, including low-performing students, to continually learn and achieve.

MALLEABLE INTELLIGENCE, MOTIVATION, AND EFFORT

The word *motivation* derives from a Latin verb meaning "to move" and refers to "the processes that lead to the instigation, continuation, intensity, and quality of behavior" (Kaplan, 2009, p. 13). Since the early 1900s, psychologists have put forth various theories about what drives motivation. Recent theories have come to focus on cultural and social contexts as well as the cognitive concepts of "self" and "goals"—that is, how a person perceives his or her own level of competence, control, and autonomy and how a person sets goals that allow him or her to measure success or failure.

Attribution Theory

Weiner's (1980, 1992) attribution theory focuses on how people explain their own behavior, particularly as it relates to achievement. In terms of student motivation, Weiner's theory holds that students explain success or failure according to their beliefs along three dimensions:

- *The locus of control*—whether the student believes success or failure is based on an internal cause (such as his or her ability level) or an external cause (such as the way in which the teacher presented the material).
- *Stability*—whether the student thinks the cause of success or failure is likely to remain the same every time or to vary and produce a different outcome next time.
- *Controllability*—whether the student thinks he or she can control the cause of the outcome. A controllable cause might be the amount of time a student spends on his or her homework, while an example of an uncontrollable cause is a student's belief that he or she does not have the "math gene."

How people attribute their successes or failures (their beliefs about why they succeeded or failed) influences the amount of effort they will put forth for the same activity next time. Students are more likely to be motivated to put in effort if they believe that they have control over an outcome and that the situation is unstable—that is, likely to vary in outcome each time.

In Sum

When students learn that they are in control of their own learning, their motivation to work hard and succeed increases.

Goal-Setting

Goal-setting has also been shown to be effective in increasing motivation (Wilson & Conyers, 2020). Locke and Latham (2002) outlined four main benefits of goals:

- They increase and focus our attention on the project or activity at hand.
- They are energizing and increase our effort level.
- They help us persist over time.
- They help us create strategies and alternative routes to achievement.

Achievement Goal Orientation Theory

Achievement goal orientation theory (Ames & Archer, 1988; Dweck & Leggett, 1988) explains motivation by distinguishing between the types of goals toward which people are working. People with a mastery goal orientation are focused on building skills and increasing understanding; mastery goals are internally driven. Those with a performance goal orientation, on the other hand, focus on external goals, such as how teachers, peers, and others will judge or critique their work. Recently, researchers have further segmented a performance goal orientation into two types—performance approach orientation, in which people will work hard in order to be the best and show they're competent, and performance avoidance orientation, in which people try to avoid making mistakes or appearing incompetent (Svinicki, n.d.).

Connection to Malleable Intelligence

Dweck (1999) has argued that students who have an incremental, or malleable, view of intelligence are more likely to have a mastery goal orientation, while those who have an entity view are more likely to have a performance goal orientation. People are more likely to persist and work hard if they are driven by mastery goals—and more likely to enjoy what they are doing (Brophy, 2005; Dweck, 2016; Halvorson, 2012). While performance goals can also be very motivating, especially under a performance approach orientation, they are often tied to feelings of self-worth and can lead to a loss of self-confidence and a tendency to give up when things become too challenging. Those with a performance avoidance orientation may shy away from taking academic risks; students with this orientation, in particular, need to learn that making mistakes is an important part of learning rather than a potential source of embarrassment.

It is possible to change the goal orientation of students, classrooms, and schools to a mastery goal orientation and thereby have a positive impact on student achievement (Anderman, 2009; Dweck, 2016). Studies focused on the elementary and middle grades have demonstrated that student motivation to learn increases when students are directed to become more oriented toward mastery goals (Maehr & Midgley, 1996).

Both attribution theory and achievement goal orientation theory propose that believing in and focusing on one's ability to improve provides

---

In Sum

Mastery goals are internally driven, with a focus on building skills and increasing understanding. Performance goals are externally focused on how others will judge one's work.

---

the motivation needed to work hard—and that "students who see the value of effort and hard work in achieving their goals are more likely to be motivated and to push themselves" (Sternberg & Williams, 2010, p. 377). Dweck sums it up succinctly: "For students with the growth mindset, it doesn't make sense to stop trying" (2016, p. 59).

Clements and Sarama, writing specifically about mathematics, reach a similar conclusion:

> One deeply embedded belief is that achievement in mathematics depends mostly on *aptitude* or *ability*. . . . In contrast, people from other countries believe that achievement comes from *effort*. . . . *Even more disturbing, research shows that this U.S. belief hurts children and, further, that it is just not true.* Children who believe—or are helped to understand—that they can learn if they try, work on tasks longer and achieve better throughout their own school careers than children who believe you either "have it" (or "get it") or you do not. (2009, p. 212; emphasis in original)

Two Views of Intelligence

People who believe that intelligence is a single, predetermined attribute (g-factor) tend to . . .	People who believe that intelligence is multifaceted tend to . . .
Believe intelligence is fixed	Believe intelligence is dynamic or malleable
Have an entity view or fixed mindset	Have an incremental view or growth mindset
Have a performance goal orientation	Have a mastery goal orientation
Attribute their successes and failures to external, stable, and uncontrollable causes	Attribute their successes and failures to internal, unstable, and controllable causes

Students with a fixed mindset are sometimes afraid to put in effort. As Dweck explains, these students believe that the need to put in effort indicates that they don't have the inherent intelligence and skills to succeed; this viewpoint holds that people who are good at something don't have to try hard. Furthermore, if they do try, they won't have any excuses to fall back on if or when they fail. Therefore, Dweck writes, "students with the fixed mindset tell us that their main goal in school—aside from looking smart—is to exert as little effort as possible" (2016, p. 58).

REHEARSAL: TALENT VS. DELIBERATE PRACTICE

The fixed mindset can prevent students from ever gaining real expertise in a subject. Research by Ericsson and Ward (2007) on expert performance in fields ranging from surgery to musical performance emphasizes the fact that individuals have to practice a good deal to become an expert at something (Ericsson & Pool, 2016). In fact, this research has shown that top performers undertake thousands of hours of "deliberate practice"— practice in which an individual engages in a training activity, typically planned with the objective of improving performance beyond the current level and characterized by full concentration, feedback and analysis, and repetitions with an eye toward refinement (Ericsson & Pool, 2016).

Ericsson and Ward conclude that "the commonly held but empirically unsupported notion that some uniquely 'talented' individuals can attain superior performance in a given domain without much practice appears to be a destructive myth" (2007, p. 349). The implication for educators is that we should never underestimate the importance or power of practice or assume that someone cannot do something if he or she has not had an opportunity for extended practice. For example, we should recognize that becoming a proficient reader requires spending many hours in silent reading—and give students as many opportunities as possible to put in those hours reading books they enjoy. Furthermore, it is imperative to provide students with opportunities to practice through creative and innovative tasks, both to maintain interest and to accommodate a diverse range of students across a broad range of subjects.

Experts in a particular field have several advantages over novices, including an ability to remember information more easily, see the big picture, and problem solve more efficiently while making fewer mistakes.

It takes a good deal of willpower and time to focus on and commit to the deliberate practice required to develop expertise, especially given that willpower and time are limited resources—that is, people have only limited amounts of willpower and time to devote across all activities in their lives. Fortunately, research on endeavors such as study habits and physical fitness has shown that it is possible to increase willpower (Baumeister & Tierney, 2012). Setting both short-term (or proximal) and long-term (or distal) goals is a key part of the process of staying focused to achieve desired outcomes. These findings suggest that teachers can guide students to succeed by helping them set both long- and short-term goals and helping them find the right levels at which to set these goals in a zone that reflects the "analysis after feedback, and repetitions with refinement" elements reported by Ericsson and Ward (2007) as steps in the development of expertise.

Willpower in this context can be seen as a determination on the part of a student to overcome obstacles, difficulties, or delay in learning school-based content or skills, either in general or related to specific content or processes. Teachers can help students to develop this kind of willpower or determination to learn by guiding them to do the following:

1. *Stay focused.* People have a limited amount of willpower, so spending it to accomplish one goal will deplete the supply for other endeavors.
2. *Make a list of tasks* they need to complete to support or accomplish their learning goals, so they can monitor their progress.
3. *Celebrate milestones.* For example, once they finish a project, students could treat themselves by playing a favorite game or reading a book they've been looking forward to.

In Sum

Both teachers' and students' beliefs about intelligence can have a profound impact on the level of motivation and effort students exhibit—and their overall level of achievement. Current theories about motivation, effort, and the role of deliberate practice provide useful frameworks for educators who are intent on increasing student learning and helping all students realize their potential to get smarter.

USING FORMATIVE ASSESSMENT FOR INTELLIGENCE-BUILDING

Formative assessment refers to a diverse range of procedures employed throughout the learning process to gauge students' progress and identify the need to modify teaching and learning activities to improve achievement. The focus is on qualitative feedback for both students and the teacher about what is and is not working in facilitating learning. Formative assessment is continuous and dynamic; it is used by teachers and students as partners in learning to gather evidence that students have gained knowledge and that learning goals have been achieved. The use of frequent, low-stakes assessments also provides students with opportunities to enhance their memory. In contrast, summative assessment tends to be a quantitative measure of student outcomes.

Teachers are conducting formative assessment when they check in with students to verify understanding of the content they are teaching so they can provide additional instruction on lesson content for the whole class or selected students, if necessary. This form of assessment may involve quizzes and tests, but it also relies on classroom discussions, interviews with individual students, consultations on draft works, and observations of how students are applying what they have learned. Performance tasks and rubrics are common tools used in these ongoing evaluations; students may also use self-assessments such as journal entries and personal checklists where they can be prompted to monitor their own progress and reinforce learning strategies that they find especially useful.

A fundamental aim of formative assessment is to provide opportunities for students to exhibit their "true understanding" of what they have learned by explaining their new knowledge logically and with appropriate evidence, by interpreting new information and connecting it with what they already know, by exploring and appreciating other perspectives, and by applying what they have learned in other lessons and outside the classroom (McTighe & Willis, 2019; Wiggins & McTighe, 2005).

The aim of formative assessment is to foster students' learning. In that regard, it connects with current theories of cognition and instruction, including views on malleable intelligence. Lane and Tierney note that this form of measuring academic progress is "capable of evoking meaningful reasoning and problem-solving skills" and provides "results that help guide instruction" (2008, p. 469). It is also consistent with research on the importance of explicit instruction on metacognition and equipping students with cognitive and metacognitive strategies to encourage them to take charge of their own learning, which we will explore in Chapter 5.

EDUCATIONAL LEADERSHIP: BEYOND THE CLASSROOM

Teachers with the growth mindset love to learn themselves. Georgia teacher leader Susan Hyzer identifies herself as a lifelong learner and asserts that "most teachers are lifelong learners. Right now, I'm learning about interactive whiteboards and how to use them in classroom. . . . It's not easy, but you learn by doing."

Productive individuals focus on improving what they can control—and getting enough nurturance in life to do their work. For teachers, this nurturance needs to come from the policymakers, administrators, teacher educators, and professional developers responsible for facilitating ongoing teacher learning. Teacher educators can assist teachers-in-training to better understand the concept of malleable intelligence as it relates to human potential and brain plasticity and the importance of teaching thinking and reasoning skills.

Teachers must then be allotted adequate planning time—and time to plan lessons with their colleagues—to translate what they've learned into practical lessons. Through these efforts, teacher educators may empower practicing professionals with the vision, understanding, and tools with which to help their own students graduate prepared to learn and think well across their lives and careers.

FROM RESEARCH TO CLASSROOM PRACTICE: INTELLIGENCE AND A GROWTH MINDSET FOR 21st CENTURY SUCCESS

No matter how we define intelligence, the evidence indicates that education affects it. In an example tested in research, consider two children of the same age who enroll in different grades at the same time—one in 4th grade and the other in 5th grade. The child who enrolled in 5th grade will have a verbal IQ that is more than 5 points higher at year-end and up to 9 percentiles higher in 8th grade (Nisbett et al., 2012). In another study, researchers found that at-risk 1st-graders posted higher achievement scores if their teacher was considered to be within the top third of teachers (in terms of quality) as opposed to the bottom third: "Indeed, the performance of the children with the better teachers was not significantly worse than that of children with well-educated parents" (Nisbett et al., 2012, p. 9), which is a reliable predictor of student success. The conclusion that can be drawn from these findings is that effective instruction and support for learning can help children who arrive unprepared to "do school" catch up to their peers.

Such research points to the potential for teachers to have a significant impact on students' intelligence and achievement—and reinforces how important it is that teachers bring the right mindset to their work. As Dweck contends, "teachers with the fixed mindset create an atmosphere of judging" (2016, p. 200). These teachers assess students' performance at the beginning of the school year, deciding which students are smart and which are not, and use those labels as their guide throughout the year—in effect, giving up on the students for whom they have low expectations. Dweck describes a study conducted by Falko Rheinberg in Germany of teachers with different mindsets. Teachers with fixed mindsets made statements such as "'According to my experience students' achievement mostly remains constant in the course of a year'" and "'As a teacher I have no influence on students' intellectual ability'" (Dweck, 2016, p. 66).

On the other hand, teachers with a growth mindset—those who believe that intelligence is malleable or changeable—model this mindset in the classroom and foster the growth mindset among their students, leading to greater student motivation and effort. Working from this mindset, students can become smarter.

Classrooms of teachers with a growth mindset exhibit seven major characteristics:

1. High standards. Leanne Maule is a high school English teacher in Georgia. Her excellent teaching is evidenced by the high standards to which she holds *all* students, not just the high achievers. For example, she had her 9th-grade remedial English students act out the same scenes from *Romeo and Juliet* that gifted students in the same grade did—but instead of acting out the scenes in a traditional fashion, her students performed them in modern contexts they developed themselves. Students were able to increase and demonstrate their understanding of Shakespeare's language by putting it into their own words (Maule, 2009). Maule was named Georgia Teacher of the Year in 2009 in recognition of her success in the classroom, her emphasis on high expectations for all, and her refusal to give up on any student.

Clements and Sarama (2009) assert that high standards can be attained by encouraging students toward more abstract and complex understandings and by helping them "develop more efficient and elegant solution strategies" (p. 259). For example, when teachers solve problems aloud in the classroom, they help students learn to think at higher levels through effective modeling.

Dweck writes about Marva Collins, a teacher who held students from poor neighborhoods in Chicago to exceptionally high standards; her class of 2nd-graders began the year with the lowest-level reader but had graduated to the middle of the 5th-grade reader by the end of the year, "studying Aristotle, Aesop, Tolstoy, Shakespeare, Poe, Frost, and Dickinson along the way" (2016, p. 65). Later, Collins started her own school for children who were unable to make it in regular public school classrooms. Rather than "dumbing down" her curriculum, Collins had the 3- and 4-year-olds in her school using *Vocabulary for the High School Student* as they learned how to read; the 7-year-olds reading *The Wall Street Journal*; and older students reading Orwell, Chekhov, Shakespeare, and Chaucer. Collins made her high expectations clear from day one, telling students, "You must help me to help you. If you don't give anything, don't expect anything. Success is not coming to you, you must come to it" (p. 195).

2. A nurturing environment. High standards must be coupled with a nurturing environment to promote student motivation; as Kaplan summarizes, "Quality achievement motivation among all students is facilitated by caring and safe environments . . . in which the emphasis is on personal development and collaboration rather than on competition and social comparison" (2009, p. 16). Holding classroom discussions about the enjoyment that can come from working hard to solve challenging tasks can help promote such an environment, as can allowing students to select books for independent reading and to choose topics for class projects that align with their interests.

At the same time that Marva Collins held high standards and maintained strict discipline, she created a caring environment by making it clear that she was invested in her students' growth and success. When addressing a student who seemed determined not to try, for example, Collins said:

I am not going to give up on you. I am not going to let you give up on yourself. If you sit there leaning against this wall all day, you are going to end up leaning on something or someone all your life. And all that brilliance bottled up inside you will go to waste. (Dweck, 2016, p. 203)

3. Guidance for deliberate practice. Growth-minded teachers who believe in malleable intelligence understand that students must work hard to improve. As Ericsson and Ward's work (2007) has shown, hard work is most beneficial if it takes the form of deliberate practice—planned activities that require full concentration, include feedback and analysis on completion of practice activities, and are subsequently improved and repeated. Providing students with various opportunities to continually engage in such deliberate practice supports steady gains, particularly when it is possible to give students some choice in the way in which they practice.

4. Praise for effort and strategy use. Attribution theory demonstrates that motivation levels depend on how individuals view the locus of control, stability, and controllability of the situation. Teachers can promote attributions that increase motivation by focusing their praise on students' efforts and improvements, rather than the outcome alone (i.e., success or failure). The following are examples of statements that focus on effort and the use of effective strategies:

- "All that effort you put into your homework has really made a difference—look how much your grade improved on this week's quiz."
- "I can tell that you put a lot of work into this project; tell me about what you did."
- "You did a nice job on this project. I think you could have done even better if you had tried . . . "
- "I like how you looked up the definition yourself rather than just asking what the word means."
- "If you work on your note-taking skills, you will have better materials to use when studying for the next test."
- "You could have done even better on this test if you had spaced out your study sessions over a number of days instead of doing all your studying the night before."

5. A focus on mastery goals. Classrooms that focus on mastery goals also increase motivation. To help students develop mastery goals, teachers can use Epstein's (1989) TARGET acronym, as described by Anderman (2009):

- *Tasks:* Arrange classroom learning tasks so that they encourage all students to focus on personal mastery rather than competing with the performance of others. Tasks should be beyond students' current capabilities while still being achievable; they should also hold value for the students by being useful, inherently interesting, or challenging.
- *Authority:* Give students some control and choice over their schoolwork. For example, allow them to read books that interest them personally and are at an appropriate reading level.
- *Recognition:* Acknowledge the effort individual students have put into a task, their level of progress, and their accomplishments; refrain from comparing students to one another.
- *Grouping:* Identify students' individual interests rather than focusing on their perceived ability and then group students according to their interests rather than ability, when possible.
- *Evaluation:* Base evaluations on mastery rather than comparisons to others—for example, rather than comparing the amount of time it took students to complete the same task, consider how far each student has progressed since the last time his or her work was assessed.
- *Time:* Structure the classroom schedule so that all students are allowed time to master tasks rather than leaving tasks incomplete and assignments only superficially absorbed.

6. The use of formative assessments. Measuring what children are learning on an incremental basis and using that information to guide classroom practice supports an understanding of malleable intelligence. Teachers who share this understanding might use formative assessments to help students achieve their mastery goals. These assessments also help students understand how their hard work is translating into improvement.

Teachers with a growth mindset understand that standardized and intelligence tests provide only one piece of information about a student's intelligence. They should not be relied on as the only indication of a student's ability and should never be used as an excuse for lowering expectations about what students can achieve.

7. An emphasis on thinking skills. A large longitudinal study showed that only 5% to 10% of elementary school classrooms emphasize the development of cognitive skills (Pianta, Belsky, Houts, & Morrison, 2007). Yet teachers who hold malleable conceptions of intelligence understand that thinking skills as well as knowledge are required to be successful in the 21st century, both in work and in life (see Chapter 5 on metacognition for a further discussion of thinking skills). According to the WICS model (Sternberg et al., 2015), educators should provide explicit instruction on five specific types of thinking skills:

- **Memory skills.** Students must be able to retain and apply information. To maximize long-term memory skills, "it is better to give students several opportunities to study and review the same material. Ideally, the opportunities would be different in kind" (p. 20). *Long-term memory skills* involve the conscious identification of information and use of tools to retain that information for a long period of time. Sternberg and colleagues (2015) suggest spacing out reviews of material over a period of time and using mnemonic devices. For example, Edna Gibson, an 8th-grade science teacher in Whittier, California, provides explicit instruction on the use of different memory strategies, many of which also support student attention and focus, while helping them to build creative skills. For example, she uses pictograms to help students recall new concepts; students draw pictures to better understand chemical reactions and physical changes, concepts they are required to learn under California state science standards. "They keep them with them, and I post the best ones on the wall as a basis to discuss what we're learning in class. The kids love them," she says.
- **Analytical or critical thinking skills.** Analytical thinking, such as comparing/contrasting, critiquing, interpreting data, and making predictions, is more often emphasized in the classroom than other thinking skills. D'Jon McNair, a special education teacher in Acworth, Georgia, has designed an activity that emphasizes both practical and analytical skills. He has students study advertising fliers from three different stores to compare prices and calculate potential savings from coupons and other offers.
- **Creative skills.** Creativity does not belong just in art class; creative skills allow students to come up with new ideas and deal with new problems in any field. Kelly Rose, a teacher at Sarasota (Florida) Outdoor Academy, uses a variety of lessons to help her 2nd-graders think creatively and analytically. After reading a book about tornadoes and hurricanes, for example, she asks students

to create a new name for each and also engages them in a debate about which they would rather experience. In another lesson, when learning about the different types of camouflage animals use, students are asked to identify which kind of camouflage they would want to have and why.

- **Practical skills.** Practical skills help students apply knowledge to real-world situations, explore ideas from a personal perspective, and build their own metacognition. Gretchen Vermiglio, a former accountant who now teaches high school business education in Macomb, Michigan, focuses on creating lessons that build practical thinking skills among her students and promote metacognition—often by modeling improved metacognition herself. For example, she changed one of her lessons on income tax forms to be more student-centered and less teacher-driven. In the new version of the lesson, she no longer provides students with the basic information they need to compute values—now students do research on the computer to learn it for themselves. This simple shift in emphasis has enhanced learning.
- **Wisdom-based skills.** Sternberg and colleagues (2015) describe three types of wisdom-based thinking skills that educators can teach: *reflective thinking*, when students self-monitor their thinking and strategies and thereby increase their metacognition; *dialogical thinking*, when students strive to understand different perspectives and various points of view surrounding a topic and to consider alternatives; and *dialectical thinking*, when students

---

In Sum

Teachers can help their students maintain the motivation and effort they need to improve their academic performance by

1. setting high standards,
2. fostering a nurturing environment,
3. providing guidance for deliberate practice,
4. praising effort,
5. focusing on mastery goals,
6. employing formative assessment, and
7. emphasizing development and use of thinking skills.

learn how to integrate two perspectives that are at odds with one another.

The seven characteristics described here encompass some of the major strategies teachers can employ to create a growth mindset among their students and increase student motivation, effort, and achievement. When these strategies are put in place, both teachers and students find greater enjoyment and inspiration in their day-to-day work.

> ### From Teachers for Teachers
>
> Allison Groulx, who teaches high school students online, says, "Every person, every student, every parent is somewhere in their learning process and in their understanding of the cognitive assets [thinking and learning strategies]. If you meet them where they are and then you help them understand and grow in their thinking abilities, anyone is capable of anything. And that has really influenced every decision I make with students."

WHAT'S THE BIG IDEA?

While there are many different views on and definitions of intelligence, both among the general public and psychologists, perhaps the most useful view for educators is the idea that intelligence can be changed and shaped based on one's environment and experiences. After all, teachers are in the classroom to help students learn—why engage in a complex endeavor like teaching unless you believe that your efforts can and will make a positive difference?

As we look back on the preceding three chapters and consider our exploration of plasticity, potential, and intelligence, we can see that a solid foundation is emerging for approaching the rewarding and difficult work of teaching. We have learned that research supports the idea that people can learn new things across the life span—meaning that both students and teachers can expect to grow and develop through experience and hard work. Potential and intelligence are not fixed at birth; genetics plays a role in everyone's development, but genes do not determine what a person can ultimately accomplish. The concept of experience-dependent synaptogenesis suggests that people learn and develop based on their environment and the experiences they have in life.

These findings underscore the importance of a safe, nurturing classroom environment in which all students have the opportunity to fulfill their potential and increase their intelligence. The ability of any individual to grow in intelligence, or "get smarter," makes it clear that educators have both an enormous responsibility and an excellent reason to believe they can help all students learn—in other words, to deploy the growth mindset. Instruction in thinking skills as well as content is critical for students to become lifelong learners and engaged citizens in today's world; a further discussion of how teachers can guide students to develop cognitive and metacognitive skills forms the basis for Chapter 5. In the next chapter, we explore how the body and brain work together to support learning.

Questions for Reflection

Some education professionals adhere to a general factor (*g*-factor) theory of intelligence, others to a multifaceted theory, and still others to a combination of the two.

- In which camp would you feel most comfortable? Why? Have you changed your thinking about how intelligence is defined?
- Do your colleagues or others you spend time with have a fixed mindset or a growth mindset? What about your students? How can you tell?
- Whom do you know who most embodies the growth mindset? What behaviors illustrate this mindset to you?
- Aside from the examples offered in this chapter, what else might teachers with a growth mindset say about and to their students? What about teachers with a fixed mindset?
- What roles do effort and practice play in determining success in achieving a learning goal?
- What is an example of a strategy you have used or intend to use that builds thinking skills? Which of Sternberg's five types of thinking skills does your strategy build?
- What kind of training or professional development on the topic of intelligence would be useful to you? Are there ways you could try to ensure you can receive such training?
- Describe four people you respect for having practical intelligence, creative intelligence, analytic intelligence, and wisdom.
- What are your prime areas of intellectual strength, based on the discussions in this chapter? Describe.

Key Terms

Achievement goal orientation theory: A theory that explains motivation by differentiating between two types of goals that individuals might pursue—mastery goals and performance goals.

Attribution theory: A theory of motivation, developed by Bernard Weiner, that focuses on how people explain their own behavior, particularly in regard to achievement—that is, whether success is determined by effort or ability.

Entity view: A view of intelligence, suggested by Carol Dweck, that treats intelligence as fixed and stable.

Fixed mindset: Similar to the entity view of intelligence, the fixed mindset identified by Dweck describes a viewpoint that assumes individuals cannot increase their intelligence.

Formative assessment: A type of assessment that focuses on measuring student progress toward mastery of a concept or skill in order to identify ways in which teaching needs to be modified to promote learning.

General factor theory of intelligence: A theory of intelligence, originally developed by Charles Spearman, that defines intelligence as a single ability that is applicable across a broad range of tasks and activities.

Goal-setting: The act of setting goals in order to increase motivation.

Growth mindset: Similar to the incremental view of intelligence, the growth mindset identified by Dweck describes a viewpoint that assumes that individuals can make themselves more intelligent.

Incremental view: A view of intelligence, suggested by Dweck, that treats intelligence as changeable or malleable.

Intelligence: The capacity to understand, adapt to, and learn from our environment and experiences.

Intelligence quotient (IQ): A score on a standardized test that is meant to assess one's intelligence level.

Long-term memory skills: Conscious identification of information and use of tools to retain that information for a long period of time.

Malleable intelligence: A conception of intelligence that assumes that intelligence can be changed through the process of learning.

Mastery goals: Goals that are internally driven, such as building skills or increasing mastery of a task.

Performance goals: Goals that are externally driven, such as meeting others' expectations or achieving high grades.

CHAPTER 4

Big Idea 4

The Body-Brain System at Work for Learning

> When given adequate opportunity, support, and encouragement, children naturally think, feel emotions, and engage with their social and physical worlds. And these patterns of thoughts, feelings, and engagement organize brain development.
>
> —Mary Helen Immordino-Yang, Linda Darling-Hammond, and Christina Krone, *The Brain Basis for Integrated Social, Emotional, and Academic Development,* The Aspen Institute National Commission on Social, Emotional and Academic Development, p. 1

How do you think emotional and physical health might support the brain in learning?

Now we widen our scope to consider what research has to say about the whole child and how the brain and body work together to facilitate learning. Researchers throughout the United States and around the world have studied the impact of emotions, exercise, nutrition, and sleep on academic performance. Their findings have implications for the structure of the school day; the role of school breakfast and lunch programs; the essential nature of physical and health education; the crucial importance of an emotionally positive learning environment; and teaching strategies to incorporate movement, sensory activities, social awareness, and opportunities to collaborate with others into lessons (CDC, 2014).

We use the term *Body-Brain System* to signify how emotions, cognition, and the body influence the readiness, motivation, and ability to learn (Conyers & Wilson, 2015a; Wilson & Conyers, 2018). Human beings rely on a combination of emotional, physical, and mental health to achieve peak performance, and cognitive and physical "fitness" are closely intertwined. Research in three areas establishes the foundation for the Body-Brain System of learning:

1. Studies on the role of emotional health, the harmful effects of toxic stress, and social and emotional learning.
2. School-based studies on the impact of physical activity on academic performance;
3. Research on how physical activity, healthy nutrition, and sleep help to optimize cognitive processing, sharpen attention to learning, and enhance retention of what is learned.

This chapter examines the evidence for the connection between emotional, physical, and cognitive functioning.

SOCIAL AND EMOTIONAL LEARNING

As we have taught our BrainSMART® approach to educators over the past 2 decades, they have responded positively to learning how to increase student achievement by focusing on the fundamentals for effective learning.

The first component of our SMART framework is state, which refers to "the power to produce results by helping students switch on positive, low-stress/high-challenge frames of mind" (Wilson & Conyers, 2018, p. 81). Teachers can develop an optimal learning state in a classroom environment that is low on stress and high on practical optimism and appropriate levels of challenge by undertaking the following practices:

- Encouraging students to look forward to new learning experiences with anticipation and excitement instead of fear. Students who are practically optimistic are often better equipped to learn the skills needed to achieve their learning goals.
- Talking to students about age-appropriate and healthy ways to deal with stress. Among the strategies that teachers enjoy sharing are physical exercise, yoga, tai chi, journaling, peer support groups, and meditation.
- Reinforcing positive behavior helps students to strive for positivity and calm.

- Modeling a love of learning by sharing your excitement about something you are learning and telling your students why you are pleased to be learning it.
- Assisting students to think about a positive experience they had the day before, which can help even struggling students begin their day on a more upbeat note.
- Making adjustments with how you work with students to ensure their personal level of learning is being targeted, thus helping to motivate them to exert effort on challenges that are appropriate.

This type of environment fosters learning where students feel secure, safe, accepted, and encouraged to take intellectual risks.

The role of emotions in learning has been recognized for decades, even centuries; some modern educators point to Plato's writings linking positive emotions to educators. However, some school systems have not yet incorporated emotion comfortably into the classroom and curriculum. Further, our profession hasn't yet fully addressed the important relationship between an emotionally positive and stimulating classroom experience and the overall health of both staff and students. This observation reflects a consensus among teachers we have worked with that, while many students have the capacity for academic success, they often lack the positive mindset, focus, and dedication that fuels the hard work and persistence required to produce learning gains.

The antidote to this disengagement is forging connections in classrooms and schools through individual and group learning that engages emotions and guides students to develop emotional and social competencies. Emotional engagement activates regions of the brain involved in cognition, memory, and meaning-making (Immordino-Yang, 2016). The more students care about the subjects they are studying, from literature and social studies to math and science, the better they will perform academically when supported with effective learning strategies. Learning begins with emotion—and cannot happen without it.

In addition to the direct role of emotions in learning, explicit instruction guiding students to develop their abilities to acknowledge and manage their emotions in a healthy way and to interact in positive ways with others can improve academic outcomes. Schools play an essential role in raising well-adjusted children and youth by cultivating not only their cognition and achievement, but also their emotional and social development. Fostering positive emotions, an optimistic outlook, and fulfilling social relationships is a central aspect of optimizing the Body-Brain System of students for learning. When students are positively engaged in learning tasks, their brains operate at a peak level—focused, alert, and creating positive changes in their brains (Merzenich, 2013).

Scientific and educational research in recent decades (e.g., Durlak et al., 2011; Gilman, Huebner, & Furlong, 2009; Jackson, 2018; Zins, Bloodworth, Weissberg, & Walberg, 2004) has identified strong links between social and emotional learning and success in school. Durlak and colleagues define social and emotional learning (SEL) as "the process of acquiring core competencies to recognize and manage emotions, set and achieve positive goals, appreciate the perspectives of others, establish and maintain positive relationships, make responsible decisions, and handle interpersonal situations constructively" (2011, p. 2). School-based SEL programs have been shown to improve students' social skills, mental health, and academic achievement, with resultant benefits that may extend throughout their school years (Durlak et al., 2011; Taylor, Oberle, Durlak, & Weissberg, 2017). A meta-analytic study of 213 such programs involving 270,034 kindergarten through high school students found that, compared to control groups, SEL participants demonstrated significant improvements "in social and emotional skills, attitudes, behavior, and academic performance that reflected an 11-percentile-point gain in achievement" (Durlak et al., 2011, p. 1).

A follow-up study published 6 years later of 82 school-based programs involving 97,406 students from the same grades examined data collected 6 months to 18 years post-intervention. Results of this second meta-analysis showed that "participants fared significantly better than controls in social-emotional skills, attitudes, and indicators of well-being. Benefits were similar regardless of students' race, socioeconomic background, or school location" (Taylor et al., 2017). Yet another study analyzing data on more than 570,000 students found that guidance and modeling by teachers on developing social-emotional skills can have a positive impact on behaviors other than test scores, including reduced school absences and suspensions, higher grades, reductions in high school dropout rates, and improvements in graduation rates (Jackson, 2018).

As with intelligence, social and emotional skills are malleable and can be enhanced through explicit instruction, teacher guidance and encouragement, and practice over time. Attending to students' social and emotional development, in addition to their cognitive abilities, benefits children and youth individually, fosters a positive and productive learning

environment, and supports classroom management by reducing the inci-
dence of conduct problems. According to a research brief from the Aspen
Institute National Commission on Social, Emotional, and Academic Development, "studies indicate that classroom instruction and academic activities that connect rigorous cognitive challenges with social interaction
or that spark students' emotions result in deeper, longer-term learning"
(n.d., para. 2).

The Collaborative for Academic, Social, and Emotional Learning
(CASEL, 2019) recommends a framework for school-based SEL programs to help students develop five interrelated cognitive, affective, and
behavioral competencies: self-awareness, self-management, social awareness, relationship skills, and socially responsible decisionmaking. Guiding
students to understand and develop these competencies supports social
and emotional learning. These skills and abilities are also critical aspects
of metacognition, the big idea explored in Chapter 5. The strategies presented in this chapter to prime the Body-Brain System for learning and the
cognitive and metacognitive strategies presented in the next chapter are all
useful in supporting SEL goals.

In Sum

In addition to teaching students to wield their cognitive abilities, schools have
a fundamental responsibility to support social and emotional learning so
that students learn to recognize and manage their emotions, set and achieve
positive goals, appreciate the perspectives of others, establish and maintain
positive relationships, and make responsible decisions.

To Learn More

CASEL shares the core competencies at the foundation of its framework
for school-based SEL programs at casel.org/core-competencies. The
Aspen Institute National Commission on Social, Emotional, and Academic
Development offers its vision for incorporating SEL components in
classrooms, schools, and communities in its report *From a Nation at Risk to a
Nation at Hope* (nationathope.org).

MODELING AND TEACHING PRACTICAL OPTIMISM

Over the years our approach to fostering SEL and positive learning states has been informed by psychologists such as Martin Seligman, one of the founders of the positive psychology movement, whose research links optimism to cognition. For example, Seligman (1998) reported on a study focused on classroom outcomes for 4th-graders involved in learning tasks at a high level of challenge based on their current abilities. As the students struggled to solve the problems, two distinct responses to the challenge emerged. One group of children exhibited optimism about their capacity to succeed; they asked questions and tried different strategies, persisting until they completed the task. The other group of students exhibited pessimism and gave up quickly as the tasks became harder. Their attitudes conveyed a lack of confidence in their abilities to succeed, and their problem-solving skills, as assessed by researchers, dropped by as much as three grade levels.

Neuroscientist Richard Davidson describes just a few of the many contexts in which developing and maintaining an upbeat, optimistic outlook can benefit students' cognitive abilities and social interactions: "When positive emotion energizes us, we are better able to concentrate, to figure out the social networks at a new job or new school, to broaden our thinking so we can creatively integrate diverse information, and to sustain our interest in a task so we can persevere" (2012, p. 89).

A growing body of research supports the importance of students' believing that they can succeed as the fuel that powers the persistence necessary to make learning gains (Boman, Furlong, Shochet, Lilles, & Jones, 2009; Dweck, 2019; Hattie, 2009, 2012; Seligman, 1998, 2002, 2011, 2018b; Yeager et al., 2019). This research underscores how essential it is for teachers to model and provide explicit instruction on the value of an optimistic outlook. Put simply, the difference between the attitudes that "I can't do this" and "I can if I work harder" is often the difference between failure and success. The good news is that teachers can guide students to become more optimistic through modeling and encouragement.

We use the term *practical optimism*, which refers to an approach to life that relies on taking practical positive action to increase the probability of successful outcomes (Conyers & Wilson, 2015b; Wilson & Conyers, 2020, 2016; Wilson, Conyers, & Buday, 2013). The major advantage of developing practical optimism is a boost in perseverance in achieving what you set out to do. Adopting this approach enhances critical thinking and problem-solving abilities. A positive outlook may lead to greater student motivation. It can enhance engagement in learning and determination to tackle challenging tasks and material.

People with an optimistic outlook are more likely to be undaunted by setbacks and to keep trying until they succeed. Their tenacity is fueled by their belief that they will prevail over adversity, learn from their failures, and overcome plateaus in performance and progress. On the other hand, pessimists are more likely to give up, drop out, and doubt their abilities. They tend to internalize setbacks and view challenges as permanent and insurmountable. Where pessimists see obstacles as a reason to quit, optimists see one more task to complete, one more puzzle to solve on the road to success. As Achor notes, "When we are happy—when our mindset and mood are positive—we are smarter, more motivated, and thus more successful. Happiness is the center, and success revolves around it" (2010, p. 37).

Guiding students to develop practical optimism about their learning ability is not about conveying that anyone can succeed without effort. The message is that when students set learning goals, identify and carry out strategies to meet their goals, monitor their progress and adjust strategies as needed, and persist when the going gets tough, they will accomplish what they set out to do. Thus, an important component of practical optimism is *self-awareness*, which can be described as the skill of recognizing one's own emotions, thoughts, and beliefs, as a necessary step in students' development in influencing their learning behaviors. As an important aspect of social and emotional learning, this key competency works as a "tool for monitoring and controlling our behavior and adjusting our beliefs of the world, not only within ourselves, but, importantly, between individuals" (Price-Mitchell, 2015, para. 4).

Self-awareness encompasses the ability to accurately assess one's limitations and strengths, with a well-grounded sense of one's mindset about the learning task as well as confidence and optimism to take on an appropriate learning challenge. The essential skill of self-awareness is sometimes understood as taking a step back to observe one's thoughts, actions, and beliefs about learning. This type of reflective thinking is an aspect of metacognition, which is the subject of Chapter 5.

In Sum

Practical optimism is an approach to life that relies on taking positive action to increase the probability of successful outcomes. When teachers model and encourage this approach, students learn that when they think they can succeed, they often do—through persistent effort and hard work.

MANAGING STRESS

Guiding students to recognize the impact of stress on their capacity to learn is an important component of self-management within the SEL framework. Outside of school, some students may be coping with difficult situations, including poverty, violence in their neighborhoods or homes, or family problems such as divorce or illness. In school, they may feel threatened by being bullied or have feelings of alienation or confusion over incomprehensible lessons and learning materials. Anxiety over tests, fear of being ridiculed for giving "wrong" answers, feelings of isolation as the result of physical or language differences, frustration over the inability to understand information presented in lessons—all of these negative feelings are sources of stress that may impair learning.

Stress is not inherently bad; in some forms, it can even have a positive impact in making students feel alert, engaged, and ready to respond to a challenge, such as finishing a big class project, preparing for a test, or competing in an academic bowl. But high levels of chronic stress and high-threat situations can have a toxic effect, impairing cognitive processing and students' ability to learn and thrive. When the brain feels threatened and is focused on survival, its capacity for other types of learning is reduced.

While teachers cannot eliminate the stresses in their students' lives outside the classroom, they can foster a positive learning environment in which all children feel safe and secure, valued and accepted, and encouraged to take intellectual risks. In contrast to situations where students feel threatened or intimidated, having learning experiences that they find interesting, relevant, and enjoyable may stimulate the production of neurotransmitters that promote increased attention and stimulate the brain's memory centers. Teachers can provide explicit instruction on stress reduction strategies and on the power of persistence and belief in one's ability to succeed. In addition, educators can and should advocate for a safe and supportive environment in the homes and communities where children grow up. To paraphrase a popular axiom: it takes a community approach to maximize children's educational potential.

In Sum

Emotional health is an essential component of the Body-Brain System. In optimal learning environments, students feel safe, secure, accepted, free from severe life stresses, and optimistic about their ability to learn.

From Teachers for Teachers

A kindergarten teacher participating in a qualitative study involving educators enrolled in a graduate program (Germuth, 2012b) spoke about the connection between a positive classroom environment and learning success. "When you model it and transfer positive thinking, [students] really learn to set their goals higher [and] improve their self-esteem," the teacher explained. In a school with a high proportion of disadvantaged students, "for some of the kids the best part of the day is being at school," she added. "When you can make it a positive day and a goal to look forward to, it impacts their future and how positive they can be with their goals" (p. 9).

STRONGER BODIES, SHARPER MINDS

Cognitive, social, and emotional learning are reinforced and refreshed by incorporating physical activity into the school day (CDC, 2014). Research on the role of physical education in optimizing both body and brain functioning dates back to the 1950s (Sibley & Etnier, 2003). These findings make a solid case for supporting physical education programs, but also have implications for classroom teachers in emphasizing the benefits of incorporating movement into lessons and transition periods.

In their meta-analysis of 44 studies on the connection between physical activity and academic performance, Sibley and Etnier (2003) note that in the 1970s, PE programs were touted largely for their physical health benefits, but more recently, requirements that students in elementary, middle, and high school participate in regular physical education have dwindled. In many districts, phys ed programs, along with art and music, have been cut back in the name of budgetary belt-tightening and increased time spent on core academic subjects with the aim of improving performance on mandatory standardized tests. In response, the focus of research has swung back to gauge the effects of reduced opportunities for students to engage in physical activity during the school day and the extent to which exercise may support students' attention to and success in learning.

Sibley and Etnier report on four large-scale studies in which schools expanded the time allotted for physical education during the school week:

> In each of these studies, time spent by students in PE was significantly increased at the expense of time spent in academic classes. In three of the studies, significant improvements were found . . . and in the fourth . . . there were no significant differences in performance. (2003, p. 244)

In other words, at worst, expanding phys ed did not decrease academic achievement, and there was a great deal of evidence that it had a positive impact on learning. The researchers' larger analysis of studies involving a wide variety of physical activity (resistance/circuit training, traditional physical education, aerobic exercise, and perceptual-motor training) found gains across the board in math and verbal tests, perceptual skills tests, and measurements of IQ and academic achievement. In short, they reported that "physical activity has a positive relationship with cognition across all design types, for all participants, and for all types of physical activity" (2003, p. 251). The association between exercise and cognitive gains was especially strong for younger students—those in early elementary grades—and the researchers also cited several studies identifying benefits for students with learning disabilities as well as their peers. They point out the irony of cutting back on opportunities for physical activity with the aim of improving academic performance when, in fact, many studies indicate that physical activity supports learning gains.

One of the studies cited in the meta-analysis was undertaken by the California Department of Education (CDE) involving hundreds of thousands of 5th-, 7th-, and 9th-graders. That research assessed students' level of physical health using the Fitnessgram (a battery of assessments to measure aerobic capacity, muscle fitness, and body composition) along with their performance on the Stanford Achievement Test. That research found a "consistent positive relationship between overall fitness and overall achievement" on math and reading tests, but Grissom (2005) cautions against the conclusion that physical fitness automatically leads to academic gains; rather, "it is more likely that physical and mental processes influence each other in ways that are still being understood" (p. 11).

These links between fitness and academic achievement are borne out in research from other countries as well. For example, Swedish medical researchers (Aberg et al., 2009) connected a heart-healthy diet and exercise to improved school performance for teenagers and young adults.

In their analysis of research on the interactions between physical fitness and cognitive abilities, Tomporowski, Davis, Miller, and Naglieri (2008) note that exercise training seems to have the most obvious impact on executive function, which involves higher-order thinking skills that help to control other abilities and behaviors. *Executive function* is an umbrella term that encompasses the cognitive abilities needed to set and work toward goals, such as planning, organizing, developing strategies, identifying and remembering important details, and managing time and space. These abilities are useful in processing complex stimuli and novel situations and environments (see Chapter 5 for more discussion on executive function and metacognition). Thus, the researchers note that "exercise training programs may prove to be simple, yet important, methods of enhancing aspects of children's mental functioning that are central to cognitive and social development" (first paragraph under Conclusions).

Other researchers have looked more closely at what type of physical activity might be most beneficial in supporting academic gains. Castelli, Hillman, Buck, and Erwin (2007) corroborated the results of the California study in similar research among 3rd- and 5th-graders at four Illinois schools, two of which were considered academically effective (more than three-fourths of students met or exceeded math and reading standards) and two of which were not. Two of the schools were also in high-poverty areas, with two-thirds of students receiving free or reduced-price lunches. At all four schools, the researchers noted generally that "physical fitness was related to academic performance." More specifically, "aerobic fitness was positively associated, and BMI [body mass index] was negatively associated, with total academic achievement, reading achievement, and mathematics achievement, whereas muscle strength and flexibility fitness were observed to be unrelated to achievement test performance in this data set" (p. 248). Sattelmair and Ratey also make the distinction that "the quality of physical education is vitally important to cognitive and academic outcomes" (2009, p. 369); they advocate for daily aerobically demanding activity and physical education "that focuses on personal progress and lifelong fitness activities by encouraging modes of physically strenuous play that are engaging, challenging, and enjoyable to students" (p. 370). However, there is also growing evidence that even less intense activity can have a positive impact on learning. For example, one study found that when students walked for just 10 minutes prior to engaging in memory and mathematical reasoning tasks, there was significant improvement in their results (Mualem et al., 2018).

In Sum

A wide body of research suggests a connection between physical fitness and academic achievement. To learn more from the authors on this topic, see "Smart Moves: Powering Up the Brain with Physical Activity" (*Phi Delta Kappan* online, 2015), kappanonline.org/smart-moves-powering-up-brain-physical-activity-conyers-wilson).

THE SEARCH FOR CAUSAL CONNECTIONS

How does physical fitness contribute to cognitive functioning? Researchers have suggested a number of mechanisms that fit into two broad categories: physiological mechanisms and learning/developmental mechanisms (Entin, 2012; Sibley & Etnier, 2003). The first category is based on the premise that physical changes in the body produced by exercise enhance the brain's ability to learn. These mechanisms might include increased oxygen in blood flow to and in the brain, alterations to neurotransmitters, structural changes in the central nervous system, and arousal of the senses to enhance engagement in and attention to the tasks of learning. Along these lines, Castelli and colleagues report:

> Greater aerobic fitness has been associated with changes in neurocognitive function . . . as higher fit children exhibited a more effective neuroelectric

profile than lower fit children on a stimulus discrimination test. The higher fit children also performed better along behavioral measures of reaction time and response accuracy, perhaps stemming from greater allocation of attentional resources to working memory. (2007, p. 249)

The second category encompasses theories that "movement and physical activity provide learning experiences that aid, and may even be necessary for, proper cognitive development" (Sibley & Etnier, 2003, p. 244). As just one example, the researchers cite the work of Piaget, who theorized that "skills and relationships learned during physical activity carry over to the learning of other relationships and concepts" by young children (p. 244). More generally, Sattelmair and Ratey suggest that physical activity has a positive impact on healthy child development and contributes to memory, concentration, and a positive mood, all of which have "a significant bearing on a student's academic performance" (2009, p. 365). A recent summary of research states:

The neurological impact of movement on the brain can be understood at three levels: increased vascularization—oxygen and glucose to the brain— augmenting brain activity; the release of neurotransmitters and Brain Derived Neurotrophic Factor (BDNF) which favor neurogenesis, memory, attention and motivation; and the development of complex movement-related neural circuits and their interconnection with the executive brain functions (Doherty & Forés Miravalles, 2019, p. 105)

One likely mechanism for this connection is that regular aerobic exercise facilitates better blood flow and oxygen intake throughout the body and brain, which supports both physical and mental exertion. And Begley notes that "walking 30 minutes a day five times a week stimulates production of BDNF (brain-derived neurotrophic factor), a molecule that

---

To Learn More

To learn more about the relationship between physical activity and cognition, see *Physical Activity and Cognition: Inseparable in the Classroom* (Doherty & Forés Miravalles, 2019) at the following link: frontiersin.org/articles/10.3389/feduc.2019.00105/full

nurtures the creation of the new neurons and synapses that underlie learning" (2012, p. 33).

Thus, whether the mechanism for exercise-enhancing learning is primarily physiological or developmental, a wide range of classroom studies support the role of regular physical activity and physical fitness in increasing academic performance. Later in this chapter, we will present several recommendations for how classroom teachers can apply this research.

In Sum

Aerobic activity at certain intensity levels has been shown to facilitate cognitive functioning. As research continues to explore cause and effect, the clear message is that physical fitness, exercise, and healthy BMI have positive results for learning. To learn more, see a meta-analysis of the research on academic achievement and physical activity at the following link: pediatrics.aappublications.org/content/pediatrics/140/6/e20171498.full.pdf

---

HIGH-OCTANE FUEL FOR LEARNING

Hand in hand with how physical activity supports the ability to learn is the need to fuel the Body-Brain System with healthy eating habits. Much of the research on the connection between nutrition and school performance has focused on the impact of skipping breakfast or starting the day with sugar-laden cereals and drinks. Several large-scale studies conducted in the United States in the 1980s and 1990s among students from low-income families showed significant improvements in reading comprehension, test scores, classroom behavior, and school attendance following the introduction of a school breakfast program (CERI, 2007). Another study compared test scores involving attention to and working memory of learning tasks following no breakfast, a glucose drink, and a bowl of cereal rich in complex carbohydrates; only the final breakfast choice was found to facilitate mental performance over an entire morning in the classroom (Wesnes, Pincock, Richardson, Helm, & Hails, 2003).

Beyond breakfast, several components of healthy nutrition may have implications for fueling students' attention to learning tasks and ability to learn—and to their teachers' health and energy levels as well:

From Teachers for Teachers

During the home stretch of guiding her middle school students to prepare for standardized state tests in the spring, Georgia teacher Meg Norris finds it helpful to take short breaks—5 minutes of fresh air outdoors or a quick stretch followed by a high-protein snack—to help students stay focused and energized. Ms. Norris provides explicit instruction on healthy nutrition to maintain the brain in peak working order, but she was still surprised when a student handed her a piece of candy he had earned in another class and told her, "Here, this isn't good for my brain."

Up with "good" fats. In an article entitled "Food for Memory," Mehmet Oz and Michael Roizen (2012) cite research that foods high in saturated fats and sugar may play a role in reduced cognitive functioning and memory loss as people age. On the other hand, monounsaturated and polyunsaturated fats have been found to have positive effects on blood cholesterol levels by reducing LDL and increasing HDL (a.k.a., "good cholesterol"). Monounsaturated fats are found in seeds, nuts, olive oil, and avocados, while salmon, albacore tuna, mackerel, and sardines are good sources of polyunsaturated fats. These nutrients are good for the brain as well. In particular, the omega-3 fatty acids found in fish oils are powerful nutrients that may help transmit signals between brain cells. CERI editors (2007) report on studies showing that children with a learning disability called developmental dyspraxia, or developmental coordination disorder (DCD), made significant improvements in reading and classroom behavior as a result of taking a dietary supplement with omega-3 and omega-6 fatty acids.

Fatty foods may make brains sluggish. In addition to the links between a diet high in saturated fats to weight gain and cardiovascular disease, recent animal experiments show that eating fatty foods over the course of several days can impair cognitive functioning as well (Parker-Pope, 2009). Researchers fed rats low-fat chow (7.5% fat content) and trained them to navigate a complex maze with a treat of sweetened condensed milk waiting at the end. The researchers kept the maze clean, so the rats would need to rely on memory rather than smell. After two months, half the maze-trained rats began dining on feed with 55% fat content. After just four days of increased fat intake, these rats had a much tougher time making it through the maze than they did when they were on a low-fat diet. All of them took much longer to get to the end. The rats who remained on the low-fat diet continued to navigate the maze efficiently.

Antioxidant power of fruits, vegetables, and whole grains. Nutrients such as vitamins C and E, beta carotene, and selenium—all found in fruits, vegetables, nuts, and whole grains—help to stave off the damage caused by a process known as *oxidative stress*, which is related to mental decline and other age-related degenerative diseases. Research funded by the U.S. Department of Agriculture reveals that these antioxidants not only counter brain decline but may also help head off cancer. In addition, researchers for the American Society for Nutrition (Jonnalagadda et al., 2010) summarized the substantial medical evidence that adding whole grains to one's diet can lower the risk of chronic diseases, including coronary heart disease, diabetes, and cancer, and contribute to weight management and gastrointestinal health.

The staying power of protein. Substituting lean protein for breakfast and lunch choices high in fat or sugar may help to enhance attention to learning tasks. Excellent sources of lean protein include fish (which, depending on the type of fish, may also supply omega-3 fatty acids), white-meat poultry (without the skin), low-fat dairy products, eggs, beans, and soy.

Importance of adequate hydration. Water helps to keep the Body-Brain System functioning at peak capacity. Like the rest of the body, brain matter is composed primarily of water, which is essential in facilitating neuronal transmission. Drinking plenty of water, especially as an alternative to sugary sodas and sport drinks, is a smart idea.

In Sum

A healthy breakfast, proper nutrition, and hydration may help students stay focused on learning. For a summary of current research on nutrition, see *Eat, Drink, and Be Healthy: The Harvard Medical School Guide to Healthy Eating* (Willett & Skerrett, 2017).

PREPARING FOR LEARNING WITH A GOOD NIGHT'S SLEEP

Lisa Meltzer, principal investigator of a large sleep study at National Jewish Health and the Cherry Creek School District in Greenwood Village,

Colorado (Meltzer, McNally, Wahlstrom, & Plog, 2019), reports, "biological changes in the circadian rhythm, or internal clock, during puberty prevents teens from falling asleep early enough to get sufficient sleep when faced with early school start times" (quoted in American Academy of Sleep Medicine, 2019, para. 3).

These findings are important given that the quantity of learning that occurs in the classroom owes to some extent to the quality of sleep students get the night before. The propensity among some adolescents of middle and high school age for late nights is in direct conflict to school days that begin at 8:00 a.m. or earlier. As Lamberg (2007) says, the need for adequate sleep is part of the human condition; in studies that take place in "time-isolation laboratories"—facilities with no clocks, windows, or other clues about the time of day—participants naturally sleep about one-third of the time. In other words, 8 hours of sleep is part of our natural equilibrium. The mental sluggishness that characterizes inadequate sleep may be related to an imbalance of neurotransmitters involved in the sleep-wake cycle.

When students are chronically sleep-deprived, their attention to and memory of lesson content suffers. Researchers at the University of California at Berkeley (Anwar, 2010) conducted a variety of experiments demonstrating that sleep helps to clear the brain's short-term memory and make room for new information. One study by this group on the impact of pulling all-nighters to cram for exams showed that this practice actually decreases the brain's capacity to recall facts by nearly 40%. Support is building for delaying middle and high school start times so that students can get enough sleep to improve their chances for academic success (American Academy of Sleep Medicine, 2019).

Health education should encompass proper "sleep hygiene" alongside information about the role of physical activity and good nutrition in nurturing the Body-Brain System due to the fact that getting enough sleep is crucial to adolescent development, health and well-being, and academic growth. The National Sleep Foundation (sleepfoundation.org) is a resource for those who wish to learn more about the importance of sleep.

FROM RESEARCH TO CLASSROOM PRACTICE: PUTTING THE BODY-BRAIN SYSTEM TO WORK

The proper care and feeding of the Body-Brain System contribute in myriad ways to learning success. CASEL (n.d.) shares a case study from Cunningham Elementary School in Austin, Texas, where teachers and administrators are working together to create a formal social and emotional learning program. In monthly staff meetings, the principal and teachers share best practices for fostering social and emotional learning in classrooms, develop schoolwide SEL activities, and discuss how to incorporate instruction on social and emotional competencies into existing lessons. For example, in art class, students created posters that are displayed throughout the school depicting strategies they can use to solve problems and interact positively with peers. The school also created "peace paths" to guide children in conflict with peers to begin on opposing sides and follow a resolution process square by square until they meet in the middle with a solution. SEL strategies have also been shared with parents to incorporate and model at home. School climate surveys and a playground survey administered at Cunningham School measuring staff and students' perceptions have found a positive impact on these continuing efforts.

Physical education has also earned a place in the school day alongside math, science, language arts, and social studies. The authors of this text, in partnership with the Winter Park Health Foundation, were involved in a coordinated health improvement program with students of the Orange County (Florida) Public School District (Conyers & Wilson, 2015a). The program encompassed physical and health education, health promotion for students and staff, nutrition lessons and services, and parent-community involvement. Student participants reported healthier eating habits, adding more vegetables and fruits to their regular diet and reducing sugar intake; increased regular physical activity; and improved hydration during the school day. An analysis found that these changes in eating and exercise habits helped students maintain a healthier body weight (Wang & Ellis, 2005). In addition, an assessment of the program cited measurable academic gains, a decrease in absenteeism, and reports from teachers of improved classroom management (Conyers & Wilson, 2015a; Watson, 2010).

In another example of exercise at work in an educational setting, the "culture of fitness" adopted by Naperville (Illinois) Community Unit School District 203 demonstrates the connection between physical fitness and academic success. Naperville is a well-to-do Chicago suburb, which is notable because socioeconomic status correlates to test score trends, but the gains reported by this school district as a result of incorporating physical fitness alongside core classes are remarkable. Eighth-graders achieved the highest scores in science and sixth-highest in math among 38 nations participating in the Third International Mathematics and Science Study (TIMSS) in 1999, and the school district continues to study how to sustain this level. In one attempt to boost academics through physical activity, a group of struggling students at Naperville Central High School was scheduled to take phys ed right before these students' most challenging classes. In the 6 years since launching that initiative, students who took phys ed directly before English have read on average a half-year ahead of those who didn't, and students who took gym class right before math posted big gains in standardized tests (Iskander, 2011). Naperville schools have also been recognized by the Centers for Disease Control and Prevention for their commitment to encourage students to be fit for life.

Beyond this direct connection between body and brain fitness, incorporating movement and physical activity in the school day supports learning in several other ways:

Enhancing attention. Experienced teachers see firsthand the benefits of short exercise or stretching breaks or an active recess on the playground in helping to resharpen the focus on learning. Research also suggests that short breaks may aid memory consolidation in the brain (Bönstrup, Iturrate, Thompson, Cruciani, Censor, & Cohen, 2019).

Supporting cognitive flexibility. You may have experienced this phenomenon yourself. When you are dealing with a perplexing problem, try taking a break and going for a run or walk or stopping by the gym. Physical movement has the power to free the mind of clutter and help fresh ideas and possible solutions "click" into place.

Fueling creativity through playful physical activity. In his book *Shine*, Hallowell suggests that "people at play produce creative results and leap from the humdrum to the exceptional" (p. 36). He defines *play* as "any activity that engages the imagination. You can play while solving a geometry problem or giving a speech. You can play doing anything. . . . Play is the most creative activity of the human brain. In play the brain totally lights up" (2011, p. 132).

Engaging the senses. The visual, tactile, auditory, and olfactory senses gather the input that sends signals to the brain, which in turn causes the rest of the body to react and engage with the world. An especially effective way to engage the senses is to get outside every day, if possible. Taking a break outside can help students refresh and refocus. Even "opening the windows from time to time and taking a pause to stretch and breathe in fresh air is beneficial to the performance of students" (CERI, 2007, p. 67).

> ### From Teachers for Teachers
>
> In teaching Spanish to students of Parsons Elementary School in Gwinnett County, Georgia, Joe Frank Uriz infuses lessons with sensory experiences to "bring language learning to life." For example, Mr. Uriz engages 3rd-graders with various fruit hidden in a "mystery bag," which students touch and manipulate as they try to put a name to what's hidden inside in their new language. Taste tests also incorporate other senses into lessons introducing the vocabulary of tropical fruits of the Americas, along with the addition of music and movement with a clapping chant song called "Frutas." These varied approaches enhance attention, meaning-making, and retention of new Spanish words for students.

Darla Castelli, a University of Illinois professor of kinesiology and community health who has studied the connection between physical activity and cognition, recommends that outdoor recess be part of every school day and that teachers look for opportunities to integrate movement into their lessons. As just one example, when reading a poem about the changing season, Castelli suggests encouraging students to act like falling leaves (University of Illinois at Urbana-Champaign, 2009).

As Lamberg summarizes the complex interactions of the Body-Brain System:

> The brain is connected to every part of the human body, and to the outside world, by a communications network dominated by two major components, nerves and messenger chemicals, primarily neurotransmitters and hormones. . . . These busy communications circuits—and we have quite a few of them, often performing simultaneously—make up, in effect, an intricate "brain-body loop" [that] orchestrates the most familiar routines of our lives. . . . The interaction of brain and body managed by this system is also proving to be an important influence on the state of our overall health and mental vitality, often in ways we modify. (2007, para. 4)

WHAT'S THE BIG IDEA?

Key implications of research about how learning must involve the "whole child" lend support for incorporating guidance of social and emotional

To Learn More

Positively Smarter: Science and Strategies for Increasing Happiness, Achievement, and Well-Being (Wiley, 2015) by Marcus Conyers and Donna Wilson discusses research and presents strategies for enjoying the benefits of greater happiness, well-being, and success over the lifespan.

learning systems into classroom instruction. Additional aspects of priming the Body-Brain System for learning include physical activity in the school day, school meal programs that offer nutritious choices, and school and community environments in which all students feel safe, protected, and accepted. Educators may choose to model practical optimism, to teach healthy habits for lifelong fitness, and to convey to students that their life-style choices can offer short-term benefits and longer-term dividends in de-laying heart disease and stroke. They can encourage emotionally healthy habits to manage stress and stave off depression and remind their students of the need for adequate exercise and rest. As the CERI editors note:

> Many of the environmental factors conducive to improved brain functioning are everyday matters—the quality of social environment and interactions, nu-trition, physical exercise, and sleep—which may seem too obvious and so eas-ily overlooked in their impact on education. They call for holistic approaches which recognize the close interdependence of physical and intellectual well-being and the close interplay of the emotional and cognitive. (2007, p. 76)

In our work with educators, we have found that the framework of the Body-Brain System is effective in empowering teachers with a practical way of thinking about the dynamic relationships among emotional health, life-style, and learning. This concept is useful in helping them to develop a great-er understanding about factors influencing student learning, and they often share what they have learned in their interactions with parents, which may have a wider impact of creating a healthier environment in students' lives outside school. In addition, teachers can apply knowledge of the brain-body connection to cognition and well-being to have more energy for teaching, to support a more positive emotional state, and to manage stress with the aim of maintaining a higher level of effectiveness in their personal and profes-sional lives (Conyers & Wilson, 2016, Germuth, 2012a, 2012b; Harman &

Germuth, 2012). Equipped with an understanding of the interconnection of the body and brain in support of learning, teachers may be empowered to share this knowledge with parents and with their own families as well.

Key Terms

Body-Brain System: The way in which the body and brain work together to promote learning; primary supports for optimal functioning of the Body-Brain System include healthy nutrition, regular physical activity, adequate sleep, and attention to the role of positive emotions in supporting learning.

BDNF: Brain-Derived Neurotrophic Factor, a protein secreted in the brain that supports neuronal and synaptic growth; exercise has been found to increase production of this chemical, which may enhance learning.

Movement in the classroom: Incorporating movement in the classroom to help students stay focused and energized.

Physical fitness: Research demonstrates that physical fitness supports increased cognitive functioning and academic achievement.

Practical optimism: Focusing on practical, positive actions to achieve successful outcomes.

Proper nutrition: Emphasis on healthy eating (a diet that relies more on fruits, vegetables, lean protein, and whole grains with fewer fatty and high-carbohydrate foods) to help students stay engaged and focused on learning.

Self-awareness: The skill of recognizing one's own emotions, thoughts, and beliefs.

Social and emotional learning (SEL): Explicit instruction with the aim of guiding students to recognize and manage their emotions, set and achieve positive goals, appreciate the perspectives of others, establish and maintain positive relationships, make responsible decisions, and handle interpersonal situations constructively.

Stress management: Strategies to relieve unhealthy levels of stress that can impair cognitive processing; classroom environments that are safe, positive, and accepting can help reduce stress and allow students to focus on learning.

Questions for Reflection

- Can you recall examples from your professional practice when students' emotional engagement with the subject matter seemed to enhance their learning?
- How might guiding students to develop social and emotional competencies such as managing their emotions, setting positive goals, and developing positive peer relationships improve the classroom learning environment?
- Have you seen evidence in your professional practice or time spent in the classroom of the positive impact of physical activity on learning? Explain.
- Have you noticed personally how dietary choices can either make you feel alert and energized or sluggish and less attentive? Describe.
- How do you feel after encountering stressful situations? What techniques or strategies do you use to deal with stress in your life?
- How can educators best model and teach "the proper care and feeding of the Body-Brain System" to optimize learning?
- How could you use research about the impact of physical activity and proper nutrition on learning in your teaching practice, in educating parents, and in your personal life?

CHAPTER 5

Big Idea 5
Metacognition as a Path to Becoming Functionally Smarter

It is clear that there is strong evidence indicating that when metacognition is
effectively taught in schools then there is a very positive effect on pupil outcomes.

—John Perry, David Lundie, and Gill Golder, from the abstract for
Metacognition in Schools, *Educational Review*, Vol. 71, Issue 4

*How might you become functionally
smarter and guide your students to be the same?*

The title of this text promises five big ideas for teaching and learning, foundational concepts that are closely intertwined—from neuroplasticity to potential to the malleability of intelligence to the way the body and brain work together to support learning. This chapter explores the fifth component, that of *metacognition*, which we define as thinking about one's thinking with the goal of enhancing learning (Wilson & Conyers, 2016, p. 8). In its simplest terms, metacognition involves being mindful of one's thinking processes, such as strategies to puzzle out the meaning of an unfamiliar word or improve recall of specific facts. The goal of teaching students to be metacognitive is to guide them to consciously recognize when and how to employ the thinking and problem-solving strategies that work best for them. Decades of research across contexts (Baas et al., 2015; Donker et al., 2014; Dunlosky & Metcalfe, 2009; Hacker, Dunlosky, & Graesser, 2009; Hattie, 2009, 2012; National Academies of Science, Engineering, and Medicine, 2018; Perry, Lundie, & Golder, 2019; Wang, Haertel, & Walberg, 1993; Winne & Azevedo, 2014) analyzing hundreds of studies offer support for explicit instruction on metacognition and cognitive strategies as one of the most effective ways to improve school performance and to help students achieve their academic potential by managing their own learning. Arguably, guiding students to become metacognitive may be one of the most important aspects of schooling if we are engaged in education that supports those aims. However, research indicates that relatively few educators are taught to explicitly teach this vital skill in some countries, for example, in the U.S. (Baker, 2013) and England (Perry, Lundie, & Golder, 2019); a report from the American Council on Education notes that "the majority of students are not prepared to manage their own learning or to be self-regulated learners when left to their own devices" (Jankowski, 2017, p. 8).

However, in some of the world's highest-performing educational systems, policymakers have encouraged the development of a variety of approaches to ensure that students are explicitly taught to use cognitive and metacognitive strategies (Perry, Lundie, & Golder, 2019). For example, in Shanghai, students and teachers are supported to use creative thinking strategies (Retna, 2016); Hong Kong is encouraging schools to adopt critical thinking (Cheng & Wan, 2017) and other higher-order cognitive strategies in the classroom (Yeung, 2015); and Finland has put significant effort into the development of curricula for teaching thinking skills across academic subject areas (Vainikainen, Hautamäki, et al., 2015; Vainikainen, Wüstenberg, et al., 2015).

Teaching students to think about their thinking—about what worked and didn't work as they learned new material and how they can improve their cognitive processing in the future—makes them more independent, effective, and self-directed learners. Explicit instruction on metacognitive strategies supports the *process* of learning and can be applied across *content* areas and in students' lives outside school. Teaching and modeling these strategies helps students to become more independent and self-directed learners. An apt metaphor is teaching students "to drive their brains" (ASCD, 2018; Wilson & Conyers, 2016).

METACOGNITION THROUGH THE AGES

The idea that we can enhance our ability to learn through the conscious employment of thinking strategies can be traced back to the teachings of philosophers in ancient Greece. Socrates believed that knowledge comes from within ourselves, and he exhorted his students to reflect on their own thinking through what we now call Socratic questioning. The word *mnemonics* also has its roots in ancient Greece; people have long relied on rhymes, phrases, acronyms, and symbols to aid in remembering important

---

From Teachers for Teachers

Donna Garland, who teaches 2nd-graders at Hamilton Crossing Elementary School in Cartersville, Georgia, includes daily exercises for maintaining a positive learning state and focusing attention on metacognitive strategies to enhance learning. Mrs. Garland's students have each colored and personalized a "brain car" cartoon, which they keep posted at their desks as a reminder that they have the power to drive their brains.

---

facts. As just one example, in the Middle Ages, people were taught the Abbey Memory System, in which a series of objects were memorized in specific locations of an abbey as a way to support recall (Dunlosky & Metcalfe, 2009). The 17th century British philosopher John Locke proposed that we gain knowledge by reflecting on our experiences and our perceptions of the world around us.

The term *metacognition* dates back to Flavell's work in the 1970s (Flavell, 1979), but the study of how cognitive processes develop is best known from the work of theorists in the field of psychology over the greater part of the past century. Jean Piaget's theories of cognitive development explored how children reflect on problems and consider different possibilities (Piaget, 1977). Russian psychologist Lev Vygotsky (1962) examined the deep connection between speech and cognitive development and was among the first to propose that deliberate mastery of higher-order thinking skills is crucial to the development of knowledge. Reuven Feuerstein (Feuerstein et al., 1980, 2015) is also known for an approach that assists educators and psychologists to guide youth with learning challenges to "learn how to learn" and to become better thinkers through the use of cognitive and metacognitive processes. In addition, neuroscientists have begun to identify the areas in the prefrontal cortex that are associated with metacognition (Fleming, 2014).

THINKING ABOUT THINKING: TWO LAYERS OF LEARNING

Much has been written about the impact of explicit instruction on metacognition on students' academic success. Dunlosky and Metcalfe (2009) summarize the research on emphasizing self-regulation, or teaching children to monitor and control their learning. Markman (1979), who studied monitoring as a comprehension strategy, reported that if students double-check what they learned and what they didn't understand when listening to a presentation or reading a passage, for example, their understanding and recall are better than those of students who are not taught to monitor.

In his synthesis of more than 800 meta-analyses focused on student achievement, Hattie differentiates between two layers of problem solving: (1) applying a strategy to solve a problem and (2) selecting and monitoring that strategy. That second layer is metacognition, which Hattie describes as "higher-order thinking which involves active control over the cognitive process engaged in learning" (2009, p. 188). As just one example, teaching students to use the HEAR strategy (one of several cognitive tools presented later in this chapter) to improve their listening and selective attention involves the first layer of problem solving, while teaching them to know when to use this strategy and to monitor how effectively they use it constitutes the second layer—the realm of metacognition. Hattie (2009, 2012) identifies several areas where teaching students to think about their use of thinking strategies has been demonstrated to have significant positive impact on school performance:

- Organizing and transforming, such as creating an outline before writing a paper;
- Self-consequences, such as rewarding oneself with an enjoyable activity after completing an assignment;
- Self-instruction, such as verbalizing the steps in solving a math problem;
- Self-evaluation, such as rereading and correcting an essay exam before submitting it; and
- Seeking help, such as looking up unfamiliar words or organizing a study group.

An earlier meta-analysis by Wang, Haertel, and Walberg (1993) also assembled research showing that the most fundamental learning characteristic of high academic achievers is the use of metacognition. The authors classified 28 categories related to student learning into 6 broad themes, including school organization, board policy, classroom instruction, and student characteristics, and scored those themes based on evidence of their

---

In Sum

A wide range of educational research indicates that explicit instruction on cognitive and metacognitive strategies improves school performance.

positive influence on learning. Students' use of metacognition and effective instruction by teachers on the use of those strategies were found to be crucial in increasing student achievement across grade levels. More recently, a study by Veenman and colleagues (2014) indicates that the ability to use a metacognitive approach to learning may account for some 40% of the variation in academic achievement across a variety of outcomes.

Metacognition, in the form of self-monitoring and self-teaching, is a necessary prerequisite for learning content knowledge and skills, such as those needed for reading and writing. Reliance on these critical thinking abilities helps students become independent learners. In addition, metacognition can aid students in enhancing the crucial emotional and social competencies of self-awareness, self-management, social awareness, relationship skills, and decisionmaking that will aid them in school and in their personal and future career endeavors.

Equally important are decades of findings indicating that these skills can be taught and that students who learn how and when to use them may outperform those who do not (Cawelti, 2004; Brown, Pressley, Van Meter, & Schuder, 1996; Education Endowment Foundation, 2019; Feuerstein et al., 2010, 2015; Graham, MacArthur, & Schwartz, 1995; National Academies of Science, Engineering, and Medicine, 2018). Palincsar and Brown (1984) led a classic study to teach 7th-graders to improve their reading comprehension through the use of study strategies, including summarizing, questioning, clarifying, and predicting; the researchers used reciprocal teaching, in which tutors and students took turns modeling and discussing how to use the strategies to monitor comprehension. A metacognitive approach to instruction that guides students to define their individual learning goals and monitor their progress in achieving them can help develop a variety of essential skills. Table 5.1 on the next page provides practical examples of metacognition in action based on key strategies identified by National Academies of Science, Engineering, and Medicine (2018).

CONNECTING METACOGNITION AND EXECUTIVE FUNCTION

Executive function is a term used to describe the brain processes and mental faculties that support metacognition. Roebers (2017) indicates that both executive function and metacognition play important roles in cognitive development and that the relationship between the two is dynamic. Goldberg describes the prefrontal cortex as the brain's "chief executive officer" for its role in "forming goals and objectives and then in devising

Table 5.1. Practical Examples of Metacognition in Action

Metacognitive Strategies	Examples of Strategies in Action
Gathering the information necessary to understand print	Looking for clues about the meaning of unfamiliar words in the text and then looking up the words online or in a dictionary to verify and clarify meaning
Assessing thinking and behavior they are using to obtain meaning from print	Asking questions such as: Does this passage make sense? How can I look at this in a new way to understand it better? How does it connect with what I already know about this subject? Where can I find out more information?
Using adequate planning behavior as they prepare to complete learning tasks	Developing a to-do list for researching and writing a paper; finding a space free of distractions for reading
Requiring precision and accuracy in their work and studies	Double-checking the operational symbols and calculations in math equations to verify the answers. Reviewing writing to see if word choices are the best and most specific to convey meaning and if ideas are expressed well enough to be fully understood.
Adequately attending to a given task	Listening carefully and taking notes during a presentation; paraphrasing what the speaker has said to ensure understanding
Finishing tasks on time	Devising a step-by-step schedule for a research project
Learning from feedback and spontaneously monitoring and correcting their own mistakes	Revising a paper based on constructive comments from a teacher or peers; reviewing answers on a test before handing it in
Using self-regulation while learning	Summarizing the action and interaction of characters in each chapter of a novel and predicting what will happen next. Noticing when one's mind wanders while reading informational content and developing strategies to maintain focus.

plans of action required to obtain these goals. It selects the cognitive skills required to implement the plans, coordinates these skills, and applies them in correct order" (2009, p. 23). The prefrontal cortex, located in the brain's frontal lobes, is also active in monitoring and evaluating the achievement of goals and in assessing the relative success in executing plans of action, which are tasks central to metacognition. Thus, by teaching students to be more metacognitive, teachers aim to help them harness the power of their brains' executive function. Research by Diamond and Ling (2015) indicates that executive function is critical for success in all aspects of life and is sometimes more predictive than even socioeconomic status or IQ.

Diamond (2013) states that core skills comprising executive function are responsible for success in life across contexts. These core interrelated skills include inhibitory control, cognitive flexibility, and working memory. Developing these core mental faculties can help students improve their attention to learning, flexibly adjust to changed demands or priorities, see things from new and different perspectives, and delay gratification (such as rewarding themselves with a favorite activity after completing a school assignment). From these faculties, higher-order executive function can be built, like planning and reasoning.

Carlson (2011) used imaginative storytelling to encourage preschoolers to engage in symbolic play as a way to stimulate flexible and abstract thinking—with the aim of demonstrating that it is possible to measure and begin promoting executive function in very young children. She cited other studies indicating that the degree of executive function demonstrated as children mature and progress from reflexive to reflective behavior may be evident in different academic and social outcomes in adulthood, ranging from criminal behavior to personal health habits to collegiate achievement. Guidance from parents, teachers, and other influential adults and an environment conducive to developing these higher-order thinking skills are crucial aspects of this maturation process.

In Sum

Teaching students to be more metacognitive may harness the power of their brains' executive function, which is responsible for making, monitoring, and evaluating the achievement of goals and for assessing the execution of plans of action.

TEACHING AND FACILITATING THE USE OF COGNITIVE STRATEGIES

Thus, a crucial finding in the research about metacognition and executive function is that the skills and strategies that permit students to take charge of their learning can be taught. Through explicit instruction, modeling, and encouragement, students can learn to identify and overcome deficiencies in comprehension, reasoning, problem solving, and communication. The aim is to equip students with a "toolbox" of specific cognitive strategies and to teach them how and when to use these tools to successfully master learning and problem-solving challenges inside and outside the classroom. Students can go beyond their zone of proximal development—the difference between what they can do independently and what they can do with the guidance of a teacher or more advanced peer—if they are taught strategies for learning.

Wilson and Conyers (2016) define useful "cognitive assets," or thinking strategies to enhance the probability for student success throughout the learning process. Earlier in author Donna Wilson's career when she worked as a classroom teacher and then as a school psychologist, her experience was that most struggling learners had not received explicit instruction in strategies that could help them overcome their difficulties. She began to focus her professional pursuits on identifying the cognitive and metacognitive strategies that could help all students improve their school performance and on supporting teachers to provide explicit instruction on strategies to prepare students:

- To ask questions, gather the information and evidence needed to answer them, and set learning goals;
- To define a problem, analyze the information they have gathered, assess the validity of the available evidence, consider and test different possibilities, and connect existing knowledge with new information; and
- To communicate and apply their new knowledge by writing essays, delivering reports, and demonstrating their understanding in tests, informal assessments, and real-world applications.

In each of these areas, students benefit from learning to use specific cognitive and metacognitive strategies. Explicit instruction on the use of these strategies and on the "language of learning" and cognition helps to enable students to use the skills they need to master learning challenges across the curriculum. Talking about the importance of metacognition and thinking about their thinking underscores that students are in charge of their learning and that they have the tools they need to set and accomplish learning goals.

Consider the example of an assignment to write an essay. Preparing students for that task entails instruction on both the process of writing (gathering and analyzing information; developing a thesis statement or argument; organizing and writing; and finally, editing and proofreading) and the components of an essay (the introduction setting out the thesis statement, body, and conclusion). This explicit instruction sets out learning challenges as a series of executable tasks and equips students with a common vocabulary they can use to assess their progress, pinpoint areas where they may need to improve, and identify the strategies to help them do so.

CONNECTING COGNITIVE STRATEGIES
TO CURRENT RIGOROUS STANDARDS

Educational systems around the world have adopted rigorous standards. Teaching the use of cognitive and metacognitive strategies is consistent with and supportive of preparing students with the learning skills they will need to master such standards. In this section, some of the many examples are linked to the U.S. *Common Core State Standards* for language arts and mathematics. The strategies described here are relevant not only to assist students to meet the rigorous *Common Core State Standards*, but also for helping them meet other demanding requirements set elsewhere. Beyond this set of standards, these strategies are important for supporting students to reach criteria set forth in other sets of standards.

The Common Core State Standards for English Language Arts and Literacy in History/Social Studies, Science and Technical Subjects (National Governors Association Center for Best Practices & Council of Chief State School Officers, 2010a), which have been adapted by many states as part of their own state standards, acknowledge that students may benefit from "the full range of metacognitive strategies . . . to monitor and direct their thinking and learning" (p. 4). The following sections offer specific examples of just a few of the many ways in which teaching students to use these types of strategies aligns with the aim of the Common Core State Standards. These connections involved in guiding students to master standards by equipping them with useful and versatile cognitive strategies clarify an important point: While the standards themselves have been developed relatively recently, the instructional strategies that support them are not new. The research foundation for the effectiveness of teaching metacognitive strategies has been building for decades, and many educational standards that may be seen as the precursors to the Common Core State Standards and new state standards emphasized the importance of explicit instruction of cognitive and metacognitive strategies.

One additional benefit of approaching the act of learning as a process of (1) gathering information, (2) exploring and elaborating on that information, and (3) communicating what has been learned is that it can help to give teachers a clearer view of where struggling students may need additional support as part of formative assessments. If a student seems to understand the lesson content but does poorly on tests, for example, the teacher may decide to focus on strategies that support communicating what has been learned. On the other hand, if a student's essay is well-written but marred by factual errors or faulty logic, the problem may lie in the exploration and elaboration stage, and the teacher can focus on cognitive strategies useful in analyzing and understanding the learning material. The following sections offer examples of useful cognitive strategies at each of these stages, along with some implications for classroom instruction.

Cognitive strategies may be specific to one domain, such as skills to support reading, math, or science, or they may be more general. The strategies presented here can be applied to most areas of study and thus will aid students in learning across the curriculum and in their lives outside school and in their future careers.

In Sum

Learning how and when to use cognitive and metacognitive strategies can help students master the Common Core State Standards for language arts and mathematics by honing their abilities throughout the learning process as they (1) gather information and set learning goals, (2) explore and elaborate on new information, and (3) communicate what they have learned.

GATHERING INFORMATION

Learning begins as students exhibit curiosity about a topic and then seek out information and evidence to satisfy that curiosity. Input is gathered through the senses, primarily in the school setting through the visual, auditory, and kinesthetic-tactile systems. For example, when conducting a science experiment, a student's visual system "sees" print and graphic presentations with instructions about the steps in the process; the auditory system "hears" the teacher's guidance and discussion with lab partners; and the tactile system "experiences" the acts of conducting the experiment. (Some experiments may even yield pungent results for the olfactory system.) All the information gathered through the senses is transmitted to the brain for processing.

The quantity and quality of information students gather sets the stage for further learning, so it is essential that they be equipped with strategies to guide these efforts. Teachers can help students get the most out of their information-seeking by introducing and modeling several strategies and encouraging students to incorporate these tools and outlooks into their schoolwork and lives.

Clear Intent

Students must identify what they want to accomplish and set goals toward that end. In many cases, the more specific students can be in establishing their learning intentions, the more successful they will be in tracking down the most useful information. Consider the difference between these two examples:

- "I'm looking for books about bears."
- "I want to learn about polar bears and their habitats, to explore whether and why they may be an endangered species, and what humans might do about that."

Establishing clear intent helps students to identify the tasks they will need to complete to accomplish their goals and to pinpoint the evidence they will need to track down. Marzano (2017) reports on research showing that effectively teaching students how to set their own learning goals can increase achievement by 18% to 41%.

Related to this idea of encouraging students to set learning goals is that of choice. Giving students choices—on which books to read and report on, for example, or which topics to research or learning activities to complete—permits them to pursue their own interests and satisfy their curiosity about subjects they find interesting and intriguing.

Initiative

Hand in hand with developing clear intent about one's learning goals is the willingness to take the necessary action to achieve one's goals. Students should come to understand that they are in charge of their learning and thus are responsible for taking the steps needed to complete learning tasks. They should be encouraged to pursue lines of inquiry that arise naturally during the school day and to take action on their ideas—and they should be recognized when they do so. Fostering initiative is at the essence of supporting students to become self-directed learners, which will serve them well throughout their years in school and later in the working world. The Common Core State Standards offer as one example of initiative students independently tracking down reliable sources of information to answer questions that arise as they

---

From Teachers for Teachers

One way to encourage students to take charge of their learning experiences is by offering them choices to pursue their individual interests and preferences. In her classroom, teacher Diane Dahl let 2nd-graders choose where to sit and what to read in independent reading, for example. When they feel they have choices, students have a more interesting and interactive school day (Wilson & Conyers, 2020).

---

are learning new lesson content, such as consulting with teachers, finding relevant library books, and identifying objective online content.

Information-Gathering Skills

The world is full of information, and the Internet puts much of it at our fingertips. The challenge is in teaching students where to find the evidence they want and need, how to assess its validity and the point of view of the sources presenting it (the *quality* of the information), and why it is useful to collect evidence from multiple sources (the *quantity* of information). For example, many sources cite statistics to support their claims; the *Common Core State Standards for Mathematics* (National Governors Association Center for Best Practices & Council of Chief State School Officers, 2010b) calls for students to "understand and evaluate random processes underlying statistical experiments" (p. 81) so that they can assess this evidence and compare it to other sources. As essential as online information-gathering skills are today, students should learn to consult more traditional sources as well, such as browsing the library shelves and asking experts in their schools and communities.

Honing information-gathering skills must be an ongoing process so that by 11th and 12th grade, students can "gather relevant information from multiple authoritative print and digital sources, using advanced searches effectively; assess the strengths and limitations of each source in terms of the task, purpose, and audience; [and] integrate information into the text selectively to maintain the flow of ideas" (National Governors Association Center for Best Practices [NGACBP] & Council of Chief State School Officers [CCSSO], 2010a, p. 46). Explicit instruction on information-gathering should also address how to avoid plagiarism, why it is important not to rely exclusively on a single source, and how to cite sources using standard reference formats.

Selective Attention

A final example of useful cognitive strategies at the information-gathering stage and throughout the learning process is the ability to identify what is important in any situation and to attend to it with appropriate focus. Explicit instruction on the HEAR strategy (Wilson & Conyers, 2016) can help students improve their listening abilities and hone their selective attention:

- *Halt:* Stop whatever else you are doing, end your internal dialogue on other thoughts, and free your mind to pay attention to the person speaking.
- *Engage:* As a sign to the speaker (and yourself!) that you are occupied by the act of listening, turn your head slightly toward the speaker.
- *Anticipate:* By looking forward to what the speaker has to say, you are acknowledging that you will likely learn something new and interesting, which will enhance your attention.
- *Replay:* Think about what the speaker is saying. Analyze it and paraphrase in your mind or in discussion with the speaker and other classmates. Replaying the information will aid in understanding and remembering what you have learned.

Meta-analyses exploring data from a large number of studies have found that mindfulness programs for teachers and students alike show promise for promoting learning and well-being in schools (Jennings, 2019). Jha's research (2011) finds support for "mindfulness practice" as a way to improve attentional control. Her work with adults involves daily practice of 30–45 minutes of purposeful selection of a focus of attention, with awareness and redirection back to that focus when the mind wanders. Jha uses the metaphor of a flashlight illuminating what is of interest and shining light on potential problems or dangers that demand our attention. Mindfulness training improved the efficiency with which adult subjects directed their attention, and Jha suggests it might also be effective at improving executive function and attention control with children.

As with many of the cognitive strategies introduced here, selective attention and the HEAR strategy are useful throughout the learning process. Although we have grouped these strategies generally by stage, they transcend strict classification. Students will revisit their clear intent, maintain initiative, and assess the quantity and quality of information throughout the learning process. They will need to be aware of point of view, which is introduced at the communicating stage, as they gather information at the beginning of a learning project. Making logical inferences, introduced in the next section, is also crucial in all stages of learning.

In Sum

Purposeful instruction and practice in establishing clear intent, marshaling initiative, gathering information from multiple reliable sources, and focusing selective attention starts the learning process on a productive path.

EXPLORING AND ELABORATING

Once students have gathered information, they explore and elaborate on it. They conduct a critical analysis of the available evidence, evaluating its validity and making inferences. They consider new information in the context of what they already know and further define problems and possible solutions. As they explore and elaborate, students engage in deep thinking and make meaning by "connecting the dots," devising and testing hypotheses, and identifying the most important information they need to tuck away in memory. They must also assess their understanding of what they are learning to determine if they need additional information to aid in full comprehension. Several cognitive strategies support learning at the processing stage.

Problem Definition

Defining a problem correctly is often the first best step toward ultimately identifying the optimal solution. Teaching this strategy effectively may involve modeling it with a variety of content lessons: Examine all aspects of the situation to identify cause-and-effect relationships and separate one from the other. Systematically identify who and what are affected by the problem. Assess the "costs" of the problem to determine their relative importance and connections to possible solutions and the potential gains in solving the problem. Finally, develop several problem definitions and then narrow them down to the one most likely at the core.

Making Inferences

This strategy involves elaborating on information students have gathered to arrive at logical and useful conclusions. It is about "thinking beyond the given." What conclusions can we draw from the available information, and how do those conclusions aid in comprehension and problem solving? How can we verify the validity of the conclusions we have made? Making inferences is the act of making meaning—of learners creating new information based on what they have learned and what they already know. The first anchor standard for reading in the Common Core State Standards is that students should be able to "read closely to determine what the text says explicitly and to make logical inferences from it" (NGACBP & CCSSO, 2010a, p. 10); these skills are useful when citing evidence from other texts in one's own writing and when formulating conclusions to include in an oral presentation, for example.

Teaching students the strategy of making inferences offers a prime example of the importance of helping them to developing their "learning vocabulary." The following exchange provides an example of learning about inferences as part of a cognitive toolkit.

Teacher: What did we observe in our experiment?

Samuel: When we boiled the water, it turned into steam.

Tanya: But then when it cooled down, it turned back into water.

Teacher: Do you remember what we learned about different states of matter?

Tanya: Solid, liquid, and gas. So, water is a liquid, but it can be a gas, too!

Teacher: Does your observation and data from this experiment confirm what we learned from our science book?

Samuel: Yes! We confirmed by experimentation and observation that water can be liquid or gas—and it can be solid, too, when it turns to ice!

Michaela: Can other things turn from liquid to gas or from solid to liquid?

Teacher: That's a great question. Can we infer from our experiment that other liquids might also change state from liquid to gas?

Samuel: Yes, we can infer that if we heat other liquids they would turn to gas.

Teacher: Maybe we will test this. Can we infer anything else?

Michaela: Maybe we can infer that other solids besides ice can also turn to liquids, but I think it would take more heat to turn some things to liquid than others, because sunlight melts ice and chocolate but not bricks or cars, and maybe some things would not melt at all.

In this example, the teacher guides the students not only to connect information from what they read to the results of their experiment but also to think about what and how they learned as the act of making an inference. Developing this strategy will serve them well in other subjects, such as inferring the relationships between characters in a story or inferring that there may be several ways to solve a math problem.

Comparing, Classifying, and Making Connections

Comparing and classifying new information is a useful way of analyzing it and connecting it with what one already knows. In contrast to traditional approaches to learning, including rote memorization, these strategies facilitate meaning-making and continued exploration. Guiding students through the process of classification—identifying attributes that are useful in grouping, comparing elements, and recalling and looking up other elements in the same categories—encourages students to use their existing knowledge about a topic, to branch into new areas, and to expand and extend what they know.

Here's an example from language arts: The English language is complex and often confusing, so classifying words by the way they are used can help establish meaning. For example, *desert* refers to an arid region when used as a noun, but it has a very different meaning when used as a verb. *Appropriate* and *minute* are other examples of *heteronyms*, or words that are spelled the same but have different pronunciations and meanings. By learning the different parts of speech, students can develop a strategy to determine the meaning of these words by classifying them as nouns, verbs, or adjectives in the context of a passage.

Another example, from science, involves the classification of animals. When students know the differences between mammals and fish, they should be able to specify what sets dolphins and whales apart from other sea creatures when they learn they are mammals. Likewise, when students discover that koala bears are marsupials, they can infer that they belong in the classification of mammals alongside kangaroos rather than black bears.

A final example of the usefulness of this strategy, from the Common Core State Standards for Mathematics, specifies that kindergartners should be able to "analyze and compare two- and three-dimensional shapes, in different sizes and orientations, using informal language to describe their similarities, differences, parts . . . and other attributes" (NGACBP & CCSSO, 2010b, p. 12). By 3rd grade, students should be able to "understand that shapes in different categories . . . may share attributes . . . and that the shared attributes can define a larger category" (p. 26).

In each of these examples, it is useful to point out the strategy students are using to underscore the need to be mindful of categories and classifications as a way to establish meaning:

- "In what category of parts of speech is *bow* used in this sentence? Is it a noun or a verb?"
- "Is a gecko a reptile or an amphibian, and what can we infer from its classification?"
- "How is a rectangle like a square? How is it different?"

Note from these examples how cognitive strategies often work in tandem. Comparing and classifying can help students to make more accurate inferences. And as we saw previously, inference leads to hypothesizing.

Planning and Organizing

The old adage that "people who fail to plan plan to fail" is certainly appropriate in executing complex learning tasks, such as writing a paper, devising and carrying out a science project, or working on a team presentation. Whether students are working independently, in pairs, or as part of a team, explicit instruction on how to plan and organize can be extremely useful and widely applicable inside and outside the classroom.

There is a widespread misperception that some people have a "talent" for organization—that they are naturally organized, while others are inherently prone to chaos, clutter, and forgetfulness. Applying the research from earlier chapters on plasticity and potential, the reality is that all students can learn how to plan and to get and stay organized, a strategy that will serve them in their adult lives as well. Organizing a plan for a learning project involves answering questions like these:

- What form will this project take, and what are its components (e.g., a three-page essay with introduction stating thesis, at least three supporting paragraphs, and a conclusion; a dramatization with characters, a script, costumes, and props)?
- What steps do I need to take to finish this project?
- When is this project due, and are there any earlier deadlines I need to meet (e.g., for review of an outline and first draft)?

- Where can I get the information I need (e.g., books, magazines, Internet sites, local museums, interviews with experts in the field, surveys of peers and community residents)?
- What materials will I need for this project (e.g., art supplies, scientific equipment, models, photographs)?
- How can I best keep my notes, outlines, and drafts organized?
- What types of problems have I had with organization and planning in the past, and how might I correct those problems with this project?

Note that this final question represents one aspect of metacognition—learning from past problems with planning and organization. Students will benefit from reminders to think about their thinking throughout the process of planning—in assessing whether they can improve the way they take and organize notes, for example, and in doing a final assessment of how this project came together and what they might improve on their next assignment. These types of self-assessment and reflection will serve students well in all subjects and in future educational and vocational endeavors.

Working and Long-Term Memory

Working memory is a powerful predictor of learning (Maehler & Schuchardt, 2016), and may be a better predictor of school achievement than IQ, according to educational neuroscience research, and teachers can guide students to enhance their working memory through explicit instruction and opportunities to practice supportive strategies (Alloway & Alloway, 2013). Fortunately, teachers can guide students to enhance their working memory through explicit instruction and opportunities to practice supportive strategies. The term *working memory* "is our ability to work with information. More precisely, working memory is the conscious processing of information" (Alloway & Alloway, 2013, p. 4). Students rely on working memory as they retain the key points they want to convey in the introductory paragraph of an essay, mentally calculate a math problem, or learn the steps in a dance routine.

As with other cognitive strategies, students can improve their working memory with practice—and reap a variety of benefits by doing so, including the ability to think faster and adapt to new situations and to maintain attention to work through more complex learning tasks. In fact, selective attention and working memory are closely related: Students are more likely to hold information in working memory if they can avoid distractions and stay focused on the learning at hand.

Consciously choosing what to retain in long-term memory and selecting useful tools to retain and recall information to achieve desired results are two additional learning tasks in the processing stage. A wide variety of strategies can be used to support retention. For example, teachers can guide students to organize their notes into memorable "chunks" of no more than seven key elements. Along the same lines, when students are studying on their own, they may find it helpful to stop at the end of every section, summarize what they have read, and think about how it might connect with the material in the next section based on its subtitle.

Creating graphic organizers, acronyms, and other mnemonic devices are all effective ways to help improve recall of important facts. These memory exercises support retention because they involve analysis (in how concepts connect in graphic organizers, for example), identification of key words to assemble into short, memorable chunks, and repetition of information as students work out lyrics and acronyms. Based on research helping children with attention deficit disorders to improve their working memory, Klingberg (2011) reported success with training that incorporates repetition and feedback and that is designed to be adaptively difficult so that the memory task becomes more challenging as performance improves. As their working memory improves, students are better able to remember and execute instructions and stay on task for learning.

Summarizing and Synthesizing

Identifying the key points in a book, chapter, or lesson and communicating them in verbal or written form succinctly is a complex, but useful, task. It engages sophisticated analytical skills, gauges and aids in understanding of the material, and identifies the most important information to "wire" into long-term memory. Like many of the other cognitive strategies outlined in this chapter, learning to summarize will prove a helpful skill for students throughout their years in school and college and on the job as well. Teaching and reinforcing summarizing skills can be a regular part of content lessons and reading activities.

Practice in learning to summarize can begin in the early grades. For example, 2nd-graders should be able to "ask and answer such questions as who, what, where, when, why, and how to demonstrate understanding of key details in a text" and "recount stories . . . and determine their central message, lesson, or moral" (NGACBP & CCSSO, 2010a, p. 11). The

Speaking and Listening Standards K–5 call on 5th-graders to "summarize a written text read aloud or information presented in diverse media and formats, including visually, quantitatively, and orally" and to "summarize the points a speaker makes and explain how each claim is supported by reasons and evidence" (p. 24).

Synthesizing takes the process of summarizing further. Rather than just restating the important points from a lesson or text, synthesizing involves combining ideas and coming to an evolving understanding of the material. Through the process of synthesizing, students are encouraged to reflect on the various texts they are reading and merge various ideas to come up with original thoughts, insights, and understanding that would not have been possible by viewing the material in isolation. It's a way for students to see how various pieces fit together, allowing them to view the subject matter in a whole new light.

In Sum

Useful cognitive strategies include instruction on and practice in defining problems, making inferences, comparing and classifying, planning and organizing, remembering key information, and summarizing oral presentations and passages from reading.

COMMUNICATING WHAT YOU HAVE LEARNED

In the third stage of learning, students may communicate what they have learned in a variety of ways. They effectively apply the information they have gathered, explored, and analyzed in the form of a research project, an oral or written report, a test, a group project, the culmination of a learning activity, or a real-world application outside the classroom. The application of reading, math, and science skills and learning across core subjects is readily evident in everyday thinking and problem solving. The cognitive strategies useful in communicating what one has learned include effective writing and presentation skills, the ability to accept feedback and apply it in a constructive way to further enhance learning, and the persistence and follow-through necessary to complete learning tasks.

It is notable that the Common Core State Standards for English Language Arts and Literacy in History/Social Studies, Science, and Technical Subjects set out guidelines for proficiency in speaking and listening in addition to reading and writing. The standards seek to prepare students for communicating effectively in both formal presentations and everyday conversations by developing "a range of broadly useful oral communication and interpersonal skills":

> Students must learn to work together, express and listen carefully to ideas, integrate information from oral, visual, quantitative, and media sources, evaluate what they hear, use media and visual displays strategically to help achieve communicative purposes, and adapt speech to context and task. (NGACBP & CCSSO, 2010a, p. 8)

The following cognitive strategies will be useful to students in improving and assessing the quality of their verbal and written communications and interactions with others.

Understanding Others' Points of View

The need to understand the perspectives of others is an essential cognitive strategy that runs through many threads of current learning standards. The 6th-grade College and Career Readiness Anchor Standard for Reading, for example, states that students must be able to "assess how point of view or purpose shapes the content and style of a text" (NGACBP & CCSSO, 2010a, p. 10). Along these lines, the reading standards for 5th-graders specify that they should be able to "describe how a narrator's or speaker's point of view influences how events are described" (p. 12). In classroom discussions, 8th-graders should be able to "pose questions that connect the ideas of several speakers and respond to others' questions and comments with relevant evidence, observations, and ideas" (NGACBP & CCSSO, 2010a, p. 49).

Teaching students to identify, respect, and seek to understand points of view that differ from their own and to tailor their communications to their intended audience are valuable lessons that will pay significant dividends throughout their lives. To facilitate students' curiosity about how others see the world, teachers can model listening actively to students, paraphrasing what they say to verify understanding, using examples that are relevant to students' lives, and encouraging all students to share their thoughts and views. Explicit instruction on the impact of point of view in literary, historical, and political writing also underscores the importance of understanding writers' perspectives in assessing their message, and these discussions can help make students more aware of their own points of view when they are writing or speaking.

Effective Expression

Whether they are speaking or writing as a means to persuade or inform, students' effective expression relies on the information they have gathered and analyzed. As the Common Core State Standards for Language Arts note,

> Students cite specific evidence when offering an oral or written interpretation of a text. They use relevant evidence when supporting their own points in writing and speaking, making their reasoning clear to the reader or listener, and they constructively evaluate others' use of evidence. (p. 7)

From Teachers for Teachers

A key aspect of effective expression is choosing one's words carefully. Specifically, the College and Career Readiness Anchor Standards for Writing call for students to be able to "write narratives to develop real or imagined experiences or events using effective technique, well-chosen details, and well-structured event sequences" (p. 18). To guide her K–5 students learning English as a second language to adhere to these standards in their work, Georgia teacher Melissa Smith uses a variety of strategies to develop higher-order thinking skills that aid in understanding the complexities of their new language.

In one writing activity focused on the effective use of participles and onomatopoeia, Ms. Smith shared Debbie Allen's book *Dancing in the Wings* as an example of writing so vivid it evokes mental imagery (Allen's book is featured as a "mentor text" by the Northern Nevada Writing Project, writingfix. com). She stopped after descriptive passages to encourage her students to visualize the scenes as a strategy to enhance comprehension and recall of the text and to appreciate the author's writing technique and word choices.

The visualizing strategy helped them to recall many more details from the text and demonstrated the importance of thoughtful word selection to convey action and set the scene, Ms. Smith notes. Her students then applied those strategies in their own work, choosing active words to convey personal stories they imagined by applying the "brain movies" visualizing strategy (Wilson, 2012b). The older students wrote independently and edited each other's work, while the kindergartners collaborated on a story, taking turns to contribute ideas and "stretch spelling" words to fill in the descriptive details of passages such as: "Bump went the heads! The ball flew to the goal. Pretty cheerleaders say, 'Go, Ryan!' Passing the ball, the quarterback threw the ball to the player. He caught it! He ran to the goal. TOUCHDOWN!"

To help students use evidence in their own work more effectively, teachers can point out how social studies and science texts do so. The Reading Standards for Informational Text K–5 call on 5th-graders to "explain how an author uses reason and evidence to support particular points in a text, identifying which reasons and evidence support which point(s)" (p. 14).

In addition, students' contributions to classroom discussions, written assignments, and responses in essay exams can be improved if they are encouraged to respond thoughtfully and to double-check their work. The fifth College and Career Readiness Anchor Standard for Writing emphasizes the importance of guiding students to strengthen their writing by planning, reviewing, and revising their work—and sometimes even starting over with a whole new approach. Teachers can help underscore the need to "think twice to think smart" with some simple approaches: (1) build "wait time" into questioning, giving students a few seconds to compose responses in their heads before calling on them to share their thoughts; (2) build an editing/rewriting stage into all writing assignments so that reviewing and improving their written work becomes second nature; (3) remind students to double-check their work before handing in assignments and tests; and (4) share examples of how famous authors revise their work—and sometimes even scrap it and start over.

Finishing Power

A common concern among teachers is that some students start new projects with a great deal of enthusiasm but finish them halfheartedly or not at all. Reinforcing the tasks needed to complete a learning activity—to "finish strong"—can help students bring together a number of cognitive

From Teachers for Teachers

Douglas Stewart, who teaches at two design schools in Tennessee, finds that even at the college level, students need explicit instruction on thinking and learning skills. He begins an information literacy course with instruction on systematic search and planning, critical thinking, and organizational skills before assigning a project-based/peer-assisted assignment to develop presentations on the impact of their chosen design discipline on people's lives. Students' diverse and creative projects allow them to hone the cognitive skills they will need to plan and carry out design assignments in their professional lives.

strategies, including careful planning, organization, and time management. It is helpful to introduce rituals of celebration at the end of successful classroom projects and lessons to underscore feelings of pride in a job well done and to model for students the usefulness of treating yourself, perhaps with an activity you enjoy, after completing important tasks.

In Sum

Communicating what students have learned may take many forms and may be supported by learning cognitive strategies such as understanding others' point of view, effective expression, and finishing power.

TEACHING COGNITIVE AND METACOGNITIVE STRATEGIES BY EXAMPLE

One theme underlying our exploration of cognitive strategies and metacognition is how effective it can be for teachers to model the use of cognitive strategies. By thinking aloud about the author's perspective after reading a passage, the teacher underscores the importance of understanding point of view. By developing a checklist of tasks for a class project with students, the teacher exemplifies planning and organization. By celebrating the successful completion of that project, the teacher reminds students of the value of finishing power. As teachers model their thinking aloud daily, students learn the cognitive processes an "expert" uses.

Another effective way of modeling cognitive strategies is to demonstrate working through mistakes aloud. Students may giggle when their teacher makes a mistake—and they will remember how she worked through the problem. As students become more metacognitive and able to identify and work through their own problems, this strategy may be extended to include student-to-student problem solving aloud. For example, a teacher might summarize how they came to an incorrect prediction about what was going to happen to a character in a favorite novel. An example for older students might be to discuss how they felt they were led to develop an incorrect conclusion about what has really happened in the news after reading a piece of print from a biased source.

At the forefront of research on the positive impact of teaching metacognition is the clear message that it is important to explicitly teach, model, encourage, and celebrate the use of cognitive strategies. Many people assume that children come to school naturally equipped with the skills needed to learn the lessons put before them. In reality, all students benefit from explicit instruction in learning how to learn—from struggling students to those who excel in many areas but may give up when presented with challenging material or who may have a hard time completing projects. Thus, explicit teaching in the area of metacognition is an effective way to differentiate instruction by identifying the stage of learning where students struggle and equipping them with strategies they can use in every content area. Providing opportunities for students to discover and practice using cognitive strategies also enhances learning motivation and engagement.

Just as the industrial, mass-production engine of our economy has shifted to a reliance on knowledge, so must our emphasis on education shift to supporting engaging, thoughtful labs for learning about learning the skills that will be useful throughout life. For example, the Common Core State Standards for Mathematics list a variety of real-life situations in which modeling, the "process of choosing and using appropriate mathematics and statistics to analyze empirical situations" (NGACBP & CCSSO, 2010b, p. 72), might be used in making the case that these higher-order thinking skills must be taught to high school students:

- Estimating the amount of food and water that might be needed for a given population in the aftermath of a natural disaster;
- Planning a sports tournament for a group of friends;
- Designing the layout of a school fair to maximize the number of stalls and funds raised;
- Analyzing the stopping distance for a vehicle in inclement weather;
- Projecting savings and investment growth; and
- Relating population statistics to individual predictions.

The ultimate goal of current standards for learning is to provide a "staircase" of learning so that students advance steadily in learning and using higher-order skills such as mathematical modeling. As more school districts begin applying these standards to their curriculum, one result could be that students receive explicit instruction in the use of cognitive strategies they can apply in all content areas. These new directions should help to correct a widespread emphasis on basic skills to the exclusion of explicit instruction on cognitive strategies that can be used to improve learning in all content areas (Pianta et al., 2007; Baker et al., 2012).

In Sum

Modeling the use of cognitive and metacognitive strategies and using the "language of learning" while presenting lessons—including thinking aloud while correcting your own mistakes—can be an effective way to guide students to think about their thinking.

A METACOGNITIVE APPROACH TO SOCIAL AND EMOTIONAL LEARNING

Thus far, we have focused our discussion of metacognition on how students can monitor and improve their cognitive abilities, but metacognition is also invaluable in supporting social and emotional learning. And, as educational research in this area indicates (see Chapter 4), the development of cognitive, affective, and behavioral competencies that support SEL—including self-awareness, self-management, social awareness, relationship skills, and socially responsible decisionmaking—can lead to improved academic outcomes.

Guiding students to develop the cognitive strategies presented in this chapter—clear intent, initiative, selective attention, and understanding others' points of view—clearly support social and emotional learning. In addition, applying a metacognitive approach to the following competencies can help students to improve their own learning and interactions with peers and contribute to a more positive and productive classroom environment.

Self-Awareness and Self-Management

The ability to recognize and regulate one's emotions, thoughts, and behaviors has a direct impact on motivating oneself to set and work toward academic and personal goals, controlling impulses, and effectively managing stress. When students learn how to manage and direct their learning, they become more independent and successful learners. Educators can assist students to develop these competencies by guiding them to "recognize that they are in charge of their emotions, thoughts, and actions, and by equipping them with strategies and skills to steer their feelings, thinking, and behaviors in positive and productive directions" (Wilson & Conyers, 2016, p. 11).

In addition to the cognitive strategies of clear intent, selective attention, and others presented in this chapter, learning from experience can be a powerful metacognitive tool that students can wield to improve their cognitive, emotional, and social competencies over time. For example, teachers can encourage students to reflect on what went well in individual and group learning assignments and how they might make positive changes in the future. They can model effective self-reflection by thinking out-loud about how to work through hard problems and remind students that many successful people persisted through setbacks to achieve their dreams. Thomas Edison's famous statement, "I have not failed. I have just found 10,000 ways that won't work," is a great reminder of the power of persistence and thinking about new and better ways to accomplish learning goals.

Questions like these can help students take charge of their learning:

- What strategies worked best in helping me study for this test?
- What can I do to avoid distractions and stay on task when I'm working on a project?
- Looking back on my report, what are the best sections, and why? How could I have made the other sections better?
- How do I feel about my part in this group project? How can I help our team do better in the future?
- How can I use feedback from my teachers and classmates about my presentation to do a better job the next time?

Social Awareness and Relationship Skills

As a highly social species, humans use social abilities such as empathy, compassion, and perspective-taking to infer the emotions and mental states of other people, including those from diverse backgrounds (Singer & Klimecki, 2014). These capacities are key elements of what has been termed *social awareness*, which includes the ability to understand social and ethical norms for behavior, such as expectations for acceptable classroom behaviors. Guiding students to develop their social awareness and relationship skills bolsters social, emotional, and cognitive learning abilities: "Individuals' brains are critically shaped by social relationships, and the information they learn through these relationships supports both their emotions and their knowledge about facts, procedures, motivation, and interests" (National Academies of Sciences, Engineering, and Medicine, 2018, p. 29).

The emotional tone of the classroom becomes more positive when teachers encourage and model *empathy*, the capacity to share the feelings of others, and *compassion*, "feelings of warmth, concern, and care for the other, as well as a strong motivation to improve the other's wellbeing" (Singer & Klimecki, 2014, para. 2). Discussions of historical figures and literary characters provide many opportunities to highlight empathy and compassion in action. Consider, as just one example, Scout Finch's observation in *To Kill a Mockingbird*: "Atticus was right. One time he said you never really know a man until you stand in his shoes and walk around in them" (Lee, 1960, p. 294).

Teachers demonstrate empathy when they encourage students to celebrate each other's successes, which can be an everyday occurrence of a shared emotional response (Dovidio & Banfield, 2015), and when they treat everyone in the class fairly and with respect. Students often take cues on how to treat others based on their teachers' actions. Praising students for prosocial behaviors such as sharing, helping peers who are struggling with classroom assignments, encouraging others, and working together cooperatively reinforces those behaviors and helps maintain a positive classroom environment. Finally, when a teacher conducts a lesson with a smile and an upbeat, positive attitude, many students instinctively mirror that smile and positive attitude.

Teachers and students alike can adopt a metacognitive approach to social awareness by considering questions such as:

- What does it mean to be empathetic? How do I display empathy to others, and how do they respond when I do that?
- How do I feel when my classmates show empathy to me?
- How can I contribute to a group learning project in a positive way? How do I feel when I make a positive and helpful contribution?
- Do I listen carefully when others are speaking? How can I get better at trying to understand points of view that differ from mine?
- Do I learn better in a classroom where we all support each other and work together cooperatively? How can I do my part to make our classroom a positive place?

Responsible Decisionmaking

Every day, students make hundreds of decisions, consciously or otherwise, about how they spend their time and focus their attention, how they interact with others, and how they attend to their emotional and physical well-being. Proactive classroom discussions about the importance of making wise choices underscores for students that they are in charge of their thoughts and actions—and that their decisions can have a big impact on themselves and others. As Zhang and colleagues underscore, "If children are to start on the path toward becoming thoughtful decision makers, they need more time during the school day for active reasoning about significant issues" (2016, p. 218).

Sharing this basic framework for decisionmaking can equip students with a versatile guide for thinking carefully about the many choices in their daily lives:

1. Identify your desired outcome.
2. Recognize that you have a choice in achieving that outcome.
3. Consider your options.
4. List the pros and cons of each option.
5. Choose what you believe to be the best course of action.
6. Reflect on your decision.

Teachers can lead discussions on this framework by inviting students to apply these steps in a variety of situations, from choosing an after-school snack to dealing with a bullying situation on the playground to applying for a job or college admission. Suggesting a wide range of situations emphasizes that sometimes students can go through this process quickly, and sometimes they need to slow down, think carefully about their options, and consider how the outcomes of their past choices might guide this decision. For older students, a useful message is that decisionmaking is a fundamental aspect of problem solving and that there are many tools available to analyze their options to solve complex academic and on-the-job problems (Jonassen, 2012). For students of all ages—and their teachers—a metacognitive approach to thinking about how to improve decisionmaking can have a positive impact on cognitive, social, and emotional learning.

FROM RESEARCH TO CLASSROOM PRACTICE:
LEARNING BY TEACHING AND REFLECTING
ON YOUR PROFESSIONAL PRACTICE

In his follow-up to a presentation on his work on helping students become better thinkers at a conference at the University of Tennessee in the late 1980s, Reuven Feuerstein responded to an educator teacher's concern about the difficulty she might have in teaching the complex material to students and her peers in the teaching profession. Feuerstein used the metaphor of a ricochet to explain how one can deepen one's own understanding of cognitive psychology by teaching it to others: "As you teach it, you will better learn it." One nuance of this good advice is that there are many metacognitive aspects of developing lessons to teach students to think about their thinking and to employ useful cognitive strategies.

Educators hone their own metacognitive mindset as they teach and reflect on their practice. Donald Schön, one of the founders of organizational learning, wrote that reflective practice is at the center of what it means to be a professional (Hargreaves & Fullan, 2012). Schön focuses on two aspects of reflective practice:

- *Reflecting in action* refers to "the capacity to walk around a problem while you are right in the middle of it, to think about what you are doing even as you are improvising it" (p. 98). This type of reflective practice might occur in the classroom, as when a teacher quickens or slows the pace of a lesson, moves to a different location in the room, or illustrates a concept with more examples.
- *Reflection on action* refers to thinking after a lesson or learning activity has concluded about how it might be improved. For example, a teacher might reflect on the variation in responses from different students to a writing prompt or consider why one group of students seemed more engaged than others in a learning activity.

Teachers may also engage in a more structured and systematic contemplation of their practice in the form of *action research*, a term introduced by social psychologist Kurt Lewin in 1946 to describe a circular process of planning, execution, and reflection. Action research can be a meaningful and useful endeavor for educators. After studying cognition, thinking, and the brain as a school psychologist, Wilson wanted to help young students become better learners and thinkers and also to provide professional development to teachers as she modeled how to teach thinking strategies.

To do this, she co-taught while conducting her action research (Wilson, 1996a, 1996b). Teachers may identify opportunities for action research in the classroom or in collaboration with other educators with the aim of improving their practice and sharing what they've learned with colleagues (Conyers & Wilson, 2016). (See Chapter 7 for a discussion on collaborating with other educators.)

To Learn More

Check out the book *Teaching Students to Drive Their Brains: Metacognitive Strategies, Activities, and Lesson Ideas* (Wilson & Conyers, 2016) for more practical strategies from Wilson and Conyers for teaching students to use metacognition effectively. Also, elementary educators may want to view the companion video series, *Teaching Students to Drive Their Brains* (ASCD, 2018).

WHAT'S THE BIG IDEA?

Returning to the metaphor of students "driving their brains," mastering cognitive and metacognitive skills allows students to take control of defining their academic goals, monitoring their progress, and choosing the best strategies for the learning task at hand. Explicit instruction on metacognition builds on the concepts of neuroplasticity and learning potential by equipping students with strategies and critical thinking skills so that they can become "functionally smarter" and achieve their learning goals. Teaching these skills and strategies should begin in the early grades and continue throughout their years in school in order to support steady progress as core lesson content becomes more demanding. Hattie notes that "when tasks are very complex for the student, the quality of metacognitive skills rather than intellectual ability is the main determinant of learning outcomes" (2009, p. 30).

If students are in the driver's seat of their educational journey, then teachers are their driving instructors—riding alongside them, monitoring their individual progress, and teaching and modeling effective learning. Some students need more instructional support than others. However, there is strong evidence indicating that the effective teaching of metacognitive skills can make a significant difference for student outcomes across age levels and various subjects as students become more self-directed, independent learners (Perry, Lundie, & Golder, 2019; Education Endowment Foundation, 2019).

Key Terms

Action research: A term coined by social psychologist Kurt Lewin to describe a circular process of planning, execution, and reflection.

Clear intent: Developing and maintaining a clear sense of one's intention in any given situation.

Cognitive strategies: Techniques that can be used in the classroom to help students develop a variety of thinking and problem-solving abilities that will help them succeed in school, work, and life.

Common Core State Standards: These standards in language arts and mathematics are intended to provide educators with targets for helping students progress in key areas of learning.

Comparing, classifying, and making connections: Noticing similarities and differences; grouping and distinguishing between information to suit one's purpose; linking information to create deeper meaning and facilitate greater understanding.

Compassion: Sympathetic consciousness of and desire to alleviate the distress of others.

Effective expression: Expressing oneself thoughtfully based on appropriate exploration and planning on a topic or problem.

Empathy: Capacity to share the feelings of others.

Finishing power: Sustaining one's focus on a task over a period of time or in the face of challenges in order to complete it.

Higher-order thinking: Thinking skills that help one control other cognitive processes and that are critical to developing knowledge; related to metacognition.

Initiative: Displaying readiness and skill in taking action.

Information-gathering skills: Using multiple sources of information from trustworthy sources to effectively solve problems.

Making inferences: Going beyond the information given to solve problems and identify logical conclusions.

Metacognition: Thinking about one's thinking with the aim of increasing learning.

Planning and organizing: Making plans and organizing information to create a well-expressed, thoughtful response.

Problem definition: Defining a problem correctly so that one can generate an appropriate solution.

Responsible decisionmaking: Deliberate process to define a desired outcome and select the best option to achieve it.

Selective attention: Identifying and focusing on what is important in any given situation.

Key Terms (continued)

Self-directed learners: Learners who take initiative and are empowered to actively identify and use resources that can assist them in learning.

Self-management: Ability to regulate one's emotions, thoughts, and behaviors.

Social awareness: Ability to understand social and ethical norms for behavior.

Summarizing: Understanding what is most relevant or important and communicating it in a concise manner, verbally or in writing.

Types of reflection: Donald Schön, one of the founders of organizational learning, described two types of reflection for professionals: reflection *in* action, which refers to the ability to reflect on and address a problem while one is in the midst of the activity, and reflection *on* action, which refers to thinking about a problem or challenge after the activity has concluded.

Understanding others' points of view: Understanding and respecting others' viewpoints through the display of empathy and development of rapport.

Working memory: System for temporarily storing and managing information required to carry out complex cognitive tasks such as learning, reasoning, and comprehension.

Questions for Reflection

- How does the approach of equipping students with cognitive strategies to enhance the process of learning in all content areas compare with how you were taught as a child?
- Can you think of some examples of how you might use metacognition personally and professionally?
- In what ways might explicit instruction on strategies such as making inferences, classifying and connecting new information with existing knowledge, and understanding point of view be useful to students?
- How might instruction on metacognition and the use of cognitive strategies support differentiated instruction?
- Where else in your personal and professional life might the ability to recognize and respect other people's points of view prove useful?
- How might instruction and guidance for students on a metacognitive approach to self-management, social awareness, and relationship skills improve the classroom learning environment?
- In which lessons and subjects might you incorporate discussions on the importance of responsible decision making?

CHAPTER 6

Teaching, Learning, and Neuroeducation Myth Busting

The growing interest in the brain and learning has occurred so rapidly over the past two decades that gaps in understanding have emerged. Many teacher training programs still do not offer enough information about the brain, leaving teachers vulnerable to neuromyths.

—Tokuhama-Espinosa, *Neuromyths*, p. 7

What myths about teaching and learning have you encountered in your studies, teaching practice, or society in general?

Neuroscientists have greatly increased knowledge about the workings of the human brain in recent decades and continue to delve into its complex operations. From the earliest days of their profession, psychologists have honed their understanding of cognitive functioning, and educational researchers have applied a scientific framework to test what works and what doesn't in the classroom. The confluence of these diverse explorations is a science of learning on which we can rely in separating fact from fiction about how students learn best and how we can best teach them.

However, persistent myths and misunderstandings make it harder to take full advantage of the implications of these exciting breakthroughs in knowledge about how learning occurs. Some of these ideas continue to be widely accepted and repeated long after they have been disproved. A prime example is the oft-repeated statement that you use only 10% of your brain. The Society for Neuroscience (SFN, n.d.) counters with the reality check that "neuroimaging technology has conclusively destroyed this falsehood" (p. 1). For any given activity—even when you seem to be doing nothing at all—several areas of the brain are active.

And then there is the myth that listening to classical music can make you smarter. The SFN notes that this myth was born from a single, small study of college students in 1993, the results of which have never been replicated. On the other hand, learning how to play a musical instrument has been demonstrated to enhance cognitive skills such as concentration and coordination over the long term.

A final example is the widespread, but false, notion that the brain is incapable of making new neurons. This myth holds that you were born with all the neurons you are ever going to have—and once you started losing them in early adolescence, you were in for a long, steady, irreversible decline. In reality, the SFN notes, "Your brain constantly generates new cells and remains adaptable—or 'plastic'—as you age" (p. 1).

BECOMING AN "APPRENTICE" OF EFFECTIVE EDUCATION

Dispelling these and other pervasive myths among students, parents, colleagues, and policymakers and in your own mind and practice is a first step toward making the most of what we know works in teaching and learning. Another challenge is putting aside long-held, but perhaps outmoded, views about what it means to be a good teacher. As we noted in the Introduction, some prospective and practicing teachers begin their professional training with the unacknowledged assumption that they know what it takes to teach—having just spent 13 years at the receiving end of the educational system.

There are two central problems with what has been described as the "apprenticeship of observation." The first is that it ignores the reality that teaching is a complex endeavor that takes years of study and practice to master. Not even the most frequent fliers assume they could pilot a jet just because they have spent so many hours watching take-offs and landings from their business-class windows. Unfortunately, though, many people, including some who enter the teaching profession and administrative and policymaking arenas, seem to believe that because they have been students, they know what it takes to be an effective teacher.

The other problem with this mindset is that it sidesteps all the research and more recent advances in effective practice that have occurred in the intervening years. For example, a prospective teacher currently earning an education degree may have attended middle and high schools at a time when students were tracked into sections and classes based on perceived ability. This practice runs counter to this current approach in many districts today—and to the foundational concept that all students have the potential to achieve academic progress when provided effective instruction tailored to their needs. However, based on personal experiences in the classrooms of his or her childhood, the prospective teacher might harbor persistent, unacknowledged assumptions that intellectual capacity is fixed, that assessments measure individual students' ability to learn (not just their current performance), and that teachers' expectations for student achievement should be based on those assessment results.

Of course, there are many teachers who have long practiced in ways that research now supports, acting on their beliefs—borne out by their professional experience—that all students have the potential to learn, that a positive learning environment makes a difference, that incorporating physical activity into the school day enhances academic performance, and that explicit instruction of cognitive strategies helps students to take charge of their learning. In our myriad interactions with teachers, many have told us that they are thrilled to learn that cognitive psychologists, educational neuroscientists, and educational researchers are uncovering evidence of what they have seen in their classrooms for years.

Our goal in this chapter is to highlight several essential aspects of effective teaching practice and students' potential for learning success with the aim of dispelling myths that may persist just below the surface of discussion and debates about education today. We have touched on several of these concepts in previous chapters, but they are worth revisiting to underscore those claims that are consistent with the new science of learning—and to continue to erase those that are not. There are many more neuromyths than we are addressing in this chapter. Our focus is on the myths that, in our experience, can have a particularly negative impact in education.

To Learn More

To learn more about other neuromyths and, importantly, what we know now is supported by science, see Tracey Tokuhama-Espinosa's book, *Neuromyths: Debunking False Ideas About the Brain* (Norton, 2018).

THERE IS MORE TO 21st CENTURY
EDUCATION THAN THE 3 Rs—A LOT MORE

Common misconception: The best way to improve students' performance in core subjects is to go back to the basics.

Taking a deeper look: In addition to basic reading, writing, and math abilities, children today need to develop critical thinking, problem-solving, and communication skills to succeed both academically and in the working world of the 21st century. In a technologically based, global economy, workers must be able to continually learn new processes and to collaborate with colleagues to overcome new challenges, develop new products and services, and identify new efficiencies.

One aim of the Common Core State Standards for English Language Arts is "to lay out a vision of what it means to be a literate person in the twenty-first century" (NGACBP & CCSSO, 2010a, p. 3). Toward that end, the standards encompass not only the development of reading and writing skills but also effective speaking and listening abilities. As the introduction to the Common Core standards explains:

> Students must learn to work together, express and listen carefully to ideas, integrate information from oral, visual, quantitative, and media sources, evaluate what they hear, use media and visual displays strategically to help achieve communicative purposes, and adapt speech to context and task. (p. 8)

In addition to expanding the scope of their communication skills, explicit instruction on metacognitive strategies helps students to develop a systematic approach to problem identification, investigation, and resolution that will serve them well throughout their lives. The Common Core State Standards for Mathematics state that one fundamental aim of students' developing proficient skills is to prepare them "to solve problems arising in everyday life, society, and the workplace" (NGACBP & CCSSO, 2010b, p. 7). Business management embraces the Pareto principle, which holds that 20% of effort produces 80% of results. In education, metacognition fuels the 20% of effort that optimizes learning. Teaching students to employ cognitive strategies such as those presented in Chapter 5 equips them to become self-directed learners who make the most of the challenges put before them in all core subjects and in life outside school.

We would suggest that this myth about the need to focus primarily on the basics of core content goes hand in hand with another misperception about education—that teaching is a simple endeavor requiring no special skills or particular talents. In the Prologue, we discussed the commonly held belief that teacher education should focus on subject matter because of the misunderstanding that the act of teaching is simple. In fact, teaching is a complex endeavor that requires ongoing professional growth, exploration, and attention to emerging mind, brain, and education research about what works best for individual students and for an entire class. The concepts and findings from mind, brain, and education research—including neurocognitive plasticity, potential as capacity, malleable and dynamic intelligence, the intertwined Body-Brain System, and explicit instruction on metacognition—explored in this text are at the core of what 21st century education needs to look like.

YOU CAN GET BETTER AT ALMOST ANYTHING IF YOU SET YOUR MIND TO IT

Common misconceptions: Some children have a gift for math, and some children are born readers. Those students who are not naturally gifted in academics cannot excel.

Taking a deeper look: In the book, *Peak*, Ericsson and Pool share research on the development of expertise and note that a key to success in many domains is sustained deliberate practice over time. In education, that deliberate practice may take the form of intensive instruction and ample opportunities for learning to close stubborn achievement gaps (Ericsson & Pool, 2016)..

Myths about "natural talent" are particularly pervasive and insidious. As Halvorson notes, "We celebrate people who we believe have special abilities and tend to see those who work hard to succeed as less innately capable" (2012, p. 215). Ericsson and colleagues (1993) trace this predilection to attribute success to natural abilities back to the 19th century, but their research amassed extensive evidence that a key that propels expert performers, including celebrated musicians, chess players, artists, and athletes, to the top of their professions is hard work. What separates experts from others, in part, is their dedication and commitment to thousands of hours of *deliberate practice*, or activities that are designed to improve the current level of performance. Deliberate practice is focused and rigorous, aims for continuous improvement, and is tailored to the needs of the individual. It is made possible through extraordinary commitment and motivation and is supported by access to effective teachers and coaches, training materials, and facilities and to the resources necessary to learn and grow one's skills and knowledge.

This prescription for the development of expertise can be applied to the challenge of guiding children who arrive at school without the readiness to learn reading, math, and problem-solving skills to cultivate these abilities. Once we set aside the myth of natural talent and recognize that all students have the capacity to succeed academically, we can more effectively devote the necessary energy and enthusiasm needed to identify and teach the tools students need to learn.

To Learn More

For teachers interested in developing their professional expertise, K. Anders Ericsson and colleagues' "The Making of an Expert" in the July–August 2007 issue of the *Harvard Business Review* is well-written and useful.

YOUR BRAIN IS LIKE A LEARNING MUSCLE—BUILD IT

Common misconception: Intelligence is fixed and innate.

Taking a deeper look: Everyone, students and teachers alike, has the capacity to learn new things and grow smarter. As a recent study on measuring adolescent IQs demonstrates, even this single evaluation of intelligence is not unchangeable. More important, we can learn new ideas, concepts, and skills throughout our lives—and we need to be prepared to do that.

Scientists at the Wellcome Trust Centre for Neuroimaging at University College London (Ramsden et al., 2011) conducted IQ tests and MRI brain scans of 33 adolescents ages 12 to 16 in 2004 and then repeated the tests 3 or 4 years later on the same subjects, now ages 15 to 20. No specific cognitive interventions or tests were provided between the two periods; in fact, the study's participants were not even told they would be invited back for further testing. The researchers' aim was not to gauge the impact of a particular teaching approach or curriculum but to measure whether intellect, as measured by the Wechsler Intelligence Scale for children and adults, would change and to determine if IQ changes would be reflected in brain structure. They discovered significant shifts up and down in IQ—ranging from a drop of 20 points for one participant to a gain of 23 points for another in verbal IQ, a range of –18 to +17 in performance IQ (nonverbal skills, including spatial reasoning and problem solving unrelated to language), and a range of –18 to +21 in full-scale IQ. The researchers also found, through brain scans, corresponding changes in gray matter density and volume. As part of their research, the team asked participants to perform verbal and nonverbal tasks similar to those that would be performed in the IQ tests to identify neural markers in the brain associated with verbal and performance tasks.

The work of these London medical specialists supports a growing body of research behind two of the big ideas in education explored in this text: (1) intelligence is malleable and can be improved over time through learning (conversely, it can also decline), and (2) learning changes the brain. As Begley notes, mind, brain, and education research continues to develop our understanding of the capacity of all people "to know more, to understand more deeply, to make greater creative leaps, to retain what we read, to see connections invisible to others—not merely to make the most of what we have between our ears now, but to be, in a word, smarter" (2012, p. 30).

EARLY INTENSIVE READING
INSTRUCTION CAN OPEN NEW WORLDS

Common misconception: Children who arrive at school without the reading readiness skills of their peers do not have the potential to learn to read on grade level.

Taking a deeper look: Some children come to school with a head start in reading readiness, but nearly all children can learn to read fluently and to comprehend the meaning of what they are reading.

Fielding and colleagues (2007) report that on the first day of school, the gap between the highest and lowest performers in kindergarten in terms of reading readiness and ability can be as much as 6 years (4 years for math skills). These differences do not measure capacity to learn how to read; in fact, Allington (2011a) states that "studies have shown that virtually every student could be reading on grade level by the end of 1st grade" (para. 1). Instead, this gap underscores the importance of effective teaching and intensive literacy opportunities in the early elementary grades. Nancy Kerr, president of the National Children's Reading Foundation, notes that children who are read to at least 20 minutes a day from birth to kindergarten age are exposed to 600 hours of structured language, which allows them to acquire the preliteracy skills that form a useful foundation for learning to read. Children who begin school without the benefit of this regular exposure to print materials that is at the foundation of reading readiness need to experience 2 to 3 years of academic gains to learn to read and to catch up with their peers by 3rd grade (Fielding et al., 2007).

What this means for teachers is that they must be equipped with effective strategies to help children who come to school unprepared for learning to catch up with their peers and with daily opportunities to guide these students to build that foundation. As just one example, supplying struggling readers with books and other print materials that they can read with 98% accuracy—their independent reading level—helps them to experience success in reading and to become more motivated and proficient readers over time. Developing automaticity and fluency in reading is critical to students' success in all core subjects. In the United States, K–12 students spend an estimated 85% of their school day on lessons and assignments that require reading from text (Fielding et al., 2007). It follows logically that students who are not taught the reading skills they need to read on grade level do not benefit from the vast majority of instruction that goes on around them in their classrooms. But they *can* learn to read through their own dedicated efforts—and those of their teachers.

THE LITTLE ENGINE THAT COULD HAD THE RIGHT IDEA

Common misconception: Positive thinking has nothing to do with learning. Intellect and emotions do not intersect.

Taking a deeper look: A positive outlook can make a difference in how well students learn. If they are optimistic about their likelihood of succeeding at a learning task, they are more likely to keep trying and less likely to succumb to frustration and give up.

A myth related to the misconception that emotion does not play a role in intellectual development is that people's outlook on life—and, in particular, their tendency toward optimism or pessimism—is an intrinsic, unchangeable part of their personalities. Research by Martin Seligman (2018b), a pioneer in the field of positive psychology, indicates that people can change their outlooks and become more optimistic. Seligman's research also provides motivation to do so: People who maintain a "can-do" attitude actually outperform their more pessimistic peers, largely because they persist in their efforts based on their belief that they can succeed. An added incentive is that optimistic people may live longer, healthier lives on average than their pessimistic peers and tend to be more successful in their business and professional endeavors. Positive psychology has been applied directly in education: An optimistic approach to learning can be modeled and taught, with the aim of improving academic performance (Gilman et al., 2009; Wilson & Conyers, 2020). These findings are supported by Dweck's work on student "mindsets," discussed in Chapter 3. Chapter 4 presents research supporting explicit instruction and modeling of practical optimism.

Seligman (2011, 2018a) lists five elements of personal well-being, which is at the center of positive psychology, summarized by the acronym PERMA:

- *Positive emotion*, as represented by feelings of happiness and satisfaction with life;
- *Engagement*, or the pleasure that comes from being immersed or absorbed by an endeavor;
- *Relationships*, or positive interactions with other people, such as those that give the feelings of well-being that come from helping others;
- *Meaning*, as in finding purpose in your pursuits; and
- *Accomplishment*, or achieving something that you value.

This formulation is consistent with the discussion earlier in this text about the critical importance of a positive learning environment—classrooms and schools where students feel safe and secure, accepted and valued, and encouraged to take intellectual risks. When students are taught that they can get smarter by doing the work required in learning, they are more likely to persist in their efforts to master new knowledge and skills. In positive learning environments, students feel that they have positive relationships with their teachers and peers, they are engaged in learning, and they celebrate their academic accomplishments.

In the "chicken or egg" quandary of whether success produces happiness or vice versa, Achor argues that happy people are more likely to work hard and persist in their efforts until they succeed. He describes happiness as "the joy we feel striving after our potential" (2010, p. 40). Achor cites a meta-analysis by advocates of positive psychology of more than 200 studies involving 275,000 people worldwide; one common thread in that research is that happiness leads to success in virtually all aspects of life, including health, creativity, and work. Thus, he frames happiness in a way that is consistent with our formulation of practical optimism—as a realistic basis on which "to cultivate the mindset and behaviors that have been empirically proven to fuel greater success and fulfillment" (p. 24).

To Learn More

Check out Martin Seligman's three-book collection set, which provides readers with research and strategies for increasing optimism and human flourishing (Nicholas Brealey Publishing, 2019). This comprehensive collection of Seligman's works would be a good addition to an institution's professional library.

DON'T FORGET: YOU *CAN* REMEMBER

Common misconception: Having a good memory is another one of those lucky accidents for a chosen few, but that's OK because whatever we can't remember we can just search for on the Internet.

Taking a deeper look: Memory is an essential component of academic achievement—and like other cognitive skills, it can be learned.

Learning and memory go hand in hand. Memory is the mechanism by which we store what we have learned for future retrieval and use. In fact, the connection between learning and memory illustrates how inextricably linked human thinking processes are. The cognitive strategies presented in Chapter 5 of comparing, contrasting, and classifying aid in analyzing new information and connecting to what we already know. These forms of analysis aid in understanding and help to make the information more personally relevant, which also helps make it more memorable. When we understand a concept, we are more likely to remember it. Thus, teaching for meaning is also teaching for memory.

However, Thorne (n.d.) suggests that "understanding the subject matter is not enough; [students] must also actively engage in activities that will lead to the storage and ultimate retrieval of relevant information from long-term memory" (par. 15). Toward that end, a working knowledge of memory processes can help teachers design lessons and employ instructional strategies that help transfer new knowledge through short-term working memory into long-term storage, where it can be retrieved and applied in the future.

The key is to structure lessons and learning activities so that students transfer input to their fleeting sensory memory (what they hear, see, touch, and experience through other senses) to working, short-term memory, the stage where they can process and analyze the input and make meaning of this new information. Then the information must be transferred to long-term memory. The complexities of these memory processes have implications for teaching and learning. Here are just a few examples:

- "Priming" the brain for new information, or starting a lesson with a short activity or advance organizer once an idea has been introduced, gives students a chance to begin to process the new information. This can help them to recognize and remember it more easily the next time they encounter it.
- Along the same lines, presenting lesson contents in short segments (7, 15, or 20 minutes, depending on students' ages and the complexity of the content) and ending with a summing-up activity before shifting gears to a different learning activity or type of presentation may help to maintain students' attention, which is critical to learning, and aid in retention.
- Learning activities and cognitive strategies that facilitate long-term memory storage include activating students' prior knowledge about a subject, categorizing information to help give it a label for future retrieval, making lessons relevant by connecting them to students' lives, and making information more concrete by tying it to experiences through dramatic reenactments and field trips, for example.

Mnemonic devices can effectively help store "big picture ideas" for long-term retention because they key information to visual or brief verbal cues in a memorable way. We offer the particularly appropriate example of the acronym SAVE (Wilson & Conyers, 20118) as a way to remember useful tips to present lesson content in a memorable way:

See: Visual presentations are easier to receive, retain, and recall than information presented verbally for many students, which explains why graphic organizers and cartoons can be effective ways to reinforce key concepts.

Associate: Connecting new information to details that are personally relevant or visually memorable is another useful strategy. For example, remembering how many feet are in a mile is easy for a student who lives at 5280 Main Street. Recalling that there's *a rat* in *separate* provides an effective reminder for spelling the word correctly.

Vividly: The more vividly information is presented, the more memorable it will be. Dramatic, first-person accounts are a more effective means for relating history than a dry passage from a textbook. Watching a space shuttle launch in a video is more interesting—and thus more memorable—than reading a technical passage with no accompanying visual information.

Experience: As noted previously, active learning—taking a nature walk, writing and producing a play about a historical event, conducting a science experiment—is much more memorable than simply listening to a lecture.

As to the misconception that the need to train our memory is passé now that we can simply look up whatever we need to know on the Internet, heed the warning in the advice to "use it or lose it." Guiding students to hone their memory skills will help improve reading comprehension (so that they can better recall the content of the beginning of a document by the time they reach the end), note-taking in class (so that they can remember what the teacher is saying as they write it down), information processing and analysis, and test-taking.

SUPPORT PHYSICAL ACTIVITY TO SUPPORT LEARNING

Common misconception: If children spent less time in physical education and out playing at recess, they'd learn more.

Taking a deeper look: Incorporating opportunities for physical activity into the school day does not detract from learning. In fact, it may support academic achievement.

As we noted in Chapter 4, educational researchers continue to study how physical fitness and opportunities for physical activity throughout the school day enhance learning. Hattie reported in his review of more than 800 meta-analyses on student achievement that these studies

> found that the addition of physical education to the curriculum resulted in small positive gains in academic performance, and, as important, allocating time away from other subjects to physical education did not detract from achievement in other subjects. The effects came mainly from small positive effects on concentration and memory, and enhanced classroom behavior. (2009, p. 53)

Thus, regular physical education—combined with opportunities for movement incorporated into learning activities, short breaks to stretch and move about during transition times, and quick trips outside for a breath of fresh air—help to energize students and maintain their focus on learning. In addition, teachers should emphasize the importance of

From Teachers for Teachers

Allison Groulx teaches high school students taking online classes through K12 Inc. Even in this virtual learning environment, Ms. Groulx incorporates movement and encourages good nutrition to fuel the brain, emphasizing the importance of the Body-Brain System connections to learning. "I always had students do different types of movement activities, kinesthetic activities and changing activities every 10 or 12 minutes," she notes. "Now I understand why that works—movement helps us learn by bringing more oxygen to the brain."

developing good sleep habits and look for opportunities to remind students that adequate sleep supports learning success.

YOUR ROLE AS A MYTH BUSTER

In the Prologue, we touched on the need for teachers to be "adaptive experts," continually reexamining their professional beliefs and practices in the context of current research and the evolving needs of their students. The ongoing development of adaptive expertise is a surefire way to ferret out myths about teaching and learning that may continue to underlie some educational practices and policies. This approach allows teachers to make the most of their classroom experiences, to look for new ways to tackle persistent challenges, and to share what they have found to be effective and to learn from colleagues near and far. The next chapter takes up the topic of continuing your professional journey on your own and in partnership with peers.

Questions for Reflection

- Can you recall any teaching practices in the classrooms and schools of your youth that have likely been changed or discontinued in light of recent educational research?
- Have you encountered any of the myths presented in this chapter or in earlier chapters in discussions with peers, administrators, parents, acquaintances, or community members? What myth came to the surface, and in what context?
- Why do you think that myths about fixed intelligence and the potential for all students to learn are so persistent?
- How might these myths stand in the way of providing effective instruction or inhibit lifelong learning?

CHAPTER 7

Your Journey of Learning and Teaching

Classroom teaching . . . is perhaps the most complex, most challenging, and most demanding, subtle, nuanced, and frightening activity that our species has ever invented. The only time a physician could possibly encounter a situation of comparable complexity would be in the emergency room of a hospital during or after a natural disaster.

—Lee Shulman, *The Wisdom of Practice: Essays on Teaching, Learning, and Learning to Teach*, p. 504

Is it helpful for teachers to learn with others?

The big ideas about teaching and learning presented in this book should help you launch or further your teaching career and acquire the cognitive mindset that will facilitate your ongoing role as an adaptive expert. Throughout their careers in education, adaptive experts remain open to new ideas and are continually on the lookout for effective teaching approaches and strategies to add to their professional practice.

Toward that end, teachers need effective preparation and ongoing professional development. They also benefit greatly from opportunities for collaborative learning with their peers, both in the form of professional learning communities and through less formal team meetings, networking, mentoring, and idea-sharing. In this final chapter, we explore how you can continue your career-long journey of learning and teaching on your own and in collaboration with other educators.

THE IMPORTANCE OF LEARNING TOGETHER

Many people may think of learning as a solitary pursuit, but there is a great deal of support in the educational literature for *collaborative learning*, which has its roots in Vygotsky's work (Arthur & Cremin, 2006; Conyers & Wilson, 2016; Vygotsky, 1978). One well-known example is a form of *scaffolding*, of learning with a teacher or more experienced peer so that a student can move beyond his or her current level of understanding to improve knowledge and skills. *Social learning*, including collaboration in pairs and small groups and peer tutoring, has been found to boost achievement as children share what they know and expand their knowledge by comparing their perspectives and learning strategies with others' (Hattie, 2009, 2012).

More to the point for our purposes in this chapter, teachers also benefit from informal and formal cooperative learning opportunities to improve their professional practice. Scaffolding and social learning can play useful roles in professional development. Drago-Severson & Blum-DeStefano (2018) report that participating in a professional team or network may guide educators to learn from peers and to think differently about their own and others' teaching practice. Teamwork suggests a way for teachers to exchange information and feedback, to work together, and to build consensus around crucial aspects of their practice. In team meetings, teachers can learn from a variety of perspectives and mutually beneficial partnerships and change practices based on peer feedback and shared dialogue about practice. Such a collaborative approach offers a way for teachers to develop the collective efficacy that has been found to be important to schools and student achievement (Hoogsteen, 2020).

Collaborative learning in the form of professional learning communities (PLCs) is also an effective way for teachers to share what works in their classroom and to learn from their colleagues. The term *professional learning community* is fairly self-explanatory, writes Morrissey (2000), in suggesting a community of educational professionals learning together how best to teach in ways that improve student performance. In *Learning by Doing: A Handbook for Professional Learning Communities at Work* (DuFour, DuFour, Eaker, Many, & Mattos, 2016), the authors discuss envision PLCs as educators working together in a continual process of collective inquiry and action research with the aim of improving learning for all students. The members of a PLC are guided by a clear vision of what the organization should become in order to support all students to learn.

They make shared commitments clarifying what each individual member will do to create such an organization, and they use a results-oriented process to mark progress.

DuFour and colleagues (2016) identify several key elements of PLCs:

- *A central focus of the school or district functioning as a PLC on the learning of each student.* Inherent in this focus on incremental learning by students is that their teachers are learning continually as well.
- *A collaborative culture in which educators work interdependently to achieve common goals that support the learning of all students.* Both aspects of this component are essential: Collaboration is important as a means to the end of student learning, but DuFour and colleagues identify critical questions that teachers and administrators must consider and agree on to identify their common goals:
  - » What knowledge and skills must each student acquire through this instructional unit, course, or grade level?
  - » What evidence will we gather to monitor student learning?
  - » How will we provide students with extra time and support if they need it to achieve their learning goals?
  - » How will we enrich the learning of students who are already proficient?
  - » How can we use our common goals and evidence of student learning to inform and improve our practice?
- *Collective inquiry into traditional versus best practices in teaching.* This element requires all members of the learning community to be open to new information and new ways of teaching.
- *An action orientation of "learning by doing."* Members of PLCs are not content simply to agree on visions of what should be but rather commit to the hard work of discovering effective teaching approaches and strategies by reading, listening to colleagues, participating actively in professional development, planning, implementing what they have learned, and assessing the outcomes.
- *A commitment to continuous improvement.* This terminology may come from the business world but is extremely apropos for educators and the aim of professional learning communities.

To Learn More

Learning by Doing: A Handbook for Professional Learning Communities at Work, by Richard DuFour, Rebecca DuFour, Robert Eaker, Thomas Many, and Mike Mattos (Solution Tree Press, 2016), offers a practical guide for teachers and administrators working together to create a PLC in their school or district. For an overview of their approach to professional learning communities, visit the website AllThingsPLC (allthingsplc.info/about/aboutPLC.php).

As in the business environment, continuous improvement in schools involves measuring baseline performance, identifying weaknesses and opportunities for improvements in the system, implementing new strategies demonstrated to be effective, and analyzing the impact of those new strategies. This shared commitment to improving student learning is not just about process but also about attitude: Teachers who commit to learning by doing recognize that talking with colleagues about challenges in their classroom and trying new strategies are not signs that they are ineffective in their work. Rather, taking action is an acknowledgment of the "gold standard" of the profession—becoming an adaptive expert continuously learning ways to improve one's practice.

- *A results orientation.* This final element acknowledges another shared value of all members of the professional learning community—that their work and learning make a difference. Toward that end, teachers work together to identify tangible results of new teaching approaches and strategies. Formative assessments are an essential tool in helping to monitor students' ongoing progress and to help identify the types of support they may need to continue to improve. Teachers can work together to identify types of formative assessments that they can all use in their classrooms to monitor their students' progress and to evaluate the impact of teaching approaches and strategies.

Research on the Impact of Professional Learning Communities

As the opening quote to this chapter suggests, teaching is a complex endeavor, with the aim of optimizing learning among a new group of students arriving in the classroom each fall. Each student is at his or her own point along the continuum of knowledge and skills, and each has a unique background and way of viewing the world. The schools in which teachers do this work are often dealing with tight budgets, expected to do more with less year after year. And there is always something new to learn—new curricula, new teaching technology, new textbooks and learning materials, new policies and practices—all with the aim of school improvement at their core, but all adding to teachers' already busy workloads. Professional Learning Communities can help teachers rise to these challenges. Their structure can provide a context for positive and productive dialogue and collective inquiry among teachers. When time is allotted for teachers to work together to plan lessons and provide instruction, to assess student progress, and to develop and plan how to deliver curriculum, the benefit can result in greater student learning (DuFour, DuFour, Eaker, Many, & Mattos, 2016).

Exploration about the benefits of professional learning communities for teachers and their students began in the 1980s and 1990s; for example, Rosenholtz (1989) reported increased teaching effectiveness and commitment among teachers who had support for their work in the form of teacher networks, cooperation among colleagues, and opportunities for expanded professional roles. In addition, teachers were more confident about and committed to their teaching as a result of those collaborations with colleagues and were more likely to adopt new teaching strategies demonstrated to support student learning. Darling-Hammond (1996) cited opportunities to join in decisions about curriculum and new roles for teachers in their schools and districts, along with structured time for teachers to meet to plan instruction, to observe in each other's classrooms, and to share feedback, as other examples of collaborative learning that support school improvement.

Research support for the impact of professional learning communities and teacher collaboration continues to grow (Public Agenda, 2017). A major study in a Midwestern school district involving more than 450 teachers and 2,500 4th-graders found higher achievement in math and reading at schools where teachers reported more opportunities for collaboration involving the curriculum and instruction and for professional development (Goddard, Goddard, & Tschannen-Moran, 2007).

Reporting on research on collaborative learning among educators in New York City schools, Leana (2011) compares the impact of teachers' "human capital" (e.g., education levels, years in the classroom, subject matter knowledge) to that of enhancing their "social capital" (through opportunities to interact with colleagues to share teaching perspectives and strategies). The research involved 1,000 3rd- and 4th-grade teachers in 130 schools, comparing students' academic performance based on the frequency of their teachers' interactions with colleagues and level of trust among teachers. The study found a correlation between scores on math tests and the collaborative atmosphere among teachers. Researchers also concluded that teachers of low ability can perform as well as average teachers with the support of a professional learning community. As Leana put it, "When social capital is strong, student achievement scores improve" (p. 33).

A teacher participating in the study made the point that "teaching is not an isolated activity. If it's going to be done well, it has to be done collaboratively over time." She noted that teachers working individually, without opportunities to interact with their colleagues, might become overly focused in one area, such as teaching thinking skills or focusing on basic lesson content, for example. She concluded,

> A good teacher needs to help students develop all of those things, but it's easy to get stuck in your own ideology if you are working alone. With collaboration, you are exposed to other teachers' priorities and are better able to incorporate them to broaden your own approach in the classroom. (Leana, 2011, p. 34)

Another teacher shared an example of the advantages of pooling human and social capital to enhance the knowledge and skills of a community of teachers. In her California district, teachers can participate voluntarily in a program of observing in their colleagues' classrooms, which can be especially useful for beginning teachers to develop their "competence and confidence" (p. 35). Opportunities to interact with colleagues to share strategies and perspectives benefit longtime educators as well as relative newcomers.

Time to End Teacher Isolation

The limitations of teachers' practicing their profession in isolation without the support of colleagues date back to the early days of public education in the United States and have persisted through the decades. Writing in 1975, Lortie identified this isolation as a major obstacle to school reform.

Still, opportunities for collaborative learning among teachers seem to be in short supply in American schools. In a survey of 10,000 teachers (Scholastic & the Gates Foundation, 2012), 89% ranked "time for teachers to collaborate" as either absolutely essential or very important to support student achievement; at the same time, teachers reported having only an average 15 to 17 minutes per school day to interact with their colleagues. With so many new teachers entering the profession, and schools hard at work implementing rigorous mandated learning standards, it is critically important to support collaborative learning among educators today. These concurrent developments offer both challenges and opportunities; professional learning communities can help to overcome the former and take advantage of the latter. But even in schools and districts without formal PLCs, teachers can seek out opportunities to work together, share ideas, and engage in collaborative learning. Book study groups within or outside of PLCs can help teachers grow together through focus on a specific area of practice to help students succeed.

Building social capital among teachers through formal and informal professional communities builds on several big ideas from this text. Brain plasticity facilitates your ability to improve your professional practice throughout your career. The concept of incremental intelligence underscores that there is always something new to learn about teaching. And the understanding that potential is dynamic has applications for teachers in their individual careers and for schools and districts, with educational professionals working together to improve student performance.

Throughout this book, we have discussed opportunities for teachers to advocate for their students and for their professions. Supporting collaborative learning for you and your colleagues is one such opportunity. There is no census of how many districts and schools have embraced the use of professional learning communities. If you begin your career or are currently working in a district without a formal PLC, you may choose to advocate for building collaborative learning into the school day, through meeting regularly with colleagues to plan and share strategies, observing in each other's classrooms, and volunteering for teacher leadership roles, such as mentoring peers and planning curriculum and standards. Collaborative learning can also take place in a virtual environment, as the next section discusses. When teachers work together to create effective lessons and see the positive impact on student learning, they can build what is known as collective teacher efficacy. Research suggests that this makes a highly significant impact on student learning. According to Hattie's research, "based on a synthesis of more than 1,500 meta-analyses, collective teacher efficacy is greater than three times more powerful and predictive of student achievement than socioeconomic status" (Donohoo, Hattie, & Eells, 2018).

To Learn More

Smarter Teacher Leadership: Neuroscience and the Power of Purposeful Collaboration by Marcus Conyers and Donna Wilson, with a foreword by neuroscientist Immordino-Yang (2016, TCP), advances the key ideas from this book to enhancing collective teacher efficacy across schools and districts. Another resource is *Collective Efficacy: How Educators' Beliefs Impact Student Learning* by Jenni Donohoo (2017).

In Sum

The research in support of collaborative learning for students also applies to teachers. Formal and informal professional learning communities allow teachers to develop, support, and work toward realization of a shared vision—that all students can learn and succeed academically.

CONNECTING WITH A WORLDWIDE
PROFESSIONAL LEARNING COMMUNITY

When you're looking for ideas, feedback, and support in your professional practice, you can turn to the teachers down the hall—and across the country and around the world. In recent years, the virtual environment has expanded from a ready source of information about lesson plans and content to a real community of educators who want to participate in on-demand learning, access a network of educators with common interests, and often practice media literacy skills that transfer into classroom pedagogy (Coughlin & Kajder, 2009; Elliott, 2017).

Digital file-sharing and social networking sites facilitate teachers' creative and problem-solving energies put to the task of finding and sharing solutions to persistent teaching challenges, new ways of presenting lesson content, strategies to monitor and support students' learning progress, implementation of current learning standards, and support and inspiration—to name just a few of the areas where questions may be asked and answers found.

From Teachers for Teachers

In her blog "For the Love of Teaching" (fortheloveofteaching.net), Texas teacher Diane Dahl writes about how she puts mind, brain, and education research to work in her 2nd-grade classroom and how she uses technology to support her professional practice. Her blogs often begin conversations with teachers across the United States and in other countries (including Australia, Brazil, Canada, Indonesia, Ireland, Saudi Arabia, and Russia). Ms. Dahl's blog is even required reading for education students in a class at the University of Alabama whose assignments include reading, commenting on, and writing a report on a teaching blog.

Ms. Dahl is also an active member of the EdupIn Ning community (edupIn.ning.com) and the BrainSMART Facebook community. She participates in regularly prearranged virtual chats with teachers around the world via Twitter (e.g., #edchat, #techchat, #kinderchat, #educhat, #scichat, #mathchat). "It's so important to learn from educators outside of our usual connections, because we get other points of view and dynamic ideas," says Ms. Dahl, known as DahlD on Twitter.

Florida teacher Kelly Rose relies on the Internet to keep tabs on the latest in educational research. She gets regular updates on her smartphone through ASCD Smartbrief (smartbrief.com/news/ascd) and often shares those research updates with her colleagues. After sharing one recent link with fellow faculty, "I heard from colleagues from departments I don't usually work with," Ms. Rose notes. "After that, they started sending me links, videos, etc., on the same topic. It got others inspired and interested. We found ourselves sitting outside my classroom talking about different topics from links I sent out."

Georgia teacher Tonya Moore also takes advantage of collaborative learning through technology within her district and school. The district hosts webinars using the Blackboard Collaborate system so that teachers can participate actively without traveling to a distant location. In addition, teachers can share educational resources, strategies, and videos via virtual folders accessible to colleagues at each school.

Coughlin and Kajder cite a variety of qualities that set online collaborative learning apart from more traditional face-to-face professional communities:

- Online resources are readily available 24/7.
- These resources are easily searchable. Enter any topic about learning and teaching into any search engine, and you'll find a wealth of information.
- Your work and that of your peers can be easily shared, edited, reposted, and replicated.
- You have a ready audience for your ideas and questions. Tightknit online communities of teachers in your grade level or subject matter can provide constructive criticism and support for effective teaching in a comfortable environment.
- You can interact in real time—or not—as your schedule allows. Online learning communities provide a convenient medium for teachers to communicate without the need for sitting down around the same table at the same time.
- You can investigate possibilities directly related to your work and your students' learning in a virtually limitless database of information supplied by experienced practitioners.
- You can build your technology skills and facilitate learning for your students as well as helping them connect online to explore, share their work, and develop their own technological competencies.

In short, online professional development offers opportunities for professional growth to teachers who may not be able to participate otherwise due to time and travel constraints. You can even find information online about how best to advocate for and develop a professional learning community in your school and district!

To Learn More

For an online resource for research updates in the learning sciences, see the npj Science of Learning website at nature.com/npjscilearn. This site also offers access to the npj Science of Learning Community.

In Sum

Internet file-sharing, online communities, and social media provide near-endless opportunities for professional development and collaborative learning among teachers.

THE JOY OF INFORMAL LEARNING

Teachers make their living in the field of "formal education"—in classrooms and schools where the sole focus is on learning and improving academic performance. But we would suggest that the big ideas in this text also support *informal learning*, which has been identified by the Organisation for Economic Co-operation and Development (OECD, n.d.) as a component of lifelong learning. By definition, informal learning takes place outside the classroom and the formalized pursuit of knowledge. You might think of it as "accidental learning" or "learning through experience." This type of learning encompasses useful information and skills you pick up in your pursuits outside school, while reading or watching television, talking with friends, and traveling to interesting places, for example. These activities are not undertaken to satisfy formal learning objectives, but rather because one is interested and personally motivated to discover new ideas or learn new abilities. The OECD suggests that, as one aspect of developing personal and professional knowledge and skills, informal learning along with formal education "has value . . . and deserves to be made visible and recognized" (para. 5).

We include this concept of informal learning in this chapter to make the point that you may find opportunities for "professional development" in some unexpected places throughout your career. This willingness to consider new ideas is at the essence of lifelong learning and of becoming an adaptive expert.

RISING TO THE HOPE AND CHALLENGES
OF YOUR PROFESSIONAL PRACTICE

A central premise of this chapter—and of the entire book, for that matter—is that effective teachers "practice what they teach." In guiding your students to make the most of their neural plasticity, to realize their full academic potential, to continually increase their intelligence, to nurture their Body-Brain Systems, and to learn and wield cognitive and metacognitive strategies, your role is not just as a teacher. You are also the "lead learner," a role model of the pleasures and rewards of lifelong learning. You and your students will learn and grow together. As Hord and Tobia suggest:

There can be no improvement without change, and no change without learning. Change *is* learning; it's as simple and as complicated as that. . . . What we know of professionals is that they are continuous learners, always changing in order to improve their practice and to serve their clients more effectively. (2012, p. 96)

When thinking about your own potential to become the best possible educator you are capable of being, you might consider some oft-cited good advice from the psychiatrist William Glasser to "begin to act the part, as well as you can, of the person . . . you most want to become." In other words, you have the capability to excel as a teacher through continued persistent effort and learning, but you don't have to go it alone. By forming professional learning communities with teachers in your school and district and taking advantage of less formal collaborative learning locally and in the virtual environment, you can find and share new ideas for learning and teaching and the support you need to thrive in this challenging and rewarding profession.

In daily classroom practice, you can "act the part" of the learner you want your students to become. The fundamental message of explicit instruction about the power of brain plasticity and malleable intelligence is that all students can learn and succeed inside and outside school. Teaching and modeling useful cognitive strategies helps equip them with learning, thinking, problem solving, and communications skills that will serve them well throughout their years in school and in the working world of the 21st century. Adopting this mindset will also prepare you to continue learning and growing throughout your career in education.

Wherever you are on your career path, you can fortify a strong foundation for professional practice by furthering your understanding of

1. brain plasticity,
2. the potential of both students and teachers for lifelong learning,
3. the malleability of intelligence,
4. the body and brain working together to support learning, and
5. the gains that may result from using cognitive and metacognitive strategies.

These closely intertwined big ideas offer a vision for an educational system that supports all students to make learning gains—and means to help achieve that aim.

THE OPPORTUNITY

At the dawn of the second decade of the 21st century, educators stand at a unique point in history. More is known than ever before about how people learn, and about teaching practices that could increase the academic achievement of all learners. By connecting the science of learning to the practice of teaching educators around the world, teachers can have a more positive impact on the life trajectories of their students than never before.

In this book we have shared some insights from our own journeys of discovery in exploring the emerging science of learning and our experience of sharing the framework of five interconnected factors for supporting effective teaching in our graduate degree programs and in live events with thousands of teachers worldwide. The application of this framework can make a positive impact for individual teachers in developing their own

---

Key Terms

Collaborative learning: The concept that people learn better when they learn together; related to social learning.

Collective teacher efficacy: Collective self-perception among teachers in a school that they believe they can make a difference to their students above and beyond the influence of the students' homes and communities.

Human capital: Attributes that individual teachers bring to their profession (e.g., education, teaching experience, subject matter knowledge).

Informal learning: "Accidental learning" or "learning from experience" outside formal educational programs and without stated learning objectives.

Professional advocacy: Teachers' efforts to promote attitudes, actions, and endeavors that support student learning, school improvement, and the furthering of their profession.

Professional learning community: Collaborative learning by teachers, characterized in formal programs by recurring cycles of collective inquiry and action research with the aim of improving student achievement.

Social capital: Opportunities to interact and learn with colleagues to share teaching perspectives and strategies.

Social media: Internet-based applications that permit teachers to share ideas and strategies about classroom practice and to network with fellow professionals.

sense of efficacy as they see the lightbulbs switch on as their students learn more as a result of their effective teaching practice. When teachers collaborate and educational leaders support collective teacher efficacy, there is tremendous potential for an even greater positive impact at the school and school system level.

We hope that this book has stimulated your thinking about teaching and connected you to resources for continuously increasing your impact with your students, colleagues, and community. We wish you all the best on your ongoing learning journey and look forward to hearing from you in the future.

Questions for Reflection

- What do you think Lee Shulman meant when he described teaching as the "most complex, most challenging, and most demanding [and] frightening activity that our species has ever invented"? How might collaborative learning with fellow teachers and the support of colleagues help to overcome those challenges?
- How have you benefited from collaborative learning during your years in school as a student, teacher, or both?
- What might be the benefits of professional learning communities for teachers and their students?
- How might teachers advocate for professional learning communities?
- How have you used the Internet and social media in learning to become a teacher? How might practicing teachers use online file-sharing and networking to improve their practice?
- Can you identify some examples of informal learning in your life? How might informal learning support your professional development?
- How can you become the "lead learner" in your classroom?

References

Aberg, M. A. I., Pedersen, N. I., Toren, K., Svartengren, M., Backstrand, B., Johnsson, T., . . . Kuhn, H. G. (2009). Cardiovascular fitness is associated with cognition in young adulthood. *Proceedings of the National Academy of Sciences, 106*(49), 20906–20911. doi: 10.1073/pnas.0905307106

Achor, S. (2010). *The happiness advantage: The seven principles of positive psychology that fuel success and performance at work*. New York, NY: Crown Business.

Allington, R. L. (2011a, August). What at-risk readers need. *Best of Educational Leadership 2010–2011, 68,* 40–45. Retrieved from ascd.org/publications/educational_leadership/summer11/vol68/num10/What_At-Risk_Readers_Need.aspx

Allington, R. L. (2011b). *What really matters to struggling readers: Designing research-based programs* (3rd ed.). Boston: Allyn & Bacon.

Alloway, T. P., & Alloway, R. (2013). *The working memory advantage: Train your brain to function stronger, smarter, faster*. New York, NY: Simon & Schuster.

Almy, S., & Theokas, C. (2010). *Not prepared for class: High-poverty schools continue to have fewer in-field teachers*. Washington, DC: Education Trust. Retrieved from edtrust.org/sites/edtrust.org/files/publications/files/Not%20Prepared%20for%20Class.pdf

American Academy of Child & Adolescent Psychiatry. (2016, September). Teen brain: Behavior, problem solving, and decision making. *Facts for Families, 95.* Retrieved from aacap.org/AACAP/Families_and_Youth/Facts_for_Families/FFF-Guide/The-Teen-Brain-Behavior-Problem-Solving-and-Decision-Making-095.aspx

American Academy of Sleep Medicine. (2019). Teens sleep longer, are more alert for homework when school starts later. *Uncover Sleep 2019.* Retrieved from aasm.org/later-school-start-times-study

American Psychological Association. (2014, July). See brain. See brain read. . . Reading instructions change the brain. *Psychology: Science in Action.* Retrieved from apa.org/action/resources/research-in-action/reading

Ames, C., & Archer, J. (1988). Achievement goals in the classroom: Students' learning strategies and motivation processes. *Journal of Educational Psychology, 80,* 260–267. Retrieved from unco.edu/cebs/psychology/kevinpugh/motivation_project/resources/ames_archer88.pdf

Anderman, E. M. (2009). Goal orientation theory. In E. M. Anderman & L. H.

Anderman (Eds.), *Psychology of classroom learning: An encyclopedia* (pp. 437–442). Farmington Hills, MI: Gale, Cengage Learning.

Anwar, Y. (2010, February 20). An afternoon nap markedly boosts the brain's learning capacity. Retrieved from newscenter.berkeley.edu/2010/02/22/naps_boost_learning_capacity/

Armstrong, T. (2017). *Multiple intelligences in the classroom* (4th ed.). Alexandria, VA: ASCD.

Arrowsmith-Young, B. (2012). *The woman who changed her brain: How I left my learning disability behind and other stories of cognitive transformation.* New York, NY: Free Press.

Arthur, J., & Cremin, T. (2006). *Learning to teach in the primary school.* London, UK: Routledge.

ASCD. (2018). Teaching students to drive their brains [Video series], featuring Donna Wilson. Retrieved from ascd.org/professional-development/videos/teaching-students-to-drive-their-brains-videos.aspx

Aspen Institute, National Commission on Social, Emotional, and Academic Development. (n.d.). The evidence base for how we learn: Supporting students' social, emotional, and academic development. Retrieved from assets.aspeninstitute.org/content/uploads/2017/12/CDS-Brief-One-Pager.pdf?_ga=2.195504556.1848643884.1569544161-72785088.1548621396

Aud, S., Hussar, W., Kena, G., Bianco, K., Frohlich, L., Kemp, J., & Tahan, K. (2011). *The condition of education 2011* (NCES 2011-033). Washington, DC: U.S. Department of Education, National Center for Education Statistics.

Baas, D., Castelijns, J., Vermeulen, M., Martens, R., & Segers, M. (2015). The relation between assessment for learning and elementary students' cognitive and metacognitive strategy use. *British Journal of Educational Psychology, 85*(1), 33–46.

Baker, D. P., Salinas, D., & Eslinger, P. J. (2012). An envisioned bridge: Schooling as a neurocognitive developmental institution [Supplement 1]. *Developmental Cognitive Neuroscience, 2,* S6–S17.

Baker, L. (2013). Metacognitive strategies. In J. Hattie & E. M. Anderman (Eds.), *International guide to student achievement* (pp. 419–421). New York, NY: Routledge.

Barber, M., & Mourshed, M. (2007). *How the world's best-performing school systems come out on top.* New York, NY: McKinsey. Retrieved from mckinseyonsociety.com/downloads/reports/Education/Worlds_School_Systems_Final.pdf

Battro, A. M., Fischer, K. W., & Lena, P. J. (2008). *The educated brain: Essays in neuroeducation.* Cambridge, UK: Cambridge University Press.

Baumeister, R. F., & Tierney, J. (2012). *Willpower: Rediscovering the greatest human strength.* New York, NY: Penguin Press.

Begley, S. (2012, January 9 and 16). Buff your brain: Want to be smarter in work, love, and life? *Newsweek,* 28–35.

Bergland, C. (2014, February 16). Tackling the "vocabulary gap" between rich and poor children [Blog post]. *Psychology Today.* Retrieved from psychologytoday.com/us/blog/the-athletes-way/201402/tackling-the-vocabulary-gap-between-rich-and-poor-children

Berliner, D. C. (2009). Research, policy, and practice: The great disconnect. In S. D. Lapan & M. T. Quartaroli (Eds.), *Research essentials: An introduction to designs and practices* (pp. 295–326). San Francisco: Jossey-Bass.

Berninger, V. W., & Richards, T. L. (2002). *Brain literacy for educators and psychologists*. San Diego, CA: Academic Press.

Black, J. (2018). Experience-dependent, experience-expectant processes. In M. Bornstein (Ed.), *The SAGE encyclopedia of lifespan human development* (pp. 812–813). Thousand Oaks, CA: SAGE. doi: 10.4135/9781506307633.n301

Blackwell, L. S., Trzesniewski, K. H., & Dweck, C. S. (2007). Implicit theories of intelligence predict achievement across an adolescent transition: A longitudinal study and an intervention. *Child Development, 78,* 246–263. doi: 10.1111/j.1467-8624.2007.00995.x

Blakemore, S-J. (2018, February). Editorial: Why a science of learning. *Impact, Journal of the Chartered College of Teaching.* Retrieved from impact. chartered.college/article/blakemore-editorial-science-of-learning

Bloom, B. S. (1964). *Stability and change in human characteristics.* New York, NY: Wiley.

Boman, P., Furlong, M. J., Shochet, I., Lilles, E., & Jones, C. (2009). Optimism and the school context. In R. Gilman, E. S. Huebner, & M. J. Furlong (Eds.), *Handbook of positive psychology in school* (pp. 51–64). New York, NY: Routledge.

Bönstrup, M., Iturrate, I., Thompson, R., Cruciani, G., Censor, N., & Cohen, L. G. (2019). A rapid form of offline consolidation in skill learning. *Current Biology, 29*(8), 1346–1351 doi: 10.1016/j.cub.2019.02.049

Bransford, J., Brown, A., & Cocking, R. (Eds.). (2000). *How people learn: Brain, mind, experience, and school* (Expanded ed.). Washington, DC: National Academies Press.

Bredo, E. (2006). Conceptual confusion and educational psychology. In P. A. Alexander & P. H. Winne (Eds.), *Handbook of educational psychology* (2nd ed., pp. 43–57). Mahwah, NJ: Erlbaum.

Brophy, J. E. (2005). Goal theorists should move on from performance goals. *Educational Psychologist, 40,* 167–176.

Brown, A. L. (1997). Transforming schools into communities of thinking and learning about serious matters. *American Psychologist, 52,* 399–409.

Brown, J., & Fenske, M. (2010). *The winner's brain: 8 strategies great minds use to achieve success.* Cambridge, MA: Da Capo Press.

Brown, R., Pressley, M., Van Meter, P., & Schuder, T. (1996). A quasi-experimental validation of transactional strategies instruction with low-achieving second-grade readers. *Journal of Educational Psychology, 88,* 18–37.

Bruer, J. T. (1999). *The myth of the first three years.* New York, NY: Free Press.

Bruer, J. T., & Greenough, W. T. (2001). The subtle science of how experience affects the brain. In D. B. Bailey, J. T. Bruer, F. J. Symons, & J. W. Lichtman (Eds.), *Critical thinking about critical periods* (pp. 209–232). Baltimore, MD: Brookes.

Bruner, J. (1977). *The process of education.* Cambridge, MA: Harvard University Press.

Burns, M. (2019, February 19). I'm a neuroscientist. Here's how teachers change kids' brains. *EdSurge.* Retrieved from edsurge.com/news/2019-02-19-i-m-a-neuroscientist-here-s-how-teachers-change-kids-brains

Calfee, R. C. (2006). Educational psychology in the 21st century. In P. A. Alexander & P. H. Winne (Eds.), *Handbook of educational psychology* (2nd ed., pp. 29–42). Mahwah, NJ: Erlbaum.

Calfee, R. C. & Patrick, C. L. (1995). *Teach our children well: Bringing K–12 education into the 21st century.* Stanford, CA: Stanford Alumni Association.

Carlson, S. (2011, September). Session one: Early development and executive function. Summary of panel discussion at Cognitive Neuroscience of Learning: Implication for Education Symposium, New York Academy of Sciences, Aspen, Colorado. Retrieved from nyas.org

Castelli, D. M., Hillman, C. H., Buck, S. M., & Erwin, H. E. (2007). Physical fitness and academic achievement in third- and fifth-grade students. *Journal of Sports and Exercise Psychology, 29,* 239–252.

Cattell, R. B. (1971). *Abilities: Their structure, growth, and action.* Boston: Houghton Mifflin.

Cawelti, G. (2004). *Handbook of research on improving student achievement* (3rd ed.). Alexandria, VA: Educational Research Service.

Centers for Disease Control and Prevention (CDC). (2014, May). Health and academic achievement. Retrieved from cdc.gov/healthyyouth/health_and_academics/pdf/health-academic-achievement.pdf

Centre for Educational Research and Innovation (CERI). (Eds.). (2007). *Understanding the brain: The birth of a learning science.* Danvers, MA: Organisation for Economic Co-operation and Development.

Chang, Y. (2014). Reorganization and plastic changes of the human brain associated with skill learning and expertise. *Frontiers in Human Neuroscience, 8*(35). doi: 10.3389/fnhum.2014.00035

Cheng, M. H. M., & Wan, Z. H. (2017). Exploring the effects of classroom learning environment on critical thinking skills and disposition: A study of Hong Kong 12th graders in liberal studies. *Thinking Skills and Creativity, 24,* 152–163. doi: 10.1016/j.tsc.2017.03.001

Clements, D. H., & Sarama, J. (2009). *Learning and teaching early math: The learning trajectories approach.* New York, NY: Routledge.

Coggshall, J. G., Behrstock-Sherratt, E., & Drill, K. (2011, April). *Workplaces that support high-performing teaching and learning: Insights from Generation Y teachers.* Naperville, IL: American Institutes for Research; Washington, DC: American Federation of Teachers. Retrieved from air.org/files/AFT_AIR_GenY_Workplaces_April11.pdf

Collaborative for Academic, Social, and Emotional Learning. (2019). Core SEL competencies. Retrieved from casel.org/core-competencies

Collaborative for Academic, Social, and Emotional Learning. (n.d.). SEL results—Austin Independent School District. Retrieved from casel.org/sel-results-austin-independent-school-district/

Committee on the Study of Teacher Preparation Programs in the United States & National Research Council. (2010). *Preparing teachers: Building evidence for sound policy.* Washington, DC: National Academies Press.

Conyers, M. A., & Wilson, D. L. (2009). *Introduction to BrainSMART Health-Wise* (2nd ed.). Orlando, FL: BrainSMART.

Conyers, M. A., & Wilson, D. L. (2015a). *Positively smarter: Science and strategies for increasing happiness, achievement, and well-being.* Chichester, West Sussex, UK: Wiley.

Conyers, M. A., & Wilson, D. L. (2015b, May). Smart moves: Powering up the brain with physical activity. *Kappan, 96*(8), 38–42. Retrieved from kappancommoncore.org/smart-moves-powering-up-the-brain-with-physical-activity/

Conyers, M. A., & Wilson, D. L. (2016). *Smarter teacher leadership: Neuroscience and the power of purposeful collaboration.* New York, NY: Teachers College Press.

Coughlin, E., & Kajder, S. (2009). *The impact of online collaborative learning on educators and classroom practices.* San Jose, CA: CISCO; Culver City, CA: Metiri Group. Retrieved from cisco.com/web/about/citizenship/socio-economic/docs/Metiri_Teacher_Collaboration_Research.pdf

Council of Chief State School Officers, Interstate Teacher Assessment and Support Consortium (2011). *InTASC model core teaching standards: A resource for state dialogue.* Retrieved from ccsso.org/Documents/2011/InTASC_Model_Core_Teaching_Standards_2011.pdf

Craik, F. I. M., Bialystok, E., & Freedman, M. (2010). Delaying the onset of Alzheimer's disease: Bilingualism as a form of cognitive reserve. *Neurology, 75,* 1726–1729.

Cunningham, P. M., & Allington, R. L. (2010). *Classrooms that work: They can all read and write* (5th ed.). Boston: Allyn & Bacon.

Dahl, D. (2011). Reading levels jump 5 months in just 2.5 months. Retrieved from fortheloveofteaching.net/2011/03/reading-levels-jump-5-months-in-just-25.html

Dana Foundation. (2011). BrainSMART graduate programs with Nova Southeastern University. *Brain Awareness Week Partner Reports.* Retrieved from dana.org/brainweek/reports/list.aspx?keyword=BrainSMART&country=US&audience=2

Darling-Hammond, L. (1996, March). The quiet revolution: Rethinking teacher development. *Educational Leadership, 53*(6), 4–10.

Darling-Hammond, L. (2010). *The flat world and education: How America's commitment to equity will determine our future.* New York, NY: Teachers College Press.

Darling-Hammond, L., & Bransford, J. (Eds.). (2005). *Preparing teachers for a changing world: What teachers should learn and be able to do.* San Francisco: Jossey-Bass.

Darling-Hammond, L., Flook, L., Cook-Harvey, C., Barron, B., & Osher, D. (2019). Implications for educational practice of the science of learning and development. *Applied Developmental Science* (2), 1–44. doi:10.1080/10888691.2018.1537791

Darling-Hammond, L., & Oakes, J. (2019). *Preparing teachers for deeper learning.* Cambridge, MA:. Harvard University Press.

Darling-Hammond, L., & Rothman, R. (Eds.). (2011). *Teacher and leader effectiveness in high-performing education systems.* Washington, DC: Alliance for Excellent Education; Stanford, CA: Stanford Center for Opportunity Policy in Education. Retrieved from all4ed.org/files/TeacherLeaderEffectivenessReport.pdf

Davidson, R. J., with Begley, S. (2012). *The emotional life of your brain.* New York, NY: Hudson Press.

Deans for Impact. (2015–2020). What we do: Transform programs. Retrieved from deansforimpact.org/what-we-do/transform-programs

Dehaene, S. (1997). *The number sense: How the mind creates mathematics.* New York, NY: Oxford University Press.

Dehaene, S. (2009). *Reading in the brain: The science and evolution of a human invention.* New York, NY: Viking Penguin.

Deming, W. E. (1994). *The new economics for industry, government, and education* (2nd ed.). Cambridge, MA: MIT Press.

Diamond, A. (2013). Executive functions. *Annual Review of Psychology, 64*, 135–168. dx.doi.org/10.1146/annurev-psych-113011-143750

Diamond, A., & Ling, D. S. (2015). Conclusions about interventions, programs, and approaches for improving executive functions that appear justified and those that, despite much hype, do not. *Developmental Cognitive Neuroscience, 18*, 34–48 doi: 10.1016/j.dcn.2015.11.005

D'Mello, A. M., & Gabrieli, J. D. E. (2018, October 24). Cognitive neuroscience of dyslexia. *Language, Speech, and Hearing Services in Schools, 49*(4), 798–809. doi: 10.1044/2018_LSHSS-DYSLC-18-0020.

Doherty, A., & Forés Miravalles, A. (2019). Physical activity and cognition: Inseparable in the classroom. *Frontiers in Education, 4*, 105. doi: 10.3389/feduc.2019.00105

Donald, B. (2019, August 7). Stanford researchers investigate how the brain changes with different learning experiences. Stanford Graduate School of Education. Retrieved from ed.stanford.edu/news/stanford-researchers-investigate-how-brain-changes-different-learning-experiences

Donker, A. S., de Boer, H., Kostons, D., Dignath van Ewijk, C. C., & van der Werf, M. P. C. (2014). Effectiveness of learning strategy instruction on academic performance: A meta-analysis. *Educational Research Review, 11*(1), 1–26. doi.org/10.1016/j.edurev.2013.11.002

Donohoo, J. (2017). *Collective efficacy: How educators' beliefs impact student learning.* Thousand Oaks, CA: Corwin Press.

Donohoo, J., Hattie, J. A. C., & Eells, R. (2018, March). The power of collective efficacy. *ASCD Educational Leadership, 75*(6), 40–44.

Dovidio, J. F., & Banfield, J. C. (2015). Prosocial behavior and empathy. In J. D. Wright (Ed.), *International encyclopedia of the social and behavioral sciences* (2nd ed., Vol. 19, pp. 216–220). Oxford, England: Elsevier.

Draganski, B., Gaser, C., Kempermann, G., Kuhn, H. G., Winkler, J., Buchel, C., & May, A. (2006). Temporal and spatial dynamics of brain structure changes during extensive learning. *The Journal of Neuroscience, 26*(23), 6314–6317.

Drago-Severson, E., & Blum-DeStefano, J. (2018, January). *Leading change together: Developing educator capacity in schools and systems.* Alexandria, VA: ASCD.

DuFour, R., DuFour, R., Eaker, R., Many, T., & Mattos, M. (2016). *Learning by doing: A handbook for professional learning communities at work* (3rd ed.). Bloomington, IN: Solution Tree Press.

DuFour, R., & Marzano, R. J. (2011). *Leaders of learning: How district, school, and classroom leaders improve student achievement.* Bloomington, IN: Solution Tree Press.

Dunlosky, J., & Metcalfe, J. (2009). *Metacognition.* Thousand Oaks, CA: Sage.

Durlak, J. A., Weissberg, R. P., Dymnicki, A. B., Taylor, R. D., & Schellinger, K. B. (2011). The impact of enhancing students' social and emotional learning: A meta-analysis of school-based universal interventions. *Child Development, 82*(1). Retrieved from casel.org/wp-content/uploads/2016/01/meta-analysis-child-development-1.pdf

Duschl, R. A., Schweingruber, H. A., & Shouse, A. W. (Eds.). (2007). *Taking science to school: Learning and teaching science in grades K–8.* Washington, DC: National Academies Press.

Dweck, C. S. (1999). *Self-theories: Their role in motivation, personality, and development.* Philadelphia: Psychology Press.

Dweck, C. S. (2016). *Mindset, the new psychology of success: How we can learn to fulfill our potential* (updated ed.). New York, NY: Ballantine Books.

Dweck, C. S. (2019). The choice to make a difference. *Perspectives on Psychological Science, 14*(1), 21–25. doi: 10.1177/1745691618804180.

Dweck, C. S., & Leggett, E. L. (1988). A social-cognitive approach to motivation and personality. *Psychological Review, 95,* 256–273.

Education Endowment Foundation. (2019). Metacognition and self-regulation. London, UK: Author. Retrieved from educationendowmentfoundation.org.uk/evidence-summaries/teaching-learning-toolkit/meta-cognition-and-self-regulation/#closeSignup

Eggers, D. (2011, August 1). Remembering an inspiring teacher. Retrieved from salon.com/2011/08/01/dave_eggers_teacher_memory/

Elliott, J. C. (2017). The evolution from traditional to online professional development: A review. *Journal of Digital Learning in Teacher Education, 33*(3), 114–125. doi: 10.1080/21532974.2017.1305304

Entin, E. (2012, February 27). The case for recess. *The Atlantic.* Retrieved from http://38.118.71.170/health/archive/2012/02/the-case-for-recess/253549/

Entwisle, D. R., Alexander, K. L., & Olson, L. S. (1998). *Children, schools, and inequality.* Boulder, CO: Westview Press.

Epstein, J. L. (1989). Family structures and student motivation: A developmental perspective. In C. Ames & R. J. Sternberg (Eds.), *Teaching thinking skills: Theory and practice* (Vol. 3, pp. 259–295). San Diego, CA: Academic Press.

Ericsson, K. A., Krampe, R. T., & Tesch-Romer, C. (1993). The role of deliberate practice in the acquisition of expert performance. *Psychological Review, 100*(3), 363–406.

Ericsson, K. A., & Pool, R. (2016). *Peak: Secrets from the new science of expertise.* Boston, MA: Houghton Mifflin Harcourt.

Ericsson, K. A., & Ward, P. (2007). Capturing the naturally occurring superior performance of experts in the laboratory: Toward a science of expert and exceptional performance. *Current Directions in Psychological Science, 16,* 346–350. Retrieved from psy.fsu.edu/~wardlab/Peer%20Reviewed%20Articles/In%20Press/Naturally-occurring%20superior%20performance.pdf

Feigenson, L., Dehaene, S., & Spelke, E. (2004). Core systems of number. *Trends in Cognitive Sciences, 8*(7), 307–314. doi: 10.1016/j.tics.2004.05.002

Feiman-Nemser, S. (2012). *Teachers as learners.* Cambridge, MA: Harvard Education Press.

Feuerstein, R., Falik, L. H., & Feuerstein, R. S. (2015). *Changing minds and brains—The legacy of Reuven Feuerstein: Higher thinking and cognition through mediated learning.* New York, NY: Teachers College Press.

Feuerstein, R., Falik, L. H., Rand, Y., & Feuerstein, R. S. (2006). *Creating and enhancing cognitive modifiability: The Feuerstein instrumental enrichment program.* Oakland, CA: ICELP.

Feuerstein, R., Feuerstein, R. S., & Falik, L. H. (2010). *Beyond smarter: Mediated learning and the brain's capacity for change.* New York, NY: Teachers College Press.

Feuerstein, R., & Lewin-Benham, A. (2012). *What learning looks like: Mediated learning in theory and practice, K–6.* New York, NY: Teachers College Press.

Feuerstein, R., Rand, Y., Hoffman, M. B., & Miller, R. (1980). *Instructional enrichment.* Baltimore, MD: University Park Press.

Fielding, L., Kerr, N., & Rosier, P. (2007). *Annual growth for all students: Catch-up growth for those who are behind.* Kennewick, WA: New Foundation Press.

Fischer, K. W. (2009). Mind, brain, and education: Building a scientific groundwork for learning and teaching. *International Mind, Brain, and Education Society and Wiley Periodicals, 3*(1), 3–16. doi: 10.1111/j.1751-228X.2008.01048

Flavell, J. (1979). Metacognition and cognitive monitoring: A new area of cognitive-developmental enquiry. *American Psychologist, 34*(10), 906–911. doi: 10.1037/0003-066X.34.10.906

Fleming, S. M. (2014). The power of reflection: Insight into our own thoughts, or metacognition, is key to higher achievement in all domains. *Scientific American Mind, 25*(5), 30–37.

Flynn, J. R. (1987). Massive IQ gains in 14 nations: What IQ tests really measure. *Psychological Bulletin, 101,* 171–191. doi: 10.1037/0033-2909.101.2.171

Frederickson, B. (2009). *Positivity.* New York, NY: Crown.

Friedman, T. L. (2007). *The world is flat: A brief history of the twenty-first century.* New York, NY: Picador.

Friedman, T. L., & Mandelbaum, M. (2011). *That used to be us: How America fell behind in the world it invented and how we can come back.* New York, NY: Farrar, Straus and Giroux.

Fotuhi, M. (2013). *Boost your brain: The new art and science behind enhanced brain performance.* New York, NY: HarperOne.

Fullan, M. (2016). *The new meaning of educational change* (5th ed). New York, NY: Teachers College Press.

Gardner, H. (2007). *Five minds for the future.* Cambridge, MA: Harvard Business Review Press.

Germuth, A. A. (2012a). *Empowering teacher leaders: The impact of graduate programs connecting mind, brain, and education research to teacher leadership.* Orlando, FL: BrainSMART.

Germuth, A. A. (2012b). *Helping all learners reach their potential: What teachers say about graduate programs that integrate the implications of education, mind, and brain research.* Orlando, FL: BrainSMART.

Giedd, J. N. (2004). Structural magnetic resonance imaging of the adolescent brain. *Annals of the New York Academy of Sciences, 1021,* 77–85. doi: 10.1196/annals.1308.009

Giedd, J. N. (2015, June). The amazing teen brain. *Scientific American, 312*(6), 32–37.

Giedd, J. N., Blumenthal, J., Jeffries, N. O., Castellanos, F. X., Liu, H., Zijdenbos, A., Paus, T., Evans, A. C., & Rapoport, J. L. (1999). Brain development during childhood and adolescence: A longitudinal MRI study. *Nature Neuroscience, 2*(10), 861–863.

Gilman, R., Huebner, E. S., & Furlong, M. J. (2009). *Handbook of positive psychology in schools.* New York, NY: Routledge.

Goddard, Y. L., Goddard, R. D., & Tscannen-Moran, M. (2007). A theoretical and empirical investigation of teacher collaboration for school improvement and student achievement in public elementary schools. *Teachers College Record, 109*(4), 877–896.

Goldberg, E. (2009). *The new executive brain: Frontal lobes in a complex world.* New York, NY: Oxford University Press.

Goswami, U. (2019). *Cognitive development and cognitive neuroscience: The learning brain* (2nd ed.) New York, NY: Routledge.

Gottfredson, L. S. (1997). Mainstream science on intelligence: An editorial with 52 signatories, history, and bibliography. *Intelligence, 24*(1), 13–23.

Graham, S., MacArthur, C., & Schwartz, S. (1995). Effects of goal setting and procedural facilitation on the revising behaviors and writing performance of students with writing and learning problems. *Journal of Educational Psychology, 87,* 230–240.

Greenough, W. T., & Black, J. E. (1992). Induction of brain structure by experience: Substrates for cognitive development. In M. Gunnar & C. Nelson (Eds.), *Developmental behavior neuroscience* (Vol. 24, pp. 155–200). Hillsdale, NJ: Erlbaum.

Grissom, J. B. (2005). Physical fitness and academic achievement. *Journal of Exercise Physiology, 8*(1), 11–25. Retrieved from asep.org/files/Grissom.pdf

Hacker, D. J., Dunlosky, J., & Graesser, A. C. (2009). *Handbook of metacognition in education.* New York, NY: Routledge.

Hallowell, E. M. (2011). *Shine: Using brain science to get the best from your people.* Boston: Boston Harvard Review Press.

Halvorson, H. G. (2012). *Succeed: How we can reach our goals.* New York, NY: Plume.

Hammerness, K., Darling-Hammond, L., Bransford, J., Berliner, D., Cochran-Smith, M., McDonald, M., & Zeichner, K. (2005). How teachers learn and develop. In L. Darling-Hammond & J. Bransford (Eds.), *Preparing teachers for a changing world: What teachers should know and be able to do* (pp. 358–389). San Francisco: Jossey-Bass.

Hardiman, M. M., & Denckla, M. B. (2010). The science of education: Informing teaching and learning through the brain sciences. In *Cerebrum 2010:*

Emerging ideas in brain science (pp. 3–11). Washington, DC: Dana Press.

Hargreaves, A., & Fullan, M. (2012). *Professional capital: Transforming teaching in every school.* New York, NY: Teachers College Press.

Harman, A. E., & Germuth, A. A. (2012). *Bridging the gap: The impact of graduate degree programs connecting education, mind, and brain research to teaching and learning.* Orlando, FL: BrainSMART.

Harvard Graduate School of Education. (2015). Growth mindset and grit literature review. Wellington Learning and Research Centre. Retrieved from belmontteach .files.wordpress.com/2015/09/growth-mindset-and-grit-lit-review.pdf

Hattie, J. A. C. (2009). *Visible learning: A synthesis of over 800 meta-analyses relating to achievement.* New York, NY: Routledge.

Hattie, J. A. C. (2012). *Visible learning for teachers: Maximizing impact on learning.* New York, NY: Routledge.

Hebb, D. O. (2009). *The organization of behavior: A neuropsychological theory.* New York, NY: Taylor & Francis.

Hillman, C. H., Pontifex, M. B., Raine, L. B., Castelli, D. M., Hall, E. E., & Kramer, A. F. (2009, March 31). The effect of acute treadmill walking on cognitive control and academic achievement in preadolescent children. *Neuroscience, 159*(3), 1044–1054. doi: 10.1016/j.neuroscience.2009.01.057

Hinton, C., Fischer, K. W., & Glennon, C. (2012, March). Students at the center: Mind, brain, and education [Executive Summary]. Retrieved from students atthecenter.org/sites/scl.dl-dev.com/files/field_attach_file/Exec_Hinton% 26Fischer%26Glennon_032312.pdf

Hobbis, M. H., Massonnié, J., Tokuhama-Espinosa, T., Gittner, A., Arson de Sousa Lemos, M., Tovazzi, A., . . . Gous, I. (2019, November 6). Unified: Bridging the researcher-practitioner divide in mind, brain, and education. *Mind, Brain, and Education, 13*(4), 298–312. doi: 10.1111/mbe.12223

Hoogsteen, T. J. (2020). Collective efficacy: Toward a new narrative of its development and role in achievement. *Palgrave Communications, 6,* 2. doi.org/10.1057/ s41599-019-0381-z

Hord, S. M., & Tobia, E. F. (2012). *Reclaiming our teaching profession: The power of educators learning in community.* New York, NY: Teachers College Press.

Horn, J. L. (1968). Organization of abilities and the development of intelligence. *Psychological Review, 75,* 242–259.

Howard-Jones, P., Ioannou, K., Bailey, R., Prior, J., Yau, S. H., & Jay, T. (2018, February). Applying the Science of Learning in the Classroom. *Impact, Journal of the Chartered College of Teaching.* Retrieved from impact.chartered. college/article/howard-jones-applying-science-learning-classroom

Howe, M. J. A., Davidson, J. W., & Sloboda, J. A. (n.d). *Innate gifts and talents: Reality or myth?* Retrieved from users.ecs.soton.ac.uk/harnad/Papers/Py104/ howe.innate.html

Immordino-Yang, M. H. (2016). *Emotions, learning, and the brain: Exploring the educational implications of affective neuroscience.* New York, NY: Norton.

Immordino-Yang, M. H., Darling-Hammond, L., & Krone, C. (2018). *The brain basis for integrated social, emotional, and academic development: How emotions and social relationships drive learning.* Washington, DC: The Aspen

Institute National Commission on Social, Emotional, & Academic Development. Retrieved from assets.aspeninstitute.org/content/uploads/2018/09/Aspen_research_FINAL_web-9.20.pdf

Immordino-Yang, M. H., & Fischer, K. W. (2007). Dynamic development of hemispheric biases in three cases. In D. Coch, G. Dawson, & K. W. Fischer (Eds.), *Human behavior, learning, and the developing brain* (pp. 74–111). New York, NY: Guilford Press.

Iskander, M. (2011, February 8). A physical education in Naperville. Retrieved from pbs.org/wnet/need-to-know/video/a-physical-education-in-Naperville-ill/7134/

Jackson, C. K. (2018). What do test scores miss? The importance of teacher effects on non-test score outcomes. *Journal of Political Economy, 126*(5), 2072–2107.

James, K. H. (2010). Sensori-motor experience leads to changes in visual processing in the developing brain. *Developmental Science, 13*(2), 279–288.

Jammer, M. (1969). *Concepts of space.* Cambridge, MA: Harvard University Press. (Original work published 1953)

Jankowski, N. A. (2017). *Unpacking relationships: Instruction and student outcomes.* Washington, DC: American Council on Education. Retrieved from acenet.edu/Documents/Unpacking-Relationships-Instruction-and-Student-Outcomes.pdf

Jennings, P. A. (2019). *The mindful school: Transforming school culture through mindfulness and compassion.* New York, NY: The Guilford Press.

Jha, A. P. (2011, September). Session four: Executive function and attention. Summary of panel discussion at Cognitive Neuroscience of Learning: Implication for Education Symposium, New York Academy of Sciences, Aspen, Colorado. Retrieved from nyas.org

Jonassen, D. H. (2012). Designing for decision making. *Educational Technology Research and Development, 60*(2), 341–359. doi: 10.1007/s11423-011-9230-5

Jones, B. D., Bryant, L., Snyder, J. D., & Malone, D. (2012). Preservice and inservice teachers' implicit theories of intelligence. *Teacher Education Quarterly, 39*(2), 87–101.

Jonnalagadda, S. S., Harnack, L., Liu, R. H., McKeown, N., Seal, C., Liu, S., & Fahey, G. C. (2010). Putting the whole grain puzzle together: Health benefits associated with whole grains—summary of American Society for Nutrition 2010 Satellite Symposium. Retrieved from wholegrainscouncil.org/files/ASNsummary2010.pdf

Kaplan, A. (2009). Achievement motivation. In E. M. Anderman & L. H. Anderman (Eds.), *Psychology of classroom learning: An encyclopedia* (pp. 13–17). Farmington Hills, MI: Gale, Cengage Learning.

Kennedy, M. M. (1999). The role of preservice teacher education. In L. Darling-Hammond & G. Sykes (Eds.), *Teaching as the learning profession: Handbook of teaching and policy* (pp. 54–85). San Francisco: Jossey-Bass. Retrieved from msu.edu/~mkennedy/publications/docs/Teacher%20Ed/RoleofTE-LDH/Kennedy99%20Role%20of%20TE.pdf

King, A. (1993). From sage on the stage to guide on the side. *Questia, 41*, 1.

Kleitman, S., & Narciss, S. (2019). Introduction to the special issue, "Applied metacognition: Real-world applications beyond learning." *Metacognition and Learning, 14,* 335–342. doi: 10.1007/s11409-019-09214-7

Klingberg, T. (2011, September). Session four: Executive function and attention. Summary of panel discussion at Cognitive Neuroscience of Learning: Implication for Education Symposium, New York Academy of Sciences, Aspen, Colorado. Retrieved from nyas.org

Krafnick, A. J., Flowers, D. L., Napoliello, E. M., & Eden, G. F. (2011). Gray matter volume changes following reading intervention in dyslexic children. *Neuroimage, 57*(3), 733–741. doi: 10.1016/j.neuroimage.2010.10.062

Lamberg, L. (2007, November). *The brain-body loop: The Dana guide.* New York, NY: Dana Foundation. Retrieved from dana.org/news/brainhealth/detail.aspx ?id=9952

Lane, S., & Tierney, S. T. (2008). Performance assessment. In T. Good (Ed.), *21st century education: A reference handbook* (Vol. 2, pp. 461–469). Thousand Oaks, CA: Sage.

Leana, C. R. (2011, Fall). The missing link in school reform. *Stanford Social Innovation Review.* Retrieved from ssireview.org/articles/entry/the_missing_link _in_school_reform

Lee, H. (1960). *To kill a mockingbird.* Philadelphia, PA: Lippincott.

Lewin, K. (1946). Action research and minority problems. *Journal of Social Issues, 2*(4), 34–46. doi: 10.1111/j.1540-4560.1946.tb02295.x

Liu, P. Z., & Nusslock, R. (2018). Exercise-mediated neurogenesis in the hippocampus via BDNF. *Frontiers in Neuroscience, 12,* 52. doi: 10.3389/fnins.2018.00052

Lightfoot, C., Cole, M., & Cole, S. R. (2008). *The development of children* (6th ed.). New York, NY: Worth.

Locke, E. A., & Latham, G. P. (2002). Building a practically useful theory of goal setting and task motivation: A 35-year odyssey. *American Psychologist, 57,* 705–717.

Lortie, D. (1975). *Schoolteacher: A sociological study.* Chicago: University of Chicago Press.

Lusk, D. L., & Jones, B. D. (2011). The portrayal of intelligence in introductory educational psychology textbooks. *Teaching Educational Psychology, 7*(1), 40–61. Retrieved from teachingeducpsych.org/2011-volume-7

Lutz, J. (2009). Music drives brain plasticity. *F1000 Biology Reports.* doi: 10.3410/ B1-78

Lyman, L. L. (2016). *Brain science for principals: What schools need to know.* Lanham, MD: Rowman & Littlefield.

Maehler, C., & Schuchardt, K. (2016). Working memory in children with specific learning disorders and/or attention deficits. *Learning and Individual Differences, 49,* 341–347. doi.org/10.1016/j.lindif.2016.05.007

Maehr, M. L., & Midgley, C. (1996). *Transforming school cultures.* Boulder, CO: Westview Press.

Maguire, E. A., Gadian, D. G., Johnsrude, I. S., Good, C. D., Ashburner, J., Frackowiak, R. S. J., & Frith, C. D. (2000). Navigation-related structural change in the hippocampi of taxi drivers. *Proceedings of the National Academy of Sciences of the United States of America, 97*(8), 4398–4403. doi: 10.1073/ pnas.070039597

Markman, E. M. (1979). Realizing that you don't understand: Elementary school children's awareness of inconsistencies. *Child Development, 50,* 643–655.

Martinez, M. E. (2000). *Education as the cultivation of intelligence.* Mahwah, NJ: Lawrence Erlbaum Associates.

Martinez, M. E. (2010). *Learning and cognition: The design of the mind.* Upper Saddle River, NJ: Merrill.

Marzano, R. J. (2017). *The new art and science of teaching.* Alexandria, VA: ASCD. Bloomington, IN: Solution Tree Press.

Mateos-Aparicio, P., & Rodríguez-Moreno, A. (2019, February 27). The impact of studying brain plasticity. *Frontiers in Cellular Neuroscience, 13,* 66. doi: 10.3389/fncel.2019.00066.

Maule, L. (2009). The art and science of designing engaging work. *PAGE One, 31,* 24–26. Retrieved from viewer.zmags.com/showmag.php?mid=wfpprg#/page0/

McCandliss, B. D. (2010). Educational neuroscience: The early years. *Proceedings of the National Academy of Sciences of the United States of America, 107*(18), 8049–8050. doi: 10.1073/pnas.1003431107

McTighe, J., & Wiggins, G. (2004). *Understanding by design: Professional development workbook.* Alexandria, VA: Association for Supervision and Curriculum Development.

McTighe, J., & Willis, J. (2019). *Upgrade your teaching: Understanding by design meets neuroscience.* Alexandria, VA: ASCD.

Meltzer, L. J., McNally, J., Wahlstrom, K. L., & Plog, A. E. (2019, April). Impact of changing middle and high school start times on sleep, extracurricular activities, homework, and academic engagement [Supplemental Issue]. *Sleep, 42,* A328–A329. doi: 10.1093/sleep/zsz067.817

Merzenich, M. (2013). *Soft-wired: How the new science of brain plasticity can change your life* (2nd ed.). San Francisco, CA: Parnassus.

Miller, D. C. (Ed.). (2010). *Best practices in school neuropsychology.* Hoboken, NJ: Wiley.

Miller, D. C., & DeFina, P. A. (2010). The application of neuroscience to the practice of school neuropsychology. In D. C. Miller (Ed)., *Best practices in school neuropsychology* (pp. 141–157). Hoboken, NJ: Wiley.

Miller, D. C., & Maricle, D. E. (2019). *Essentials of school neuropsychological assessment* (3rd ed.). Hoboken, NJ: Wiley.

Moir, E., Barlin, D., Gless, J., & Miles, J. (2009). *New teacher mentoring: Hopes and promise for improving teacher effectiveness.* Cambridge, MA: Harvard Education Press.

Morrissey, M. S. (2000). *Professional learning communities: An ongoing exploration.* Austin, TX: Southwest Educational Development Laboratory. Retrieved from sedl.org/pubs/change45/plc-ongoing.pdf

Mortimore, P., & Sammons, P. (1987, September). New evidence on effective elementary schools. *Educational Leadership, 45,* 4–8.

Moser, J. S., Schroder, H. S., Heeter, C., Moran, T. P., & Lee, Y.-H. (2011). Mind your errors: Evidence for a neural mechanism linking growth mind-set to adaptive post-error adjustments. *Psychological Science, 22,* 1484–1489. doi: 10.1177/0956797611419520

Mualem, R., Leisman, G., Zbedat, Y., Ganem, S., Mualem, O., Amaria, M., . . . & Ornai, A. (2018). The effect of movement on cognitive performance. *Frontiers in Public Health, 6,* 100. doi: 10.3389/fpubh.2018.00100

National Academies of Science, Engineering, and Medicine. (2018). *How people learn II: Learners, contexts, and cultures.* Washington, DC: The National Academies Press.

National Council for Accreditation of Teacher Education. (2010). *NCATE glossary.* Retrieved from ncate.org/Standards/NCATEUnitStandards/NCATEGlossary/tabid/477/Default.aspx

National Governors Association Center for Best Practices [NGACBP] & Council of Chief State School Officers [CCSSO]. (2010a). *Common core state standards for English language arts and literacy in history/social studies, science, and technical subjects.* Retrieved from corestandards.org

National Governors Association Center for Best Practices [NGACBP] & Council of Chief State School Officers [CCSSO]. (2010b). *Common core state standards for mathematics.* Retrieved from corestandards.org

National Public Radio (NPR). (2011, September 6). Thomas Friedman on "How America fell behind" [Author interview transcript]. Retrieved from npr.org/transcripts/140214150

Neisser, U., Boodoo, G., Bouchard, T. J. Jr., Boykin, A. W., Brody, N., Ceci, S. J., . . . Urbina, S. (1996). Intelligence: Knowns and unknowns. *American Psychologist, 51,* 77–101. doi: 10.1037/0003-066X.51.2.77

Neuman, S. B. (2009). *Changing the odds for children at risk: Seven essential principles of educational programs that break the cycle of poverty.* Westport, CT: Praeger.

Nisbett, R. (2009). *Intelligence and how to get it: Why schools and cultures count.* New York, NY: Norton.

Nisbett, R. E., Aronson, J., Blair, C., Dickens, W., Flynn, J., Halpern, D. F., & Turkheimer, E. (2012, February–March). Intelligence: New findings and theoretical developments. *American Psychologist, 67*(2), 130–159. doi: 10.1037/a0026699

Nussbaum, A. D., & Dweck, C. S. (2008). Defensiveness versus remediation: Self-theories and modes of self-esteem maintenance. *Personality and Social Psychology Bulletin, 34,* 599–612. doi: 10.1177/0146167207312960

Nussbaum, P. (2010). *Save your brain: The 5 things you must do to keep your mind young and sharp.* New York, NY: McGraw-Hill.

Omer, S. (2011, September 26). Classroom "crisis": Many teachers have little or no experience. Retrieved from msnbc.msn.com/id/44505094/ns/today-education_nation/t/classroom-crisis-many-teachers-have-little-or-no-experience/#.T4SY mtUx43w

Online Learning™ Consortium. (2019, September). International report: Neuromyths and evidence-based practices in higher education. Retrieved from olc-wordpress-assets.s3.amazonaws.com/uploads/2019/10/Neuromyths-Betts-et-al.-September-2019.pdf

Organisation for Economic Co-operation and Development. (n.d.). Recognition of non-formal and informal learning. Retrieved from oecd.org/document/25/0,3746,en_2649_39263238_37136921_1_1_1_1,00.html

Organisation for Economic Co-operation and Development. (2018). Teaching for the future: Effective classroom practices to transform education. Paris: OECD Publishing. doi.org/10.1787/9789264293243-en

Organisation for Economic Co-operation and Development. (2019). OECD future of education and skills 2030. Concept Note: Skills for 2030. Retrieved from oecd.org/education/2030-project/teaching-and-learning/learning/skills/Skills_for_2030.pdf

Oz, M. C., & Roizen, M. (2012, January 16). Food for memory: 5 foods that age your brain. Retrieved from huffingtonpost.com/2012/01/16/food-for-memory_n_1197790.html

Pajares, M. F. (1992). Teachers' beliefs and educational research: Cleaning up a messy construct. *Review of Educational Research, 62*(3), 307–333.

Palincsar, A. S., & Brown, A. L. (1984). Reciprocal teaching of comprehension-fostering and comprehension-monitoring activities. *Cognition and Instruction, 1,* 117–175.

Parker-Pope, T. (2009, August 13). Fatty foods affect memory and exercise. *The New York Times.* Retrieved from well.blogs.nytimes.com/2009/08/13/fatty-foods-affect-memory-and-exercise/

Pellegrino, J. W., & Hilton, M. L. (2012). *Education for life and work: Developing transferable knowledge and skills in the 21st century.* Washington, DC: National Academies Press.

Pérez-Rodríguez, M., Arroyo-García, L. E., Prius-Mengual, J., Andrade-Talavera, Y., Armengol, J. A., Pérez-Villegas, E. M., . . . Rodríguez-Moreno, A. (2018). Adenosine receptor-mediated developmental loss of spike timing-dependent depression in the hippocampus. *Cerebral Cortex.* doi: 10.1093/cercor/bhy194. Retrieved from eurekamag.com/research/065/679/065679731.php

Perry, J., Lundie, D., & Golder, G. (2019). Metacognition in schools: What does the literature suggest about the effectiveness of teaching metacognition in schools? *Educational Review, 71*(4), 483–500. doi: 10.1080/00131911.2018.1441127

Piaget, J. (1977). *The grasp of consciousness.* London, UK: Routledge.

Pianta, R., Belsky, J., Houts, R., & Morrison, F. (2007, March 30). Opportunities to learn in America's elementary classrooms. *Science, 315,* 1795–1796. doi: 10.1126/science.1139719

Pickering, S., & Howard-Jones, P. (2007). Educators' views on the role of neuroscience in education: Findings from a study of UK and international perspectives. *Mind, Brain, and Education, 1,* 109–113.

Price-Mitchell, M. (2015, August 12). Self-awareness: How kids make sense of live experiences. *Psychology Today.* Retrieved from psychologytoday.com/us/blog/the-moment-youth/201508/self-awareness-how-kids-make-sense-life-experiences

Professional learning communities: What are they, and why are they important? (1997). *Issues . . . About Change, 6*(1). Retrieved from sedl.org/change/issues/issues61.html

Public Agenda. (2017). Teacher collaboration in perspective: A guide to research. Retrieved from files.eric.ed.gov/fulltext/ED591332.pdf

Ramsden, S., Richardson, F. M., Josse, G., Thomas, M. S. C., Ellis, C., Shakeshaft,

C., . . . Price, C. J. (2011, November 3). Verbal and non-verbal intelligence changes in the teenage brain. *Nature, 479*, 113–116. doi: 10.1038/nature10514

Restak, R. (2009). *Think smart: A neuroscientist's prescription for improving your brain's performance.* New York, NY: Riverhead.

Retna, K. S. (2016). Thinking about "design thinking": A study of teacher experiences. *Asia Pacific Journal of Education, 36*(sup1), 5–19. doi: 10.1080/02188791.2015.1005049

Rivera, S. M., Reiss, A. L., Eckert, M. A., & Menon, V. (2005). Developmental changes in mental arithmetic: Evidence for increased functional specialization in the left inferior parietal cortex. *Cerebral Cortex, 15*(11), 1779–1790.

Roebers, C. M. (2017). Executive function and metacognition: Towards a unifying framework of cognitive self-regulation. *Developmental Review, 45,* 31–51. doi.org/10.1016/j.dr.2017.04.001

Rosenholtz, S. (1989). *Teacher's workplace: The social organization of schools.* New York, NY: Longman.

Rosenthal, R., & Jacobson, L. (1968). Pygmalion in the classroom. *The Urban Review, 3*(1). doi: 10.1007/BF02322211

Rueda, R. (2011). *The 3 dimensions of improving student performance: Finding the right solutions to the right problems.* New York, NY: Teachers College Press.

Sattelmair, J., & Ratey, J. J. (2009, Winter). Physically active play and cognition: An academic matter? *American Journal of Play,* 365–374. Retrieved from johnratey.typepad.com/SattelRatey.pdf

Scheffler, I. (2010). *Of human potential: An essay in the philosophy of education.* New York, NY: Routledge.

Schmoker, M. (2006). *Results now: How we can achieve unprecedented achievement in teaching and learning.* Alexandria, VA: Association for Supervision and Curriculum Development.

Scholastic & the Bill and Melinda Gates Foundation. (2012). *Primary Sources 2012: America's teachers on the teaching profession.* Retrieved from scholastic.com/primarysources/pdfs/Gates2012_full.pdf

Seligman, M. (1998). *Learned optimism: How to change your mind and your life.* New York, NY: Simon & Schuster.

Seligman, M. E. P. (2002). *Authentic happiness: Using the new positive psychology to realize your potential for lasting fulfillment.* New York, NY: Simon & Schuster.

Seligman, M. E. P. (2011). *Flourish: A visionary new understanding of happiness and well-being.* New York, NY: Free Press.

Seligman, M. E. P. (2018a). PERMA and the building blocks of well-being. *The Journal of Positive Psychology, 13*(4), 333–335. doi:10.1080/17439760.2018.1437466

Seligman, M. E. P. (2018b). *The hope circuit: A psychologist's journey from helplessness to optimism.* New York, NY: Hachette Book Group.

Seligman, M. E. P. (2019). *Martin Seligman 3 books collection set (The optimistic child, Learned optimism, Flourish).* Boston, MA: Nicholas Brealey Publishing.

Serpati, L., & Loughan, A. R. (2012). Teacher perceptions of neuroeducation: A mixed methods survey of teachers in the United States. *Mind, Brain, and Education, 6*(3), 174–176.

Shonkoff, J. P., & Phillips, D. A. (Eds.). (2000). *From neurons to neighborhoods: The science of early childhood development.* Washington, DC: National Academy Press.

Shulman, L. S. (2004). *The wisdom of practice: Essays on teaching, learning, and learning to teach.* San Francisco: Jossey-Bass.

Sibley, B. A., & Etnier, J. L. (2003). The relationship between physical activity and cognition in children: A meta-analysis. *Pediatric Exercise Science, 15,* 243–256.

Singer, T., & Klimecki, O. M. (2014). Empathy and compassion. *Current Biology, 24*(18). Retrieved from ncbi.nlm.nih.gov/pubmed/25247366

Society for Neuroscience. (n.d.). Neuromyth busters: Eight myths about the brain. Retrieved from sfn.org/skins/main/pdf/neuromyth_busters/neuromyth_busters .pdf

Sparks, S. D. (2012, June 6). Experts call for teaching educators brain science: Neuro-myths seen permeating the field. *Education Week.* Retrieved from edweek.org/ew/articles/2012/06/06/33teachers.h31.html

Spector, C. (2019, July 29). "If you don't have a strong supply of well-prepared teachers, nothing else in education can work." Stanford Graduate School of Education Research Stories. Retrieved from ed.stanford.edu/news/if-you-don-t -have-strong-supply-well-prepared-teachers-nothing-else-education-can-work

Start early, finish strong: How to help every child become a reader. (1999, July). Retrieved from ed.gov/pubs/startearly/ch_1.html

Sternberg, R. J. (1988). *The triarchic mind.* New York, NY: Viking.

Sternberg, R. J. (1999). The theory of successful intelligence. *Review of General Psychology, 3,* 292–316. doi: 10.1037/1089-2680.3.4.292

Sternberg, R. J. (2010). WICS: A new model for school psychology. *School Psychology International, 31,* 599–616. doi: 10.1177/0143034310386534

Sternberg, R. J., Jarvin, L., & Grigorenko, E. (2015). *Teaching for wisdom, intelligence, creativity, and success.* New York, NY: Skyhorse.

Sternberg, R. J., Kaufman, J. C., & Grigorenko, E. L. (2008). *Applied intelligence.* New York, NY: Cambridge University Press.

Sternberg, R. J., & Williams, W. M. (2010). *Educational psychology* (2nd ed.). Upper Saddle River, NJ: Pearson.

Stine-Morrow, E. A. L., & Chui, H. (2012). Cognitive resilience in adulthood. *Annual Review of Gerontology and Geriatrics, 32*(1), 93–114. doi: 10.1891/ 0198-8794.32.93

Svinicki, M. D. (n.d.). Student goal orientation, motivation, and learning. Retrieved from education.com/reference/article/Ref_Student_Goal/

Sylwester, R. (1994, October). How emotions affect learning. *Educational Leadership, 52*(2), 60–65. Retrieved from ascd.org/publications/educational-leadership/ oct94/vol52/num02/How-Emotions-Affect-Learning.aspx

Sylwester, R. (2005). *How to explain a brain: An educator's handbook of brain terms and cognitive processes.* Thousand Oaks, CA: Corwin.

Sylwester, R. (2010). *A child's brain: The need for nurture.* Thousand Oaks, CA:

Corwin Press.

Taylor, R. D., Oberle, E., Durlak, J. A., & Weissberg, R. (2017, July/August). Promoting positive youth development through school-based social and emotional learning interventions: A meta-analysis of follow-up effects. *Child Development, 88*(4), 1156–1171.

Thorne, G. (n.d.). Memory and learning: What's the matter with Martha's memory? Retrieved from cdl.org/resource-library/articles/memory.php

Tokuhama-Espinosa, T. (2010). *The new science of teaching and learning: Using the best of mind, brain, and education science in the classroom.* New York, NY: Teachers College Press.

Tokuhama-Espinosa, T. (2011a). *Mind, brain, and education science: A comprehensive guide to the new brain-based teaching.* New York, NY: Norton.

Tokuhama-Espinosa, T. (2011b, Winter). Why mind, brain, and education science is the "new" brain-based education. *New Horizons for Learning.* Retrieved from education.jhu.edu/PD/newhorizons/Journals/Winter2011/Tokuhama1

Tokuhama-Espinosa, T. (2017). *Mind, brain and education science: An international Delphi survey.* Quito, Ecuador: Author. doi: 10.13140/RG.2.2.14259.22560

Tokuhama-Espinosa, T. (2018). *Neuromyths: Debunking false ideas about the brain.* New York, NY: Norton.

Tomporowski, P. D., Davis, C. L., Miller, P. H., & Naglieri, J. A. (2008). Exercise and children's intelligence, cognition, and academic achievement. *Educational Psychology Review, 20,* 111–131. doi: 10.1007/s10648-007-9057-0

Traver, K., & Sargent, E. K. (2011). *The healthiest you: Take charge of your brain to take charge of your life.* New York, NY: Atria.

University of Illinois at Urbana-Champaign. (2009, April 1). Physical activity may strengthen children's ability to pay attention. *ScienceDaily.* Retrieved from sciencedaily.com /releases/2009/03/090331183800.htm

Vainikainen, M.-P., Hautamäki, J., Hotulainen, R., & Kupiainen, S. (2015). General and specific thinking skills and schooling: Preparing the mind to new learning. *Thinking Skills and Creativity, 18,* 53–64. doi.org/10.1016/j.tsc.2015.04.006.

Vainikainen, M.-P., Wüstenberg, S., Kupiainen, S., Hotulainen, R., & Hautamäki, J. (2015). Development of learning to learn skills in primary school. *International Journal of Lifelong Education, 34*(4), 376–392. doi: 10.1080/02601370 .2015.1060025

Varma, S., McCandliss, B. D., & Schwartz, D. L. (2008). Scientific and pragmatic challenges for bridging education and neuroscience. *Educational Researcher, 37*(3), 140–152. doi: 10.3102/0013189X08317687

Veenman, M. V. J., Hesselink, R. D., Sleeuwaegen, S., Liem, S. I. E., & Van Haaren, M. G. P. (2014). Assessing development differences in metacognitive skills with computer logfiles: Gender by age interactions. *Psychological Topics, 23*(1), 99–113.

Vygotsky, L. S. (1962). *Thought and language.* Cambridge, MA: MIT Press.

Vygotsky, L. S. (1978). *Mind in society: The development of higher psychological processes.* Cambridge, MA: Harvard University Press.

Walberg, H. J., & Haertel, G. D. (Eds.). (1997). *Psychology and educational practice.* Berkeley, CA: McCutchan.

Wang, S., & Ellis, N. (2005). *Evaluating the BrainSMART/Health Wise/Health School Team Program at Brookshire Elementary School: An analysis of BMI trend data from 2001 to 2004.* Winter Park, FL: Winter Park Health Foundation.

Wang, M., Haertel, G., & Walberg, H. (1993). Toward a knowledge base for school learning. *Review of Educational Research, 63,* 249–294. doi: 10.3102/003465430630003249

Watson, D. C. (2010). Healthy kids make better students [PowerPoint presentation]. Winter Park, FL: Winter Park Health Foundation.

Weiner, B. (1980). *Human motivation.* New York, NY: Holt, Rinehart and Winston.

Weiner, B. (1992). *Human motivation: Metaphors, theories, and research.* Newbury Park, CA: Sage.

Wesnes, K. A., Pincock, C., Richardson, D., Helm, G., & Hails, S. (2003). Breakfast reduces declines in attention and memory over the morning in schoolchildren. *Appetite, 41*(3), 329–331.

Wiggins, G., & McTighe, J. (2005). *Understanding by design* (2nd ed.). Alexandria, VA: Association for Supervision and Curriculum Development. Retrieved from pdonline.ascd.org/pd_online/ubd_intro/wiggins98chapter4.html

Willett, W. C., & Skerrett, P. J. (2017). *Eat, drink, and be healthy: The Harvard Medical School guide to healthy eating.* New York, NY: Simon and Schuster.

Wilson, D. L. (1996a). The school psychologist as co-teacher: An example using COGNET program as a means of teaching thinking skills. *Journal of Cognitive Education, 5,* 171–183.

Wilson, D. L. (1996b, February). The school psychologist as co-teacher and staff developer: A shift in thinking. *NASP Communique,* 33–34.

Wilson, D. L. (2012a, February). Strengthening teacher effectiveness with implications from neuroeducation: A qualitative study of K–12 teachers focusing on higher needs students. Paper presented at the annual meeting of the American Association of Colleges for Teacher Education, Chicago.

Wilson, D. (2012b). Training the mind's eye: "Brain movies" support comprehension and recall. *The Reading Teacher, 66*(3), 189–194. doi: 10.1002/trtr.01091

Wilson, D. L., & Conyers, M. A. (2009). *Wiring the brain to read: Beginning reading preK–grade 3.* Orlando, FL: BrainSMART.

Wilson, D. L., & Conyers, M. A. (2010). *Wiring the brain to read: Higher-order thinking for reading.* Orlando, FL: BrainSMART.

Wilson, D. L., & Conyers, M. A. (2013). *Flourishing in the first five years: Connecting implications from mind, brain, and education research to the development of young children.* Lanham, MD: Rowman & Littlefield Education.

Wilson, D. L., & Conyers, M. A. (2016). *Teaching students to drive their brains: Metacognitive strategies, activities, and lesson ideas.* Alexandria, VA: ASCD.

Wilson, D. L., & Conyers, M. A. (2018). *BrainSMART Teaching: Science, structures and strategies for increasing student learning* (5th ed.). Moorabbin, Victoria, Australia: Hawker Brownlow Education.

Wilson, D. L., & Conyers, M. A. (2020). *Developing growth mindsets: Principles and practices.* Alexandria, VA: ASCD.

Wilson, D. L., Conyers, M. A., & Buday, M. C. (2013, April). *Impact of a graduate program connecting implications from mind, brain, and education research to teaching*. Paper presented at the 2013 annual meeting of the American Educational Research Association, San Francisco.

Winne, P. H., & Azevedo, R. (2014). Metacognition. In R. K. Sawyer (Ed.), *The Cambridge handbook of the learning sciences* (2nd ed., pp. 63–87). New York, NY: Cambridge University Press.

Woolfolk Hoy, A. E. (2010). *Educational psychology* (11th ed.). Upper Saddle River, NJ: Pearson.

Woolfolk Hoy, A. E., Davis, H., & Pape, S. (2006). Teachers' knowledge, beliefs, and thinking. In P. A. Alexander & P. H. Winne (Eds.), *Handbook of educational psychology* (Vol. 2, pp. 715–731). Mahwah, NJ: Erlbaum.

Woolfolk Hoy, A. E., Hoy, W. K., & Kurz, N. M. (2008). Teachers' academic optimism: The development and test of a new construct. *Teaching and Teacher Education, 24*, 821–835.

World Economic Forum. (2018). The future of jobs report: Key findings. Geneva, Switzerland: Author. Retrieved from reports.weforum.org/future-of-jobs-2018/key-findings/?doing_wp_cron=1559133711.9746949672698974609375

Yeager, D. S., Hanselman, P., Walton, G. M., Murray, J. S., Crosnoe, R., Muller, C., . . . Dweck, C. S. (2019). A national experiment reveals where a growth mindset improves achievement. *Nature, 573*, 364–369.

Yeung, S.-y. S. (2015). Conception of teaching higher order thinking: Perspectives of Chinese teachers in Hong Kong. *The Curriculum Journal, 26*(4), 553–578. doi: 10.1080/09585176.2015.1053818

Yoncheva, Y. N., Wise, J., & McCandliss, B. (2015). Hemispheric specialization for visual words is shaped by attention to sublexical units during initial learning. *Brain and Language, 145–146*, 23–33. doi.org/10.1016/j.bandl.2015.04.001

Zambo, D., & Zambo, R. (2009). What future teachers think about brain research. *Teaching Educational Psychology, 5*(2), 39–49. Retrieved from teachingeducpsych.org/recent-issues-1/2009

Zhang, X., Anderson, R. C., Morris, J., Miller, B., Nguyen-Jahiel, K. T., Lin, T.-J., . . . Hsu, J. Y.-L. (2016). Improving children's competence as decision makers: Contrasting effects of collaborative interaction and direct instruction. *American Educational Research Journal, 53*(1), 194–223. doi.org/10.3102/0002831215618663

Zins, J. E., Bloodworth, M. R., Weissberg, R. P., & Walberg, H. J. (2004). The scientific base linking social and emotional learning to school success. In J. E. Zins, R. P. Weissberg, M. C. Wang, & H. J. Walberg (Eds.), *Building academic success on social and emotional learning: What does the research say?* (pp. 3–22). New York, NY: Teachers College Press.

Zull, J. E. (2002). *The art of changing the brain: Enriching the practice of teaching by exploring the biology of learning*. Sterling, VA: Stylus.

Index

About the Authors

Psychologist and author *Donna Wilson*, PhD, is an international speaker on improving educational outcomes through innovative applications of mind, brain, and education research. Growing up in rural Oklahoma, Donna was the first in her family to go to college; she went on to become the Chair of Education at the University of Detroit-Mercy and later cofounded and became president of BrainSMART® and the nonprofit Center for Innovative Education and Prevention. With her passion for empowering all learners with the science and strategies for achieving academic and life success, Donna codeveloped the world's first doctoral minor in Brain-Based Leadership and the first MS and EdS degree programs in applied mind, brain, and education research (BrainSMART Programs) with Nova Southeastern University. She has shared her work with more than 60,000 participants in live events in Asia, the Middle East, Australia, Europe, and Jamaica and throughout the United States and Canada. Donna is an author of 20 books, including *Developing Growth Mindsets* (2020), *Smarter Teacher Leadership* (Teachers College Press, 2016), *Teaching Students to Drive Their Brains* (2016), and *Introduction to BrainSMART Teaching* (2018). To bring Donna to your district, state, or college, contact her at donna@brainsmart.org. View her blog at donnawilsonphd.blogspot.com or connect with her on LinkedIn under Donna Wilson, PhD and Facebook at Donna Wilson Conyers.

International keynote speaker *Marcus Conyers*, PhD, is a research supervisor for the PhD in Professional Practice: Psychological Perspectives at Canterbury Christ Church University and the lead developer of the BrainSMART and Innovating Minds® programs for improving cognitive performance and creative thinking skills. Marcus is codeveloper of the world's first doctoral minor in Brain-Based Leadership and the first MS and EdS degree programs focused on applied mind, brain, and education research (BrainSMART Programs) with Nova Southeastern University. Founder and CEO of BrainSMART and coauthor of 20 books including

Developing Growth Mindsets (2020) he has worked in 30 countries and shared his work with more than 100,000 people on five continents. In addition to ministers of education in South Africa, the United Arab Emirates, and Ontario, Canada, his audiences have included Navy SEALs, Army Rangers, counterintelligence operatives, law enforcement officers, and business leaders globally. His passion is for improving lives through innovative applications of the cognitive and implementation sciences, and he serves as the director of the nonprofit Center for Innovative Education and Prevention. To bring Marcus to your organization, contact him at marcus@brainsmart.org. Visit his website at www.innovatingminds.org, where you will also find his blog, and connect with him on LinkedIn.

Donna Wilson and Marcus Conyers are on the web at www.brainsmart. org. You can also find them on Facebook at BrainSMART and follow them on Twitter @BrainSMARTU and Pinterest at BrainSMARTU.